CHRISTOLOGY
AND THE
NEW TESTAMENT

CHRISTOLOGY AND THE NEW TESTAMENT

Jesus and His Earliest Followers

———◦———

Christopher M. Tuckett

EDINBURGH
University Press

Edinburgh University Press Ltd
22 George Square, Edinburgh

Typeset in Palatino Light
by Pioneer Associates, Perthshire, and
printed and bound in Great Britain by
MPG Books Ltd, Bodmin

A CIP record for this book is available from the
British Library

ISBN 0 7486 0869 9

CONTENTS

Part 4: Behind the Gospels

PREFACE

The genesis of this book was, in retrospect, a slightly mad suggestion by myself to Jane Feore, then of Edinburgh University Press, that there might be a place for a relatively elementary, but relatively comprehensive, student textbook on New Testament Christology. The suggestion itself may well have been a little strange. The belief that I could write such a book with any ease was very rapidly dispelled. As others will know from bitter experience, the writing of such a book always involves a far greater amount of prior reading and assimilation than can ever be put into the book itself. The end result has therefore been delayed rather longer than I had first anticipated. A change of position in the course of the writing period has further added to the delay in the final production of this book. Nevertheless, I am very grateful to all staff at Edinburgh University Press who have remained faithful to the project and have encouraged me to complete it.

Books such as this are read by a variety of different readers. It is hoped that the readers for whom this book is primarily intended, that is first/second year undergraduates or possibly those still at school, will find value in it. In line with this aim, footnoting and the citing of secondary literature has been deliberately kept to a minimum in order not to distract. Some suggestions for further reading are provided in the Bibliography at the end.

Other readers may include New Testament scholars and/or reviewers who are far more learned than I am in the subject. Many of them may also probably find some of their own ideas repeated and re-presented here. Many of these are unacknowledged. The reason is certainly not an attempt at wholesale plagiarism, but simply to try to provide a readable book for students. I am enormously grateful to those whose writings

on Christology and the New Testament I have read and tried to understand and from whom I have invariably learned a great deal. Such
authors are too numerous to name individually here: many (but by no
means all) of them are noted in the Bibliography at the end. But those
who gnash their teeth at the missing plethora of footnotes (with which
this book could easily have been adorned) are probably those who do
not need such footnotes anyway!

An academic move, from Manchester to Oxford, in the middle of the
writing of this book has forced me to expand my horizons in many
directions. I am very grateful to my colleagues in Oxford, especially Chris
Rowland and Bob Morgan, for this, even though they are probably
unaware of their influence. From my position in Manchester when I
started writing the book, my (then) colleague Martin de Boer (now of
Amsterdam) also taught me much. Various students, in a range of
lectures, classes and tutorials, have endured my strugglings with the
material and they too have helped me in many ways to clarify my
thoughts.

Finally, my family have provided that level of distraction that just
occasionally produces frustration but mostly vast relief. Without their
support, the book would have been even longer in the writing than it
has been.

Christopher Tuckett
Oxford
May 2000

ABBREVIATIONS

— ⋙⋘ —

BETL	Bibliotheca Ephemeridum Theologicarum Lovaniensum
ET	English translation
FS	Festschrift
HTR	*Harvard Theological Review*
JSNT	*Journal for the Study of the New Testament*
JSNTSup	Journal for the Study of the New Testament Supplement Series
JTS	*Journal of Theological Studies*
LukeR	Lukan redaction
LXX	Septuagint
MattR	Matthean redaction
NTS	*New Testament Studies*
NTT	*Nederlands Theologisch Tijdschrift*
SNTSMS	Society for New Testament Studies Monograph Series
TDNT	*Theology Dictionary of the New Testament*

Chapter 1

INTRODUCTION AND BACKGROUND

―――⊃⊂――――

INTRODUCTION

It is no exaggeration to say that the person of Jesus is absolutely central to Christianity. Christian belief has always made the person of Jesus of crucial significance, and it is indeed arguable that it is precisely this focus on Jesus which distinguishes Christianity from other religions. In many ways Christianity shares much of its doctrine of God with Judaism; and it shares a great deal of its ethical teaching with many of its religious neighbours, past and present. Yet a Christianity without Jesus would be impossible to conceive: it would almost be a contradiction in terms.

Yet what exactly is or was the 'crucial significance' ascribed to Jesus by Christians? Who was Jesus? That question can of course be answered at many different levels, and different people will inevitably answer it in different ways. The very fact that Jesus has become the focus of a major world religion – Christianity – means that an answer to the question 'Who was Jesus?' may well be affected by one's own religious beliefs. A Christian may well wish to answer the question rather differently from a non-Christian.

For the most part, no attempt will be made here to provide any answer to the question from the point of view of contemporary theology, Christian or otherwise. Rather, the aim will be to answer the more historical question 'Who did other people think Jesus was?', as well as raising the further question 'Who did Jesus himself think he was?' We shall be concerned with what other peoples' views were in the past. How those views might affect the views which contemporary Christians (or non-Christians) believe they *should* hold about Jesus is really a further problem which will not be considered here. (The slightly narrower question of how Jesus' own views about himself might or should affect other peoples' views about him will be considered very briefly in the final section of this book.)

Jesus lived 2000 years ago and between his own time and ours a lot of water has flown under a lot of bridges. Many people down the ages have had their say in making claims about who Jesus was. In particular, Christians have grappled with the question continuously. The focus of this book will, however, be the earliest period of Christian history: who did Jesus' earliest followers think he was? 'Early' is of course a relative word and can mean very different things to different people. I shall be taking it as covering approximately the first seventy years or so of the Christian church, that is the period of roughly the first century. And the prime – indeed probably only – evidence for discovering what Christians in this period thought about Jesus is to be found in the collection of texts which we call the 'New Testament'. The focus of this book will therefore be 'The Christology of the New Testament'.[1]

Such a statement of aims may, however, need an odd rider or two. By focusing on the New Testament I have no wish to make any claim about the normative nature for Christians about any 'New Testament Christology' which may emerge from an exercise such as this. My purpose is simply to try to discover what early Christians thought about Jesus, and/or what Jesus might have thought about himself. The fact that most (if not all) of the evidence comes from a set of documents which were subsequently claimed by the Christian church as a 'canonical' body of sacred 'scripture' can, at least in one sense, be discounted. The process by which the texts now in what we call 'the New Testament' were separated from other early Christian literature and given the status of 'scripture' alongside Jewish scripture was a long and complex one. Certainly it was not completed until at least the fourth century.[2] It seems highly unlikely that any of the New Testament authors themselves thought that they were writing a text which was to be part of Holy Scripture for a worldwide Christian church! The very idea of a specifically Christian 'supplement' being added to the Jewish Bible had simply not arisen in the first century. So, too, the nature of the 'authority' ascribed to the documents of the New Testament will inevitably vary even amongst Christians: certainly the precise manner in which any 'authority' of scripture is, or should be, related to other potential 'authorities' within the Christian church (for example the church's subsequent tradition, the pronouncements of contemporary authority figures in the church, the use of reason) is not one about which there is any unanimity amongst Christians today.[3]

Yet whatever view one takes about the nature of scriptural authority, one cannot deny that an exercise in seeking to establish what the New Testament may be saying on the question of Christology (or on anything else for that matter) must have *some* relevance for contemporary discussions. Any religious movement, in seeking to articulate its own contemporary views, will inevitably seek to be in dialogue with its own tradition and to find points of continuity with its past. Such dialogue may be critical at times; but a religious movement cannot cut itself off from its past history completely. Otherwise it will lose its very self-identity and its claim to be *this* movement and not another one. Thus contemporary Christian theologising will always involve a dialogue with earlier Christian tradition if it wishes to claim the name 'Christian'.[4] Complete novelty, with no claim to find any point of positive contact with the past, is simply not a viable option within any religious movement, Christian or otherwise.

In this context, the earliest tradition, especially the New Testament tradition, will always occupy a place of supreme importance, whatever one's views about scriptural authority. For the very fact that it is the earliest, and the fact that it was subsequently canonised, means that it forms the fountainhead and start of all subsequent tradition in the Christian church. Later theologising thus involves, explicitly or implicitly, an appeal back to the earliest form of the tradition.[5] A constant return to the earliest tradition can therefore be of vital significance, in part to see the roots of later developments, in part also perhaps to exercise a check and control on later developments which can be seen at times to have appealed to the past in ways which we would no longer find tenable today. I would not necessarily claim to have the expertise to make that kind of comparison; the remarks here are simply to highlight the significance which New Testament Christology will always have in relation, say, to the Christologies of later Christian writers and thinkers.

So far I have spoken of 'early' Christianity/Christology (interpreting 'early' as approximately first century) and 'New Testament' Christianity/ Christology as virtually synonymous. Clearly such an implied equation also needs something of a rider or qualification. In one way, of course, early Christianity and New Testament Christianity are not synonymous. It is quite clear that there are many aspects of early Christianity which are not represented, or represented only very weakly, in the New Testament. For example, we know next to nothing of the rise of early Egyptian Christianity, or of the beginnings of Roman Christianity. At the same time, I would defend here the claim (implied above) that our *prime*, if not our only, evidence for Christianity in this period is provided by the documents of the New Testament. There will always be debates about whether one or two New Testament texts can really count as 'early' in this context (for example 2 Peter may well be relatively late, from the second century), and some non-canonical Christian texts, such as the letter known as *1 Clement*, probably date from the end of the first century.[6] More controversial here may be the decision implied in the limitation to the New Testament to exclude from consideration some other texts which did not make it into the New Testament canon, but which we now have available. Some have argued, for example, that some non-canonical texts such as the *Gospel of Thomas* (now available from the Nag Hammadi library) or the *Gospel of Peter* may be just as, if not more, valuable as sources for early Christianity and/or Jesus as the canonical texts in the New Testament.[7] There is not enough time or space to debate the matter here. I can only state my own view, which is that I remain to be persuaded that any of these non-canonical texts can provide us with reliable information about 'early' Christianity or Jesus. Rather, they are more likely to be products of a rather later period of Christian history (that is second century or later).[8] As such they are invaluable resources for throwing light on many aspects of the history of Christianity about which we are otherwise very ignorant. But it is probably on a *later* period that they throw light, and not on the early period being considered here. For the first century, we are probably driven back to the documents of the New Testament itself as our primary evidence.

If then we are asking about the views of the early Christians about Jesus and/or Jesus' views about himself, we must be fully aware of the fact that the evidence available to us is in the form of texts which come to us from the first century. If then we are to be fair to the evidence, and to do justice to it, we must be aware of the fact that we are reading *ancient* texts. We must therefore be continuously aware of the dangers of anachronism, of reading back later ideas and later uses of language into earlier texts.

At a very general level we have to be aware of the fact that uses of language can change over both space and time. A word or a phrase may mean very different things in different contexts. Above all languages change over the course of time. We are all no doubt aware of this if we ever stop to think about it (though we rarely do!). Thus, for example, the adjective 'gay' in English thirty or forty years ago meant simply 'happy, cheerful', etc. Today it has largely lost that meaning and now carries clear overtones of being homosexual.[9]

The same general phenomenon applies in relation to christological language. The description of Jesus as 'Son of God' became in subsequent (that is post-New Testament) Christianity the phrase by which Christians expressed their belief that Jesus was in some sense a fully divine being, 'one in being with the Father', with 'Son' serving to distinguish Jesus from the 'Father' as two of the three 'persons' in a single undivided divine Trinity. New Testament texts also not infrequently refer to Jesus as 'Son of God'. But we cannot assume necessarily that the same thing is meant when different people use the same words. Arguably, some of the New Testament texts are using the phrase 'Son of God' to express something very different from what is being claimed by later Christians at, say, the Council of Chalcedon in the fifth century, seeking to produce a 'definition' of who Jesus was/is. Thus, if we are to do justice to the nature of the New Testament evidence as first-century documents, we must be continually wary of reading them through spectacles tinted (or tainted?!) by later Christian terminology. This is of course true for all reading of historical texts; but in relation to Christian texts, and more specifically in relation to Christology, the danger is all the more acute. For the overlap in language is certainly not coincidental. Undoubtedly, some later Christian terminology was quite explicitly borrowed from the New Testament. The language of Jesus' divine sonship was in part adopted precisely because that language was present in the formative tradition of the Christian church, that is the New Testament. But equally, it is now clear that, in the process of adopting the terminology, the ideas expressed were being changed and adapted as the same words were taken up and used in different circumstances and contexts. Thus a return to the New Testament can perhaps at times offer a *critical* reflection on the nature of the subsequent tradition which was ostensibly based upon it.

So far I have used the term 'the New Testament' or 'early Christianity' almost as if they were monolithic entities. That too clearly needs an important rider attached to it.

We are now more than ever aware of the enormous variety within the collection of texts we call 'the New Testament', and of the variety within primitive Christianity.[10] Older reconstructions of the development of Christian thinking or theology had perhaps worked with a rather monolithic model of an original, pristine and unified tradition of 'orthodoxy', only branching out into ('heretical'?) offshoots rather later, perhaps in the second century. We are now much more conscious of the tremendous variety that characterises the earliest period in Christian history to which we have access. If one wants an illustration of this, one only has to read some of Paul's letters to realise that many of Paul's communities were clearly divided – at times quite deeply – about important matters of Christian belief and conduct. Nor indeed is this surprising. Christianity started as a movement within Judaism (and indeed, arguably, stayed one throughout much if not all of the New Testament period).[11] Yet it claimed a number of novel features, and various Christians asserted the right to criticise and reject important elements within the religious system of its parent body (notably, for example, the necessity for new male members of the movement to undergo circumcision). In this process the whole question of authority, of who could say what and why, was inevitably controversial and different people had different ideas. The process of narrowing down the limits of what was acceptable, and indeed what was normative, within Christianity was long and at times painful. Thus the New Testament lets us see many different viewpoints, at times coming into conflict with each other at various levels. The conflict element is not always so evident in relation to the question of Christology, though one wonders if Paul's passing reference to some people in Corinth who were apparently 'preach(ing) another Jesus' (2 Cor. 11: 4) is not a reference to 'Christology' in some way: these people may have had such a different view of Jesus from that of Paul himself that Paul refers to their position as preaching 'another' Jesus.[12]

But even if explicit disagreement is not so evident in the pages of the New Testament over the question of Christology, it is quite clear that there is great variety. Different writers use different categories to express their beliefs about who Jesus is. Paul focuses on Jesus as in some sense 'Son of God' who is also 'Lord' and 'Christ'/'Messiah'. In the synoptic Gospels, Jesus rarely refers to himself as God's 'Son', though this is ubiquitous in the Fourth Gospel. Jesus as 'Lord' is relatively rare in all four Gospels. The author of the letter to the Hebrews develops an involved and detailed argument to show that Jesus is to be seen as a priestly figure, though a priest quite unlike the Levitical priests of contemporary Judaism: Jesus is a priest 'after the order of Melchizedek'. There is thus great variety within the pages of the New Testament and it is impossible to tie the New Testament down to a single monolithic view about who Jesus was. So too we may note that, even within the output of a single writer, we may get different views emerging. Hebrews, for example, focuses on Jesus as a priestly figure for much of the 'letter'; but elsewhere Jesus is presented as one who is greater than the angels (cf. Heb. 1), a super-Moses figure (Heb. 3), even at one point addressed as 'God' (Heb. 1: 8 citing Ps. 45: 6), but also as a human being exactly like other human beings, being the forerunner leading the way for men and women to imitate and follow (Heb. 2: 10, 17–18; 12: 2). Thus we should be wary of being able to pin down any one writer to a single 'Christology'. At best we will produce a synthesis of a range of views sitting side by side, at times not altogether happily or consistently.

At the end of a very long period of Christians' grappling with the question of Christology, the Council of Chalcedon in 451 produced a 'definition' of who Jesus was.[13] This, among other things, affirmed the claims of the Nicene creed that Jesus was/is 'God from God, Light from Light, True God from True God, begotten not made, of one substance with the Father'. It also stated that Jesus was/is 'the same perfect in Godhead, the same perfect in manhood, truly God and truly man, of one substance with the Father as touching the Godhead, the same of one substance with us as touching the manhood...'[14]

In fact it is universally recognised that this was no definition of exactly what or who Jesus was. It was simply a setting up of a number of parameters, or boundary conditions, within which it was decided that all future Christian discussion about Jesus should remain. Thus the twin claims of the full divinity and the full humanity of Jesus in the Chalcedonian Definition are effectively simply asserting that any denial of Jesus' divinity, and any denial of his humanity, are unacceptable. How one can pin things down more precisely is left open. So too (at perhaps a slightly 'lower' level) with the New Testament. The New Testament writers may want to say several things about Jesus. But we may in the end have to leave everything they say a little untidy if only because it may not be possible to synthesise everything said into a neat package. In any case, none of the New Testament writers ever offers a sustained treatise on the question of Christology. Thus we have to read off the christological beliefs of a writer at times slightly more indirectly from things that are sometimes said in passing.

We should also note here that the New Testament presents us with a great variety in relation to the *kinds* of texts which it contains. The New Testament texts form a very heterogeneous mixture in terms of their genre. Some of the texts have the form of a 'letter'. Some of these are clearly genuine letters, sent to individuals or groups of individuals, and dealing with very specific problems which have arisen. Most, if not all, of Paul's genuine letters fall into this category. Some have the form of a letter but seem to be rather more general treatises, not so clearly related to a specific situation.[15] Further, as noted earlier, the 'specific situation' does not always focus on anything directly christological, at least explicitly, and so one has to deduce the writer's Christology more indirectly.

More problems are raised in this respect by the narrative texts of the New Testament, that is the texts which purport to give historical accounts of things that have happened in the past. In the New Testament, these are the four Gospels and Acts. How far the narratives give us a reliable account of the history they are purporting to tell is a very complex question; nor is it one that can be answered with a single simple answer covering all the texts concerned: we might decide that the Gospel of Mark is more reliable as history than the Gospel of John, or indeed within one book that one part of Acts is more reliable than another part.

We have now also become aware that all these narrative texts, especially the Gospels, may represent the end-point of quite a long and complex development in the history of the tradition. Thus stories about Jesus probably circulated for some time in Christian circles before being assembled into their present form within a wider narrative by the evangelists (or possibly by a prior source).[16] So too it is seems clear that the evangelists may have had access to other sources which are now lost. Thus it is widely believed that Matthew and Luke had access to a source, usually called Q.[17] Thus we have a number of narratives, and also stages in the development of the tradition between the historical events described and the narratives, some of which may be visible to us.

Now with all narratives, it is possible, and entirely legitimate, to approach such texts in a number of different ways. We can use such texts to try to discover information about the events or people being described. Thus we could use a Gospel to try to tell us something about Jesus. But equally we could use the text to find out something about the person who actually wrote it.[18] Thus the Gospel of Mark, for example, may tell us as much, if not more, about its author 'Mark' as it does about Jesus. The way in which Mark tells the story, the nuances he gives to the narrative, the choice of the material he includes, his arrangement of the material into an ordered whole, etc., may all tell us quite a lot about Mark himself. This is supremely the case with the Fourth Gospel. The many differences between John's Gospel and the other three (so-called 'synoptic') Gospels make it all but impossible to accept that all four are reliable accounts of Jesus' ministry.[19] The portrait and story of Jesus is so different at so many levels that it is really impossible to reconcile them. In terms of historical reliability, scholars have normally opted for the synoptic picture (at least in general terms) as most likely to give us access to the figure of the historical Jesus himself. But this means that the picture in the Fourth Gospel is likely to tell us more about John and his concerns than about Jesus.

In relation to a topic such as Christology, this general state of affairs can make the Gospel accounts quite complex as texts to evaluate. How far do the Gospels show us the views of Jesus and how far do they show us the views of the evangelists? There is of course no single simple answer. Each Gospel has to be treated on its own merits, as does each part of each Gospel. But even if we want to try to discover the theology, or Christology, of the Gospel writers, there is the further complication that none of the evangelists ever addresses his readers directly. Certainly none of them writes a treatise on Christology. What they do is tell stories, making characters in the story say various things at various points, as well as having their characters do various things, *some* of which are (occasionally) 'interpreted' either by the narrator or by another character in the story.[20] It can then become a matter of some delicacy to determine how far what is said by some characters in the story directly reflects the viewpoint of the author of the narrative. In the case of John's Gospel it is perhaps easier since it seems highly likely that what John has Jesus say expresses John's own ideas well. With an author like Luke, life can be much more difficult. Luke is much more of a self-conscious historian, aware of the temporal distance between the past he is describing and his own day. Thus it is not always quite so clear that what characters in the story are made to say reflects Luke's own views. Thus, in relation to Christology, we may be able to see what some characters in the story think about Jesus and it may well be that Luke generally portrays such characters in a positive way; but whether such ideas in the story reflect Luke's own may be harder to determine.[21]

All this is simply to say that, in relation to the Gospels, the nature of the evidence for determining the Christology of the writers, or of characters in the history being recounted (supremely Jesus himself), may be rather indirect. In any case we shall have to reckon with texts that give us a 'narrative Christology', rather than a neatly ordered treatise with a logically developed argument and clearly set out bulleted points and subdivisions of the material!

Given then the rather indirect nature of the evidence in the New Testament for determining christological beliefs, how should one proceed? What is, or should be, the main focus of attention?

In some older discussions, the focus of attention has often been on the titles used of Jesus by other writers or speakers (or indeed by Jesus himself). At several points, certain key terms or phrases are explicitly or implicitly applied to Jesus. Among these are 'Son of God', 'Lord', 'Messiah', and 'Son of Man'. It is indeed one of these terms that gives us the name of the general topic as 'Christ'-ology, the Greek word *christos* being the Greek equivalent of the Hebrew *mashiah* ='Messiah'. Many older discussions of Christology focused on these titles as used by Jesus himself and other early Christians to determine both what they meant and if/how they might be adapted when they were applied to Jesus.[22]

Such an approach has come under fire in recent years, not least because this kind of investigation is in danger of ignoring quite a lot of potentially important christological material in the New Testament which does not explicitly use any of the standard christological titles.[23] Some New Testament texts say or imply things about Jesus which may have great significance without ever using one of a predetermined list of key terms. Thus the claim of the risen Jesus in Matthew 28: 17 that 'All authority on heaven and earth has been given to me' is potentially extremely significant christologically, although no title is explicitly used. (The language may echo Dan. 7: 13 and imply that Jesus is being seen as 'Son of Man', but this is at best implicit.) The phrase 'the Spirit of Jesus' used by Luke in Acts 16: 7 has been regarded by many as highly significant, possibly suggesting that the relation of Jesus to the Spirit is the same as that of God to the Spirit.[24] Yet once again no title is used, and Jesus is referred to only by his personal name. The christological use of the Old Testament, or the use of hymns about Jesus (for example Phil. 2: 6–11) may also have great significance in this context, even though no title is explicitly used. Within the Pauline (and other) letters, we may note the way in which Jesus is almost casually included alongside God in the opening greetings, for example 'Grace to you and peace from God our Father and the Lord Jesus Christ' (1 Cor. 1: 3); this too is extremely striking (and largely unparalleled in other Jewish letters), quite apart from the epithets 'Lord and 'Christ' which are attached to Jesus here. So too Paul's 'inclusive' language, whereby he speaks of Christians being 'in Christ' in some real, almost geographical, sense is potentially far more important than the term 'Christ' itself which is used in the phrase 'in Christ'.[25] So too the fact that Christians appear to have engaged in what might be termed 'worship' of Jesus has been seen by some as one of the most christologically important and influential facets of early Christian activity.[26] All of this shows that we cannot simply confine ourselves to a study of a few christological key terms such as 'Son of God' or 'Lord' in seeking to delineate New Testament Christology.

This protest against an over-concentration on christological titles has been well made by several scholars in recent debates. At the same time, one should not let the pendulum swing too far in the opposite direction. Thus we cannot ignore the use of key christological terms or 'titles' completely. In any case, many of these key terms or titles became important in subsequent Christian history when they were adapted and used as key descriptions of who Jesus was. Further, many of these terms are used in the New Testament in christologically significant ways. Hence they do constitute an important part of the evidence for the Christology of the New Testament. Thus, whilst remaining mindful of the criticisms that have rightly been brought against too 'titled-centred' an approach to the study of New Testament Christology, we cannot ignore christological 'titles' completely. In what follows, therefore, we shall not be ignoring some of the titles used of Jesus in the New Testament, as well as considering some of the other evidence which is relevant in seeking to discover what the earliest Christians thought about Jesus. However, before we start to examine the evidence of the New Testament itself, we must spend some time considering the background against which key terms or titles are ascribed to Jesus by New Testament writers.

THE BACKGROUND OF CHRISTOLOGICAL TERMS

An understanding of the background, the thought world, and the state of the language used, is essential for understanding any communication. At the crudest level, we need to know the language used. If we come across the word 'chat', we need to know at the very least if this is part of a text in English or French: does the word refer to a friendly conversation (English) or to a four-legged feline creature (French 'chat' = English 'cat')? Even within one language, we have already seen that words and phrases can change their meaning over the course of time, and hence we need to know the appropriate background against which to interpret what is said or written.

We should also note that language may change significantly across space as well as time. Thus the same words or phrases may mean different things in different geographical and/or social contexts. This is especially the case in relation to first century Christianity which started life and developed within a highly pluriform social and religious context. Thus early Christianity started from (and largely remained!) within Judaism but also spread and developed in the wider non-Jewish Greco-Roman world.

In studying 'the' background of key New Testament words, we should not, however, assume that all New Testament language has exactly the same meaning as when the same language is used in other contemporary texts. In relation to christological language, it is undoubtedly the case that some of the crucial vocabulary did change its meaning somewhat when it was taken up and applied to the person of Jesus. For example, any language about Jesus as a 'king' must have sounded more than a little strange to many in the first century, since Jesus as a 'royal' figure was, to say the least, somewhat unlike other royal figures of the time. Thus the use of royal terminology applied to Jesus involved a certain novelty in the use of such language.

Precisely because of this, it is vital to know what meanings, or ranges of meaning, were current at the time of the writing of the New Testament for key christological words or phrases. Insofar as there is continuity between the New Testament and other contemporary writings, such knowledge will enable us to understand just what the New Testament is saying (as well as what it is not saying!); and insofar as the New Testament stretches and changes language in applying it to Jesus, such knowledge may enable us to see more precisely just where and how the changes are occurring.

In assessing the background of New Testament christological language, there can be little doubt that, in general terms, the background in Judaism is of supreme importance. Early Christianity started as a movement within Judaism and, for much of the time covered by the New Testament writings, stayed within a Jewish matrix. Eventually the tensions between Christianity and Judaism became too great and the two movements diverged to become two separate 'religions'.[27] Yet it is uncertain if such terminology has ever been appropriate, at least from the Christian side. Christianity has never cut itself off from its Jewish roots.[28] Christian scripture has always included Jewish scripture as an integral part (even if it has added a 'New Testament' to the Jewish Bible which is now called by some Christians the 'Old Testament'). Certainly in the New Testament period, Christianity is clearly seen as growing out of, but remaining part of, Judaism. There are of course fierce polemics reflected at times in the New Testament documents, evidently reflecting competing claims to be the 'true' form of Judaism. Yet such polemic is not confined to debates involving Christians: the Dead Sea Scrolls now let us see very similar debates going on at about the same time as that of the start of the Christian movement between other competing groups within Judaism.

But quite apart from any polemic, it is striking how much early Christian writers assume many key aspects of Judaism as given. These are never disputed or argued for: it is simply assumed that Christians will acknowledge them without question. Thus, for example, Jewish monotheism is assumed as almost self-evident: there is one and only one God and this is never questioned, nor does the matter ever arise as a contentious issue. So too in general terms the belief in God as the Creator of the world is assumed as self-evident for Christians. All this is perhaps more surprising in relation to some of Paul's communities living in religiously pluriform cities of the Roman Empire where some kind of polytheistic belief would presumably have been regarded as the norm. Yet it is precisely in Paul's letters, writing to the church in the highly pluriform city of Corinth, that we find statements like 'all *our* fathers were under the cloud, and all passed through the sea' (1 Cor. 10: 1), referring to *Jewish* ancestors and apparently assuming as read that these can be referred to as the (Gentile!) Corinthians' ancestors as well. Similarly, it is a standard observation in relation to New Testament ethics that much of the ethical teaching of the New Testament is not that distinctive and can be paralleled in Jewish (as well as non-Jewish) texts.[29]

We should perhaps also note at this point that, whatever is said about Jesus in the New Testament, only rarely is any awareness indicated that christological claims might threaten Jewish monotheism in any way.[30] Whatever is said about Jesus, virtually no one seems to think that this in any way compromises, or affects, the fundamental belief in the uniqueness and sovereignty of God. The one exception might be the Fourth Gospel where it seems that, at least for the Jewish opponents who appear in the story, Jesus' claims about himself are regarded as blasphemous (cf. John 10: 30–9). But John at least thinks that such accusations can be answered and that even Jesus' claim to be 'one' with God (John 10: 30) is fully in line with the (monotheistic) teaching of Judaism. We must therefore constantly bear in mind that the use of what may appear at first (and second!) sight as very exalted language being applied to Jesus was rarely if ever felt to threaten the fundamental Jewish belief of monotheism. Worries on that score, seeking to reconcile claims made about Jesus with beliefs about God, were much more a feature of the time after the New Testament period.

As well as an unquestioned monotheistic belief, early Christianity also adopted, apparently without ever questioning, what were essentially Jewish ideas about history. God was the God of past history, above all of the history of the Jewish people. Thus, as we have already seen, Christian history was identified with Jewish history: the history of the Jewish people was taken over and appropriated as the history of the Christian movement.[31]

Yet Christianity also adopted another aspect of Jewish beliefs about history, an aspect which was very important in the context of christological claims. This concerned Jewish beliefs about *eschatology*, looking not so much to the past as to the future.

With the overarching belief in God as the God of history, Jews believed above all that God was the God of Israel. Within the course of history, God had chosen the Jewish people, creating a special relationship with them through the making of the covenant, and establishing them as a nation state with the promise to maintain and protect them. The fortunes of the Jewish nation reached their height at the time of the Davidic monarchy, when the nation of Israel enjoyed political autonomy and considerable material prosperity. However, the political disasters of subsequent years, including the military defeats of the nation by the Assyrians in 721 BCE and the Babylonians in 587 BCE, led to an extended period in Israel's history when the nation was no longer under its own control. It was in this situation of domination by successive foreign powers that hopes grew for God to be faithful to his promises to the nation: he would therefore at some stage intervene in history to put right all the wrongs of the present and restore the nation to its position of independence when it could once again be free of foreign domination. One thus got the rise of *eschatological* hope.

The precise nature of this hope varied considerably. In particular, there was variation in the extent to which the new conditions hoped for would be established in a line of continuity with those of the present order, or whether the new age would involve a complete break with the present. For some the new age would be continuous with the present, involving a restoration of the fortunes of the nation. For others, the new age would involve a radical break and an end of the present world order: there would be judgement on everything and everyone in the present, and then there would be a totally new world order quite different from the present.[32]

In addition (and of crucial importance for the present purposes), there was variety in the way Jews thought this new age would be established. For some, God would act entirely alone to achieve his ends (cf. *Sib. Or.* 4: 40–9, 181–2).[33] However, in other strands of Jewish eschatological thought, ideas developed whereby God would be accompanied by, and assisted by, another figure acting alongside him to inaugurate the new age. The identity and nature of this figure could and did vary considerably. Thus, in some Jewish texts, we find the belief that one of the great figures of the past would act as God's intermediary at the end of the present world order. For example, some Jews evidently thought that God would be assisted by the patriarch Enoch (*Jub.* 10: 17; *2 Enoch* 64: 5), others that Elijah would return (cf. Mal. 3: 1; Sir. 48: 10), others that a prophet like Moses would come (apparently based on Deut. 18: 15, this seems to have been important for Samaritan expectations; also cf. 4QTest), others that Enoch and Elijah together would appear (cf. *4 Ezra* 6: 26). In yet other texts God would be assisted by an angelic figure (*Ass. Mos.* 10: 1–2).[34]

In *some* (but by no means all) strands of Jewish thought the expected intermediary figure could be termed 'messianic', or a 'Messiah'. Thus as part of broader eschatological hopes, Judaism developed specifically *messianic* ideas, and some of this language was evidently applied to Jesus by early Christians. In seeking to understand what might have been meant by Christian claims about the messiahship of Jesus, we need therefore to have some idea of what messiahship might have meant in Judaism at the time of Jesus.

Messiah

First, it must be emphasised that ideas about messiahship *only* make sense against a background of Jewish categories and beliefs. The term Messiah is really meaningless outside a Jewish context. Yet within a Jewish matrix, some caution is needed.

The term 'messianic' strictly means simply an 'anointed' figure. A 'messiah' figure, a *mashiah*, is thus simply someone who has been anointed. Now in Judaism, anointing was associated with a variety of different people, supremely with three groups: kings, priests and prophets. Thus kings were anointed as part of their inauguration and installation into office (cf. 1 Sam. 10: 1; 1 Ki. 1: 39), as were priests (cf. Exod. 29: 3; 40: 13; Lev. 16: 32); so too prophets were thought of at times as anointed figures (1 Ki. 19: 16; Ps. 105: 15).

However, the use of anointing seems to have become significant in the eschatological hopes of some Jews. Thus the 'intermediary' figure (or figures – see below) who was thought of as possibly assisting God at the time of his eschatological intervention on behalf of Israel was evidently conceived of by some in 'messianic' terms, that is as an anointed figure. The precise significance of such language is not always clear since a 'messianic' figure could be a royal figure, a priestly figure, or a prophetic figure.

It is sometimes argued that messianic language must be primarily associated with a royal figure.[35] There is certainly some evidence for this in Jewish texts from around the time of the start of the Christian movement: the seventeenth *Psalm of Solomon* (c. middle of the first century BCE) describes the coming of a new Davidic ruler who will be called 'The Lord Messiah' (*Ps. Sol.* 17: 32).[36] In older discussions it was often assumed that Jewish messianic expectations were ubiquitous and uniform: Jews everywhere were looking for a royal Messiah figure to come and inaugurate the new age.[37] It is now recognised that the situation was probably far more complex and Judaism itself far more variegated.[38] The older handbooks tended to produce a rather artificial synthesis on the basis of statements culled from texts spanning a wide range both geographically and temporally. It seems very likely that 'messianic' expectations were in a state of considerable flux and development at the time of the start of the Christian movement.[39]

Nevertheless, it does seem clear that expectations of a royal Messiah figure, a new Davidic ruler, were current at the time of Jesus, or at least for some Jews.[40] The roots for such a hope lie in the Old Testament itself where the classic text is to be found in Nathan's oracle to David in 2 Samuel 7. Here the promise is made that the Davidic line will not die out and that God will establish a successor on the Davidic throne who will be to him as his son (2 Sam. 7: 14). Although no doubt originally intended as a prophecy about Solomon, the hope evidently remained alive after the monarchy ceased that God would one day restore the monarchy with the appointment of an ideal king in the form of a new Davidic ruler. The hope for a new Davidic ruler is evident in oracles attributed to some of the pre-exilic prophets: for example the prophecy of Isaiah 9: 1–6 of the child born who will sit 'on the throne of David' (v. 6), or the prophecy of Isaiah 11: 1–5 that 'a shoot shall come out of the stump of Jesse' who shall be the ideal ruler, or the promise to 'raise up the booth of David that is fallen' (Amos 9: 11). The precise dating of these oracles is disputed, and several may in fact be post-exilic. Certainly in the period around the time of the exile, the hope is still clearly alive when Jeremiah looks forward to the time when God 'will raise up for David a righteous Branch, and he shall reign as king and deal wisely and execute justice and righteousness in the land' (Jer. 23: 5–6, cf. 33: 14–26). So too Ezekiel looks forward to the come of a new Davidic ruler (Ezek. 33: 23–4; 37: 24–5). In the later period it seems that hopes for a Davidic ruler were revived with the activity of Zerubbabel and the rebuilding of the temple (cf. Hag. 2: 22–3; Zech. 3: 8; 4: 6–10; 6: 11–12).

For the period after the time of the biblical writings, there is the evidence of *Ps. Sol.* 17, as we have seen. In addition, the Qumran scrolls have shown us that such an expectation was alive in some circles at least, at a period roughly contemporaneous with the start of the Christian movement. Thus a number of texts evidently echo the language used in several of the biblical prophecies about a coming Davidic king. For example, 4QFlor (= 4Q174) contains an interpretation of 2 Sam. 7: 10–14 in which the prediction of a new ruler is evidently applied to a coming eschatological figure. So too a pesher text on Isaiah (4QpIsa^a = 4Q161) reinterprets the prophecy of Isaiah 11 in terms of an eschatological future Davidic ruler.

Many of these texts do not use the term 'messiah' as such. More often they seem to allude to other key passages in earlier prophecies within the broad stream of expectation of a new Davidic ruler (for example Isa. 11: 1–5). Nevertheless it is probably justified to speak of such expectations as 'messianic' insofar as they refer to a future eschatological royal figure, even if the term 'messiah' itself does not appear.[41]

At the same time, we must not lose sight of the fact of the very varied nature of Jewish eschatological expectations, and this variety also relates to so-called 'messianic' figures. We have already noted that anointed (that is 'messianic') figures include priests and prophets as well as kings; and it seems clear that in some strands of Judaism, the expected eschatological figure would be a priest rather than – or as well as – a king. Thus the *Testament of Levi* looks forward to the time when 'the Lord will raise up a new priest to whom all the words of the Lord will be revealed' (*T. Levi* 18: 1). Above all the Qumran scrolls have provided us with clear evidence of the expectation of a priestly Messiah by some Jews. Moreover, in a number of texts, there appears to be an expectation of *two* Messiah figures: a priestly Messiah and a royal Messiah. The classic example of this is the reference in the *Manual of Discipline* to 'the Messiahs of Aaron and Israel' (1QS 9: 11). Probably also related are the expressions 'the Messiah of Aaron and Israel' in the Damascus Document (CD 12: 23; 14: 19; 19: 10) and 'a Messiah from Aaron and Israel' (CD 20: 1). It is probable that these texts in CD also refer to two Messiahs.[42] Further, in one of the appendices to the *Manual of Discipline*, the so-called 'Messianic Rule' (1QSa = 1Q28a), there is again reference to two Messiahs with the priestly Messiah evidently taking precedence over the royal Messiah. To add a yet further complication, the text in 1QS 9: 11 speaks of a 'prophet' coming before the two Messiahs themselves.

It is thus clear that expectations about a 'messianic' figure were very fluid at the time of the New Testament. It would probably be quite wrong to think of all Jews looking forward to the coming of 'the' Messiah as if there were a well-established fixed messianic idea. Indeed the term 'the Messiah' is not attested in any pre-Christian texts so far discovered: the term 'Messiah' is always qualified by some genitive (for example 'the Lord's Messiah', or 'the Messiah of Aaron/Israel'). Later, of course, Jewish expectation did solidify into a rather more monolithic form with the hope for a Davidic Messiah, but evidence for this is later than the time of the New Testament.

In fact, ideas of a 'priestly Messiah' are not really taken up in the New Testament at all. (In Hebrews, Jesus is seen as a priestly figure, but not clearly as 'messianic' in this respect.) Insofar as any messianic ideas are taken up and applied to Jesus they seem to be royal ideas. One of the great conundrums of the study of New Testament Christology is how and why this happened: for Jesus' whole life and work are not clearly related to ideas associated with a royal figure; and yet the term *christos*/Messiah is already attached to Jesus very firmly and very early so that it soon becomes just another proper name as in 'Jesus Christ' or 'Christ Jesus' or even 'Christ' (cf. 1 Cor. 15: 3).[43] Discussion of that must, however, await our analysis of the New Testament itself.

Lord

Of all the christological 'titles' used in the New Testament, the term 'Lord' (Greek *kyrios*) is one of the most common, especially in the Pauline letters. The term could, however, be used in different first-century contexts with a very wide range of meanings.

When used in the vocative to address someone ('O Lord!', Greek *kyrie*), the term need be little more than a polite form of address. It is thus similar to addressing someone in (perhaps now slightly old-fashioned) English as 'Sir!', or opening formal letters with the stereotyped 'Dear Sir', without ever suggesting or implying by the use of such an address that the person concerned has been knighted. It is thus customary in discussions of New Testament Christology to discount simple uses of the vocative *kyrie* alone as being probably irrelevant in terms of any christological significance.

The primary meaning of *kyrios* in a Greek-speaking context is that of 'master'. A 'lord' is the master of someone else, supremely a slave. To refer to someone as your *kyrios* thus implies that the person concerned is your master, your boss, one who has rights over you and to whom you owe obedience. It is thus primarily an existential term, expressing authority and subservience. To call Jesus 'Lord' therefore expresses the fact that he is primarily acknowledged as one to whom obedience is due as master.

In some contexts, further overtones of meaning may also be present. It is now widely accepted that, within the many cults which flourished in the Greco-Roman world of the first century, a number of the cult deities were called *kyrioi*, 'lords'. This usage is prominent in, for example, the cults of Isis and Sarapis. So too a number of oriental kings were called lords. And in the developing emperor cult of the Roman Empire, which was starting in the middle of the first century and developed strongly towards the end of the century (for example under Domitian), the emperor was increasingly demanding recognition as 'Lord and God' (*dominus ac deus*).[44]

It is likely that at least some Christian claims about Jesus as *kyrios* reflect this general background by claiming that, in contrast to other alleged *kyrioi*, Jesus is the one true *kyrios*. This is, for example, probably reflected in Paul's language in 1 Cor. 8: 5 where he concedes that 'there are many so-called gods and so-called lords'in the world, whilst then affirming that 'for us there is one God the Father . . . and one Lord, Jesus Christ' (1 Cor. 8: 6).

Some have in the past argued that it is this entirely non-Jewish Greek background which lies at the origin of claims that Jesus is *kyrios*.[45] At first sight, such a claim runs into some difficulties in seeking to explain the words of Paul in 1 Cor. 16: 22, where Paul, writing in Greek, uses an Aramaic phrase *Maranatha* (= O Lord, come!), thus suggesting that the reference to Jesus as Lord was at home in Aramaic-speaking Christianity as well as in Greek-speaking circles. Bousset and others tried to get round this by distinguishing between 'invocation' and 'acclamation': Jesus was invoked as the (coming) Lord by the very earliest communities; but it was only in the context of the pagan cults that Jesus was actually acclaimed as Lord. However, it is dubious whether such a distinction can be maintained. The fact that Jesus is invoked as (coming) Lord suggests that in some sense he is already the Lord and can be acclaimed as such.[46] Thus the text in 1 Corinthians 16: 22 must cast real doubts on the claim that the non-Jewish Hellenistic world provides the primary background for determining the meaning of Jesus' 'lordship'for Christians.

One other possibly important factor should also be mentioned here as possibly relevant in discussions of the christological significance of the term *kyrios* when applied to Jesus. It is now regarded as fairly certain that Greek-speaking Jews used the term *kyrios* as their substitute to avoid uttering the divine name Yahweh in referring to God. (Jews had for a long time taken the implications of the second command of the Decalogue not to take God's name in vain as implying that the name should never be uttered: hence they adopted a variety of strategies for avoiding mentioning the name, for example when reading the Bible aloud.)

For some time such claims were heavily disputed. It was pointed out that use of *kyrios* for the divine name was primarily witnessed in copies of the LXX, the Greek version of the Hebrew Bible, which had been written by Christian scribes. Such evidence as we had from elsewhere of the work of non-Christian scribes suggests that a variety of different devices was employed, for example, the use of the Greek characters ΠΙΠΙ which is a rough *visual* equivalent of the divine name in Hebrew letters יהוה (YHWH), or the use of the tetragrammaton itself. Further, the use of 'the Lord' absolutely to refer to God was thought not to occur in non-Christian Jewish texts.

Much of this has been called into question in an important article of J. A. Fitzmyer.[47] Fitzmyer argues strongly that, although the extent of the data is small, there is enough evidence to suggest that non-Christian Greek-speaking Jews did use *kyrios* to refer to Yahweh, for example when reading the Bible aloud and being concerned to avoid uttering the divine name. Thus there is a small amount of evidence from Josephus (*Ant.* 13.68; 20.90) and the *Letter of Aristeas* (155) of the use of *kyrios* for God in reference to the Old Testament; so too one extant fragment of Aquila's translation of the Old Testament uses an abbreviation of the genitive *kyriou* for the Hebrew tetragrammaton (at 2 Ki. 23: 24).[48] In any case it seems highly unlikely in general terms that the use of *kyrios* for Yahweh would be a wholly Christian invention.

Fitzmyer has also shown that the absolute use of the Aramaic word *Mar* to refer to God is now attested in the Qumran scrolls. Thus the Targum on Job from cave 11 at Qumran uses 'the Lord' absolutely to refer to God (24: 7 paraphrasing Job 34: 12). So too the *Genesis Apocryphon* (1QapGen) at one point refers to God as 'the Lord' (20: 12–13: 'Blessed are you, O God most High, my Lord, for all ages. For you are Lord and Master over all.')

There is therefore probably sufficient evidence to suggest that the term Lord was used by Greek-speaking Jews to refer to Yahweh, and that the usage can be traced back to Aramaic-speaking Jews as well. In talking of Jesus as *kyrios*, Christians would have been using the same word that many Jews used to refer to God Himself.

How much can be deduced from this is, however, not at all certain. As we have seen, *kyrios* was a word with a very wide range of possible meanings and we cannot necessarily simply fasten on one possibility to determine what Christians meant in describing Jesus in this way. In the LXX, references to a human being as a *kyrios* can sometimes lie side by side with a reference to Yahweh as *kyrios*: for example, in Genesis 18: 12, Abraham is referred to by Sarah as her *kyrios*, and in the very next verse there is a reference to Yahweh as the *kyrios*. But this does not mean anyone thought Abraham was being equated with Yahweh himself. So then the fact that Jesus was spoken of as a *kyrios* figure should not necessarily be taken as implying that Jesus was thought of necessarily as a divine figure, on a par with Yahweh. The precise nuances that New Testament writers gave to the term *kyrios* when used christologically will have to wait our discussion of the New Testament texts themselves.

Son of God

Of all the christological 'titles' used in the New Testament of Jesus, 'Son of God' has probably had the most lasting influence in Christian history in that it is this phrase which Christians have believed encapsulates the most accurate and profound truth about the identity of the person of Jesus. In this context, the phrase is usually assumed to imply Jesus' full divinity: as 'Son of God' he is one with God the Father, 'true God from true God', and the second person of a fully divine Trinity.

Yet it would probably be extremely dangerous to transfer such a meaning lock, stock and barrel into New Testament uses of the phrase. For it is arguable that the use of the term 'son of God' in the New Testament has a meaning that in no way approaches its meaning in subsequent Christian language.

The idea of divine sonship was widespread in the ancient world in non-Jewish contexts.[49] Thus Homer and Hesiod portray the Olympian gods as a family dynasty, with Zeus the son of Kronos and Rhea and himself the 'father of men and gods' (*Il.* 1.544). The heroes of Greek mythology, for example Dionysius and Heracles, were also thought of as sons of Zeus (by mortal mothers). Egyptian rulers were termed 'son of God', 'son of Helios', or 'son of Zeus', from the time of the Ptolemies onwards. Within Stoicism, all men were thought of as children of Zeus by nature, sharing the divine seed by virtue of their reason (cf. Epictetus *Diss.* 1.3.2; 13.3; 3.22.81). In other strands of thought, famous philosophers such as Plato or Pythagoras were thought of as born of a god (Apollo). But whether such ideas have relevance in Christianity's talk of Jesus as Son of God is more doubtful. Most of such talk is far more at home in a polytheistic environment, and, as we have seen,

Christianity firmly adhered to a Jewish monotheistic 'theo'-logy.[50]

Yet, within Judaism too, talk of other beings as 'sons of God' was quite frequent. However, in no case is it implied that the person referred to by such language is in any sense divine. The term is used in the Old Testament to refer at times to angelic or heavenly beings (Gen. 6: 2; Deut. 32: 8; Ps. 24: 1; 89: 7; Dan. 3: 25). It is, however, uncertain if this terminology has any relevance in New Testament Christology. The idea of Jesus as an angelic being, or at least displaying angelic-type features, may characterise some strands of New Testament Christology,[51] but it is not clearly related to language of Jesus' divine sonship.

The term is also used to refer to the nation Israel itself. Thus in Exodus 4: 22, God says 'Israel is my first-born son'; and Hosea has God look back to the Exodus and claim 'Out of Egypt have I called my son' (Hos. 11: 1; cf. too Deut. 32: 5–6; Jer. 31: 9, 20). So, too, the righteous Israelite can be called a 'son of God'. This comes out in a number of passages in the so-called intertestamental literature. Thus Ben Sira exhorts his readers to care for those in need by saying: 'Be like a father to orphans, and instead of a husband to their mother; and you will then be like a son of the Most High' (Sir. 4: 10 LXX; Hebrew has 'God will call you his son'). So too the individual righteous sufferer described in Wisdom 2–5 is mocked by his persecutors on the assumption that he is, or has claimed to be, God's son: 'Let us see if his words are true, and let us test what will happen at the end of his life, for *if the righteous man is God's son*, he will help him . . .' (Wisd. 2: 17–18, cf. too 2: 13; 5: 5; also *Jub.* 1: 24–5). Thus Judaism clearly knows of a 'son of God' who is a loyal, perhaps persecuted, member of the true people of God. The possible relevance of this to New Testament talk about Jesus as a 'son of God' should be obvious.

It is also the case that divine sonship was predicated of the Israelite king. The *locus classicus* is the promise made through Nathan to David about David's successor(s): 'I shall be to him a father, and he shall be to me a son' (2 Sam. 7: 14). So too some of the 'royal' psalms, that is psalms thought to have been originally addressed to the king, echo the same language, for example Psalm 2: 7 'You are my son, today I have begotten you' (cf. too Ps. 89: 26–7).

Further, insofar as Jewish eschatological expectations involved the coming of a future royal figure, a (Davidic) Messiah (cf. above), 'son of God' may have been a *messianic* term as well. This has, however, been disputed, with some denying that son of God was ever used as a messianic title. Much, though, may depend on what one means by the word 'title' in this context. Certainly it is true that the phrase 'son of God' has not been found in a context where it refers clearly and unambiguously on its own to a messianic figure. Alternatively, some of the Qumran scrolls do seem to indicate a belief that divine sonship, being a 'son of God', was something that could be said of a (Davidic) messianic figure. Thus 4QFlor (= 4Q174) 1: 10–11 explicitly quotes 2 Samuel 7: 14, including the promise of God to be the Father of the coming figure as son, and then says 'This (refers to the) "branch of David" who will arise with the Interpreter of the law', a fairly clear reference to the Davidic Messiah. (The end of the column also appears to develop an interpretation of Psalm 2, though sadly the manuscript is mutilated and we cannot be certain if there was then a further interpretation of Psalm 2: 7 in messianic terms.)[52]

Other references are a little less clear. Thus an (unfortunately slightly uncertain) passage in the 'Rule of the Congregation' (the appendix to the *Manual of Discipline*) 1QSa (= 1Q28a) 2: 11–12 may read 'when God *begets* the Messiah'.[53] So too there is another text recently published (4Q246) which starts 'He will be called son of God and they will call him Son of the Most High'. Unfortunately the text is fragmentary and so we do not have the context which would clarify the exact identity of the person being described here. The subsequent part of the text seems to refer to a messianic figure and hence a messianic interpretation is certainly possible.[54] To the data from Qumran we can also add evidence from *4 Ezra* (admittedly slightly later than the New Testament, but presumably reflecting ideas of the time which did not necessarily suddenly sprout from nowhere after 70 CE). Here a messianic figure is referred to as 'my [= God's] son' in a number of passages (4 Ezra 7: 28; 13: 32, 37, 52; 14: 9).[55]

The phrase 'son of God' may not have been a fixed messianic 'title' in the sense that its usage alone would point any hearer or reader unambiguously to the idea of a messianic figure. Nevertheless, insofar as one is within a context of messianic expectations, this evidence does suggest that in some circles a messianic figure was thought of as a 'son of God'.

The term 'son of God' was thus a very wide-ranging one at the time of the New Testament. But if one thing is clear, it is that, at least within a Jewish context, the term was used not infrequently and with no overtones of divinity being ascribed to the person referred to in this way.

Son of Man

The phrase 'son of man' is one of the most widely used christological 'titles' in the New Testament, especially in the Gospels. Yet its meaning is one of the most controversial in New Testament studies today. At this point we shall consider briefly the possible background of the phrase.

The Greek phrase 'son of man' (Greek *ho huois tou anthropou*) is very strange in Greek and everyone recognises that behind it must lie the Aramaic phrase *bar nash* or *bar nasha*.[56] In Aramaic the phrase usually means 'man' in the generic sense of human beings in general, or in an indefinite sense of 'a man', 'someone'. Sometimes it appears to have been used as the substitute for the first person singular 'I', though most are now agreed that the phrase cannot really mean 'I' on its own: the usage may simply occur in contexts where a periphrasis for 'I' was felt appropriate, perhaps by making a general statement about human beings, or about a group of human beings which included the speaker.[57]

The phrase is used in this way in the Old Testament. Thus Psalm 8: 4 says 'what is man that thou art mindful of him, or the son of man that thou visitest him'. 'Man' and 'son of man' are in parallel and clearly mean the same: 'son of man' thus means 'man in general'. Similarly when the prophet Ezekiel is addressed by God as 'son of man',[58] this means simply 'you who are a man' (in contrast to God). So too in the famous vision of Daniel 7: 13, where Daniel sees a figure which he describes as 'one like a son of man', he clearly means simply that this figure looks like a human being, in contrast to the other figures he has just seen which look like various kinds of beasts (a lion, a bear, a leopard).

Nevertheless, this passage in Daniel 7, and this verse in particular, evidently caught the imagination of a number of people subsequently, both Jewish and Christian, and the figure of 'one like a son of man' seems to have taken on a life of its own, so to speak. Thus, for example, in *1 Enoch* 46, Enoch sees a figure who is clearly described in terms of the description of the Ancient of Days of Daniel 7 and also another figure 'whose face was like that of a human being', a clear allusion to the figure of Daniel 7; and thereafter Enoch refers to this figure as 'the/that' 'son of man'. The figure clearly has a role to play in the final judgement and, in an extraordinary development at the end of this section of *1 Enoch*, Enoch is himself apparently identified with this figure (*1 En.* 71: 14). A similar development occurs in *4 Ezra*, especially chapter 13, where a man appears from the sea, playing an important role in the scenes of judgement described. The description of the figure is clearly heavily influenced by the description of the human figure in Daniel 7 (cf. the note that the man 'flew with the clouds of heaven' in v. 3). The man here is referred to as God's 'Son' (13: 32, 52) who is elsewhere identified as the Messiah (7: 28).

1 Enoch and *4 Ezra* are both probably to be dated after the time of the New Testament.[59] How much of this development lies behind the New Testament uses of the phrase is not clear. But even if the two books in question are to be dated later rather than earlier, they may still preserve earlier traditions. This evidence may then show the existence of a developing exegetical tradition whereby the figure of the vision of Daniel 7 was interpreted in individualistic terms as a figure who would play an active role in the final judgement.[60] Clearly such a background may well be important in interpreting a significant number of the Son of Man sayings in the Gospels, where the Son of Man figure has a similar role. However, these will be discussed when we consider the evidence of the Gospels themselves.

The idea of messiahship in Judaism should probably be seen as part of a more wide-ranging set of ideas. We have already seen that ideas of a Messiah figure are integrally related to Jewish eschatological beliefs. But such ideas are also part of a broader spectrum of beliefs concerning what may be termed ideas of 'divine agency'.[61] It was not only in relation to eschatological activity that Jews could conceive of an idea of God having some kind of agent alongside him to assist him in various aspects of his activity. Thus some Jews evidently conceived of a variety of figures as perhaps alongside God to assist him in various capacities. Not all these are necessarily relevant to the subject of New Testament Christology (though a number have significance in relation to other aspects of New Testament texts). However some of the language related to such ideas was taken up and applied to Jesus by early Christians. The 'figures' associated with ideas of divine agency can be divided into three groups: angels, exalted patriarchs, and attributes of God.

Angels

Language about angels (messengers) of God can be found in many of the writings of the Old Testament. Thus the narratives of the

Pentateuch frequently refer to angels as beings who act as mouthpieces for God (though it is often unclear how far the narrator really distinguished between God and the angel, since very often the one seems to slide into the other).[62] So too the text in Exodus 23: 20–1 ('I am going to send an angel in front of you, to guard you on the way and to bring you to the place that I have prepared. Be attentive to him and listen to his voice; do not rebel against him, for he will not pardon your transgressions; for my name is in him') became very influential in later speculations about angels (cf. for example *Apoc. Abr.* 10: 9).

It is clear that Judaism at the time of the New Testament was developing further a rich set of ideas about the existence of angelic, heavenly beings alongside God. For example, in the book of Daniel, probably the latest of the books of the Old Testament, named angels are mentioned (for example Michael and Gabriel: cf. Dan. 8: 16; 10: 13; 12: 1); in the book of Tobit (in the so-called Apocrypha) the angel Raphael has a leading role. And the intercessory role of angels, mediating prayers of beings to God, is found not infrequently (Tob. 12: 12; *Jub.* 30: 20; *T. Dan.* 6: 2; *T. Levi* 5: 6).

The reason for such a growth in speculation and talk about angels has been much debated. In the past it has sometimes been assumed that such speculation flowered at a time when God himself was thought to be ever more transcendent and remote from the affairs of the world and of human beings. This is, however, uncertain. Hurtado has shown that such an idea is hard, if not impossible, to document. For example, he cites *2 Bar.* 48: 1–24 as a case of a writer clearly believing in a huge retinue of angelic beings alongside God; yet God can still be addressed directly. So too in the book of Tobit, Raphael and other angels play key roles, and yet human beings can still address God directly, apparently without difficulty or embarrassment. Thus Hurtado suggests that growth in angelology may be rather to do with an attempt to show how great and powerful the God of Israel was: just as other gods were portrayed as reigning over a court, so too Israel's God could be seen in the same terms.[63] But in no sense was this thought of as reflecting God's alienation or remoteness from the world.

How far such ideas affected early Christians is a matter of considerable debate in contemporary study. The idea that Jesus was regarded as an angel has often been dismissed in the past very quickly, often with reference to passages such as Hebrews 1–2, where Jesus is clearly and explicitly distinguished from angels.

It is, however, now becoming clearer that the question may not be being posed in the most appropriate way if one simply asked whether Jesus was regarded as an angel.[64] Nevertheless there may well be features which are ascribed to Jesus which could be seen as characteristic of angels, even if Jesus himself is clearly distinguished from the angels. Thus aspects of Jesus could be seen as 'angelomorphic'. Above all, such features have been seen by many to be very prominent in the book of Revelation, as we shall see. Thus an 'angelomorphic' (as opposed to 'angelic') Christology may be an important, although often largely neglected, aspect of New Testament Christology.

Exalted patriarchs

The case of exalted patriarchs will not be discussed here in much detail. Several Jews evidently developed ideas about key figures of their sacred history so that such figures were thought of as present and at times active in heaven alongside God. At times the more obscure the figure concerned, the greater the scope for speculation. Thus the mysterious figure of Enoch gave rise to a vast amount of speculation. In the Old Testament, Enoch is of course famous as one of the very few figures who did not die. All we have is the cryptic note that 'Enoch walked with God, then he was no more, because God took him' (Gen. 5: 24 NRSV). However, this led to a huge flowering of Enoch literature where Enoch passes through the heavens and is shown many of the secrets of the heavens. Potentially important for New Testament Christology in particular is the way in which, in one section of *1 Enoch*, Enoch is shown the 'son of man' figure, a feature we have already touched on in considering the use of the term 'son of man'. In the much later text known as *3 Enoch*, speculation develops even further and Enoch is identified as 'Metatron', a powerful heavenly being with his own throne, and is now called 'the lesser YHWH' (*3 En*. 12).

Other figures given exalted roles include Abel who at one point is given the task of executing judgement (*Test. Abr*. 13). Speculation also surrounded the figure of Melchizedek, the mysterious king who appears from nowhere to meet Abraham in Genesis 14. However, in one of the Qumran scrolls (11QMelch) the figure of Melchizedek appears to have the role of administering divine judgement and is even called 'Elohim', God (11QMelch 2: 9–11 citing Ps. 82: 1–2). If the figure concerned is the same as the obscure figure mentioned in Genesis 14, then we have another case of a revered (human) figure of the past raised to heaven and given a key role alongside God.

So too the figures of Moses and Adam gave rise to speculation in Judaism. Certainly, as we shall see, the ideas associated with a figure like Moses or Adam became important for early Christians in their talk about Jesus, though usually such ideas served as the basis for comparisons (positive or negative) rather than any strict identity: Jesus was *like* (or unlike) Moses or Adam – he was not necessarily to be equated with either figure.

In general, the fact that such speculations concerned specific individuals meant that such ideas were unlikely to influence New Testament Christology directly: without a belief in some kind of reincarnation, one could scarcely *identify* Jesus with one of the figures of the past.[65] Nevertheless, the existence of the speculation is good testimony to the different 'agents' which Jews could conceive of as assisting God in a variety of ways and it helps to fill in some of the background whereby Christians could claim that Jesus too could be seen in some respects as filling the same role of a 'divine agent'.

Divine attributes

The precise interpretation of divine attributes as 'beings' alongside God is rather harder to assess in Jewish thinking. What is clear is that such language was used in ways that left open the possibility that a separate being was being thought as existing alongside God. Certainly too later Christians enthusiastically appropriated some of this language and these ideas and applied them to Jesus. This was the case in particular in relation to two such 'figures': the Wisdom and the Word of God

Wisdom

It is clear that language about God's Wisdom developed significantly towards the end of the Old Testament period and in the intertestamental period, and in this development, 'Wisdom' is sometimes talked of as if she were a person in her own right. One can see the start of such a process in a text like Job 28 but the earliest clear example is probably in Proverbs 1 and Proverbs 8. Thus in Proverbs 8: 22–31, Wisdom appears as God's companion alongside him at the creation of the world.[66] This is developed further in the Wisdom of Solomon where Wisdom is spoken of as 'the fashioner of all things' (7: 22), 'an initiate in the knowledge of God, and an associate in his works' (8: 4), one 'who sits by (God's) throne' (9: 4) and who has been active in the great events of Israel's sacred history (10: 1–12: 27). In further developments, Wisdom is identified with the Law. Already in Proverbs 1, Wisdom's call is linked to the Law of God and appeals to the commandments (Prov 1: 7, 29); and in Sirach 24, the equation between Wisdom and the Law is made explicit: 'all this is the book of the covenant of the Most High God, the Law which Moses commanded us as an inheritance for the congregation of Jacob' (Sir. 24: 23).

That such language, implying some kind of idea of Wisdom as a separate being alongside God, was to hand in Judaism is undeniable. What it was actually taken as meaning is another matter. Dunn and Hurtado have both pointed out that, however similar the language is to that used in other religious traditions, there is no evidence of Wisdom ever being associated with cultic activity. Nor was such language ever felt to compromise or threaten Jewish monotheistic belief.[67] Thus it may well be that the language was never felt to be anything other than a vivid expression of God's own wise action and ordering of the creation. The psalmist could quite happily pray to God 'send out your light and your truth; let them lead me; let them bring me to your holy hill and to your dwelling' (Ps. 43: 3) without ever thinking of God's 'light' or 'truth' as personal agents sent from God capable of independent existence and undertaking a role of guiding human beings to a specific place where God was supposed to dwell. So too then perhaps with Wisdom: language about Wisdom in Judaism may have been no more than an attempt to express vividly God's own activity, based on his 'wisdom' in creating and caring for the universe. Nevertheless, it seems clear that such language was open to an interpretation that what was said was being predicated of a person other than God, and certainly early Christians exploited some of this at times when talking about Jesus.

Word

Much the same is probably also the case in relation to language about the Word (Greek *logos*) of God. In the older biblical tradition there are passages where God's 'word' could be read as having some kind of independent existence, for example Ps. 33: 6: 'By the word of the Lord were the heavens made' (although this could simply be another way of saying 'God spoke and it was done'), or Isaiah 55: 11: 'So shall my word be that goes out from my mouth; it shall not return to me empty, but it shall accomplish that which I purpose and succeed in the thing for which I sent it'. (But again this is probably vivid pictorial language for God speaking, and speaking powerfully and authoritatively).

Talk about God's Word is developed significantly by Philo who uses this language in what is at times a bewildering variety of ways. And some of Philo's language is at times open to being interpreted in ways that suggest he thought of the Word as a separate being. He calls the Logos the 'first born', 'who holds the eldership among the angels, their ruler as it were' (*Conf.* 146), 'the interpreter and prophet of God' (*Immut.* 138). The 'God' in whose image Adam was made according to Genesis 1: 27 was the Logos, who is even called a 'second God' (*Quaest. Gen.* 2.62).

How far Philo's language, let alone his ideas, were shared by others is not certain. Yet even here it is unlikely that the language was ever used within Judaism as implying anything more than a vivid metaphor. As with Wisdom, there is no hint of any cultic activity associated with the Word.[68] Yet as with Wisdom, Jewish language about the Word did give the opening to Christians at times to exploit the language used when applied to Jesus.

We have surveyed a wide range of different terminology and ideas which were evidently current at the time of the start of the new Christian movement, and which early Christians at times took up and used to express their convictions about the person of Jesus. It is though perhaps worth reiterating what was said earlier about the differences in meaning which the same terminology can have when used in different contexts. We noted earlier the dangers of anachronism, of reading back meanings which terms acquired later in Christian history into an earlier period. But we noted also the opposite danger of assuming too much continuity with the past. Just as there is a danger of assuming too much continuity (or identity) between the New Testament and what came after, there is an equal danger of assuming too much continuity (or identity) between the New Testament and what came before. Having discovered something of the meanings of key words or phrases in 'the background' for early Christianity, we should not assume that these meanings were taken as read and simply transferred to Jesus (as opposed to someone else). We have already seen something of the fluidity inherent in some of these terms anyway. But there is a real sense in which, to a certain extent, the meaning of some of the terms when applied by Christians to Jesus is determined *by Jesus* quite as much as by the term itself. A claim that 'Jesus is the Messiah' may say something about what it means to be a 'Messiah' figure (as defined now by the Jesus event) as it does about Jesus (as if messiahship were well defined and the question is simply whether Jesus 'fits' a predetermined and well-defined 'bill'). In considering the use of christological terms by Christians, we must thus be alive not only to the meaning such terms may have had in the first century outside a Christian context, but also to the changes and adaptations which Christians made when applying them to Jesus. Historical study must acknowledge elements of both continuity and innovation and we must be sensitive to both. With this in mind, we now turn to the Christian texts themselves to see how some of this language was used, as well as changed and adapted, as Christians applied it to Jesus.

NOTES

1. I shall be considering most of the New Testament writers individually. Space precludes a fully comprehensive coverage and hence I omit here discussion of 1–2 Peter, James and Jude.
2. One of the standard works on the history of the development of the New Testament canon remains H. von Campenhausen, *The Formation of the Christian Bible* (London: A. & C. Black, 1972). The main outline of the present New Testament canon was agreed by the fourth century, though there were still debates about some details (for example the status of Revelation) in some churches much later than this.
3. Cf. D. H. Kelsey, *The Uses of Scripture in Recent Theology* (London: SCM Press, 1975).
4. See Robert Morgan, 'Expansion and criticism in Christian theology', in M. Pye and Robert Morgan (eds), *The Cardinal Meaning* (The Hague: Mouton, 1973), pp. 59–101.
5. Cf. J. Barr, *The Bible in the Modern World* (London: SCM Press, 1973), p. 117.
6. Information about the possible dating of New Testament documents can be found in most *Introductions* to the New Testament. A standard work remains that of W. G. Kümmel, *Introduction to the New Testament* (rev. edn, London: SCM Press, 1975).
7. Cf. above all the work of the 'Jesus Seminar' in America. The results of much of their work is summed up in R. W. Funk and R. Hoover, *The Five Gospels: The Search for the Authentic Words of Jesus* (New York, 1993),

analysing and attempting to assess the authenticity of many Jesus traditions. The 'five' gospels are the four canonical ones together with the *Gospel of Thomas* which is often regarded as preserving authentic Jesus materials. For a high evaluation of the *Gospel of Peter* (or at least of traditions preserved in the *Gospel of Peter*) in this respect, see J. D. Crossan, *The Cross that Spoke* (San Francisco: Harper and Row, 1988).

8. In relation to the *Gospel of Thomas*, see my 'Thomas and the synoptics', *NovT*, 30 (1988), pp. 132–57; also my 'The Gospel of Thomas: Evidence for Jesus?', *NTT* 52 (1998), pp. 17–32. There is an excellent survey of the issues in J. P Meier, *A Marginal Jew: Rethinking the Historical Jesus*, 1 (New York: Doubleday, 1991), pp. 112–66.

9. For a more general discussion of these and related issues, see Peter Cotterell and Max Turner, *Linguistics and Biblical Interpretation* (London: SPCK, 1989).

10. Cf. J. D. G. Dunn, *Unity and Diversity in the New Testament* (London: SCM Press, 1977).

11. At least this was the view of Christians: whether others agreed is another matter!

12. It is in fact at one level quite surprising how uncontroversial explicitly christological questions seem to be in the debates reflected in the New Testament: the question of the level of Torah observance required by Christians, or the relation between Christian commitment and membership of the Jewish community is often quite prominent; but the explicit question of the nature of Jesus' identity does not appear to surface quite so frequently as one might expect.

13. A. Grillmeier, *Christ in Christian Tradition* (London: Mowbrays, 1975) is one of the standard works. See too J. N. D. Kelly, *Early Christian Doctrines* (London: A. & C. Black, 1960), for a shorter survey of the historical developments.

14. Text from J. Stevenson (ed.), *Creeds, Councils and Controversies* (London: SPCK, 1972), p. 337.

15. Falling into this category might be James, perhaps Ephesians (assuming [as most do] that this 'letter' is not by Paul himself but written in his name by a later admirer) and some of the other so-called 'Catholic' epistles.

16. Cf. the work of so-called 'form criticism'. On this, cf. E. V. McKnight, *What Is Form Criticism?* (Philadelphia: Fortress Press, 1969); also my *Reading the New Testament* (London: SPCK, 1987), ch. 7.

17. See below, ch. 12.

18. The work of so-called 'redaction criticism'. Cf. N. Perrin, *What Is Redaction Criticism?* (London: SPCK, 1970); also my *Reading*, ch. 8.

19. See further ch. 9 below.

20. Cf., for example, the so-called 'formula quotations' in Matthew, where the narrator provides a comment to the effect that a particular event in the story 'fulfils' very precisely a text from Jewish scripture (for example the virgin birth 'fulfils' the 'prophecy' of Isa. 7: 14 according to Matt. 1: 23). In John 2: 21, the narrator explains that Jesus' prediction about 'raising up' a 'temple' (v. 19) should be interpreted in relation to 'the temple of his body'.

21. On these issues, see my *Luke* (Sheffield: Sheffield Academic Press, 1996), and see ch. 8 below.

22. See, for example, the treatments of O. Cullmann, *The Christology of the New Testament* (London: SCM Press, 1959); F. Hahn, *The Titles of Jesus in Christology* (London: Lutterworth, 1969).

23. See especially L. E. Keck, 'Toward the Renewal of New Testament Christology', *NTS*, 32 (1986), pp. 362–77, repr. in M. C. de Boer (ed.), *From Jesus to John* (FS M. de Jonge; JSNTSup 84; Sheffield: Sheffield Academic Press, 1993), pp. 321–40.

24. Cf. H. D. Buckwalter, *The Character and Purpose of Luke's Christology* (SNTSMS 89; Cambridge: CUP, 1996), pp. 201–4 and others cited there.

25. For all these facets of Paul's Christology, see ch. 2 below.

26. See especially L. Hurtado, *One God, One Lord: Early Christian Devotion and Ancient Jewish Monotheism* (Philadelphia: Fortress Press, 1988).

27. The process was long and complicated, with not all sides necessarily agreeing about the appropriateness of the split. Cf. J. D. G. Dunn, *The Partings of the Ways between Christianity and Judaism and their Significance for the Character of Christianity* (London: SCM Press, 1991).

28. The only Christian to try to do so was Marcion in the second century, and he was judged to be heretical.

29. Cf. W. Schrage, *The Ethics of the New Testament* (Edinburgh: T&T Clark, 1988).

30. Cf. M. de Jonge, 'Monotheism and Christology', in John Barclay and John Sweet (eds), *Early Christian Thought in its Jewish Context* (FS M. D. Hooker; Cambridge: CUP, 1996), pp. 225–37.

31. Cf. above on 1 Cor. 10: 1. The same idea is reflected in much of Paul's writings (cf., especially Rom. 11), as well as the ubiquitous claim in the New Testament that Jewish scriptures point forward to, and are 'fulfilled' by, the events surrounding the new Christian movement.

32. The latter is sometimes described as a more 'apocalyptic' viewpoint, though any distinction between the two types of vision or hope for the future is probably a little artificial.

33. Given the nature of Jewish belief in the uniqueness and power of God, such a view is so obvious that it is perhaps surprising that there was ever any alternative envisaged!

34. See the short survey in N. Perrin, *The Kingdom of God in the Teaching of Jesus* (London: SCM Press, 1963), pp. 164–7. A full survey of expectations concerning eschatological figures is provided by J. J. Collins, *The Scepter and the Star: The Messiahs of the Dead Sea Scrolls and Other Ancient Literature* (New York: Doubleday, 1995); also J. Neusner, W. S. Green and E. Frerichs (eds), *Judaisms and their Messiahs at the Turn of the Christian Era* (Cambridge: CUP, 1987).

35. So G. Vermes, *Jesus the Jew* (London: Collins, 1973), pp. 130–40; C. F. D. Moule, *The Origin of Christology* (Cambridge: CUP, 1977), p. 32.

36. This is the reading of all the MSS, though some suggest that the text should be amended to read 'the Lord's Messiah'.

37. Cf. E. Schürer, *The History of the Jewish People in the Age of Jesus Christ* (revised and edited by G. Vermes, F. Millar and M. Black; 3 vols; Edinburgh: T&T Clark, 1973–87), vol. 2. pp. 488–544; G. F. Moore, *Judaism in the First Centuries of the Christian Era* (2 vols; Cambridge, MA: Harvard University Press, 1971, original 1927).

38. Hence the trend by some even to talk about 'Judaisms' (plural) rather than 'Judaism' (singular): cf. the title of the book edited by Neusner et al., cited in n. 34 above.

39. Cf. J. H. Charlesworth, 'From Messianiology to Christology: Problems and Prospects', in J. H. Charlesworth (ed.), *The Messiah: Developments in Earliest Judaism and Christianity* (Minneapolis: Fortress Press, 1992), pp. 3–35; G. S. Oegema, *The Anointed and his People: Messianic Expectations from the Maccabees to Bar Cochba* (Sheffield: Sheffield Academic Press, 1998).

40. See Collins, *Scepter*, esp. chs 2, 3.

41. So Collins who has made probably the strongest and best argued case for such a view.

42. If two figures are not meant, it is hard to see why mention is made of both 'Aaron' and 'Israel'. See Collins, *Scepter*, pp. 74–7.

43. 1 Cor. 15: 3 is almost certainly a *pre*-Pauline formula quoted by Paul: hence the development, whereby the name 'Christ' had become so firmly attached to Jesus that it had displaced the name Jesus itself, had evidently already happened by the time of this pre-Pauline formula.

44. For such 'background' usages, see W. Foerster, *kyrios*, TDNT, 3.1050–8.

45. Above all this was the theory of W. Bousset, *Kyrios Christos: A History of the Belief in Christ from the Beginning of Christianity to Irenaeus* (ET New York: Abingdon Press, 1970; German orginal 1913).

46. See J. Ziesler, *Pauline Christianity* (Oxford: OUP, 2nd edn, 1990), pp. 37–8.

47. J. A. Fitzmyer, 'The semitic background of the New Testament *Kyrios*-title', in Fitzmyer, *A Wandering Aramean: Collected Aramaic Essays* (Chico: Scholars Press, 1979), pp. 115–42 (originally published in German in the Festschrift for H. Conzelmann).

48. Ibid., p. 122.
49. See the material in P. Wülfing von Martitz, *huios*, *TDNT*, 8.335–40.
50. Cf. M. Hengel, *The Son of God* (London: SCM Press, 1976), pp. 23–41.
51. See ch. 11 below on Revelation; perhaps too the Christology of the Fourth Gospel may be influenced by such ideas (ch. 9 below).
52. See in general Collins, *Scepter*, ch. 7.
53. Though the reading 'brings' has also been proposed: see the discussion in Collins, *Scepter*, pp. 164–5.
54. So Collins, *Scepter*, pp. 154–64. However, there is a gap in the manuscript between the initial description and the subsequent continuation and so it is not clear if the later part of the fragment refers to the same person as the one referred to at the start.
55. Ibid., p. 165, for problems of interpretation and whether the Latin/Syriac references to 'son' here might reflect a Greek *pais*, meaning 'servant'.
56. The extra *a* at the end is the definite article in Aramaic.
57. The strongest advocate of the view that 'son of man' means 'I' is G. Vermes who has argued the case strongly over many years (cf. for example his *Jesus the Jew*, pp. 160–91). However, there has been fierce debate about his claim in this respect and many have argued that the Aramaic phrase cannot be forced away from some kind of a generic usage: see for example P. Maurice Casey, *Son of Man* (London: SPCK, 1979); B. Lindars, *Jesus Son of Man: A Fresh Examination of the Son of Man Sayings in the Gospels* (London: SPCK, 1983).
58. E.g. Ezek. 2:1 and several other instances.
59. *4 Ezra* is certainly to be dated after the fall of Jerusalem in 70 CE. *1 Enoch* is much harder to date, and the final version of the book may well be relatively late. At the same time, it may well preserve earlier traditions.
60. See Collins, *Scepter*, ch. 8, a reworking of his earlier 'The Son of Man in First Century Judaism', *NTS* 38 (1992), pp. 448–62.
61. On this, see especially Hurtado, *One God, One Lord*, ch. 1.
62. Cf. Gen. 16, where Hagar encounters an 'angel of the Lord' (v. 7) who speaks to her; and yet by v. 13 it is assumed that it is God himself who has been speaking all the time.
63. Hurtado, *One God, One Lord*, pp. 26–7.
64. In any case it is clear that Jesus was regarded in this way by a number of Christians in the period after the New Testament. See Justin, *1 Apol.* 63; Origen, *Comm. Joh.* 1.217–19, 277; the Ebionites according to Epiphanius, *Pan.* 30.16.3–4; *Ep. Apost.* 14, and the discussion in P. R. Carrell, *Jesus and the Angels: Angelology and the Christology of the Apocalypse of John* (SNTSMS 95; Cambridge: CUP, 1997), ch. 5; also C. A. Gieschen, *Angelomorphic Christology: Antecedents and Early Evidence* (Leiden: Brill, 1998), chs 7–10.

65. Although, as we have already noted earlier, some Jews apparently expected the return of a past figure such as Elijah (cf. Mal. 3: 1; Sir. 48: 10). Such an expectation may lie behind the speculations that Jesus might be Elijah, as articulated in Mark 6: 15; 8: 28.
66. In part the use of such language may be intended as an attempt to counter rival claims associated with the Isis cult in Egypt.
67. Hurtado, *One God, One Lord*, 42–8; J. D. G. Dunn, *Christology in the Making* (Grand Rapids: Eerdmans, ²1996) 168–76.
68. Hurtado, ibid.; Dunn, *Christology*, 215–30.

Part 1

NEW TESTAMENT EPISTLES

Chapter 2

PAUL

In any discussion of early Christian responses to Jesus, the figure of Paul will always occupy a key position. For Paul is the earliest Christian writer to whom we have any direct access. In terms of literary activity, he was extremely prolific, writing letters to various communities; he was also highly influential, at one level at least, in that his letter-writing activity was imitated by others who wrote letters in his name after his lifetime. Thus in order to discover Paul's own views, we have to discount the evidence of these later, so-called deutero-Pauline, letters. It is widely held that seven of the letters attributed to Paul are genuine letters by Paul himself: these comprise Romans, 1 and 2 Corinthians, Galatians, Philippians, 1 Thessalonians and Philemon. The other letters in the New Testament attributed to Paul are, with varying degrees of certainty, regarded by many as deutero-Pauline. These include Colossians, Ephesians, 2 Thessalonians and the so-called Pastoral Epistles (1 and 2 Timothy and Titus).[1] For the present purposes, I shall stick to the universally accepted Pauline letters as the sole evidence for Paul himself.

Paul is very often regarded as a theological 'giant' in the early Christian church, whose intellectual activity raised him above all his contemporaries. At one level, this might have an element of truth in it in that Paul's ideas may not have been shared by many other people at the time. But equally, we should not necessarily assume that Paul influenced many other people very significantly, at least during his lifetime. Despite the support he engendered (as evidenced in the existence of the deutero-Pauline corpus), it is clear that Paul was at times engaged in bitter disputes with other Christians in the communities with which he was involved. Indeed it is precisely those disputes for the most part which generated his letters.

On the other hand, Paul was not a completely isolated individual. As already noted, Paul is the earliest Christian writer whose writings have survived. But even his letters probably date from the early 50s (or thereabouts), i.e. a good twenty years or so after the death of Jesus. Clearly Paul had predecessors within the Christian church, and the ideas and thoughts of such predecessors at times have evidently affected Paul's own thinking and writing. Thus Paul was at times influenced by the ideas of earlier traditions. In particular, in relation to Christology, there are almost certainly occasions when Paul takes up and uses earlier traditional statements about Jesus. These include what may be an early credal statement about Jesus in Romans 1: 3–4, the statement about the expectation of Jesus coming from heaven in 1 Thessalonians 1: 9–10, and the so-called 'hymn' of Philippians 2: 6–11. The pre-Pauline nature of these traditions is shown by their slightly unusual (for Paul) vocabulary or ideas as well as their separability from their contexts.

At the same time, we cannot build too much on the basis of these pre-Pauline traditions. They are all isolated units and so we cannot know how each one fitted into any broader set of traditions or ideas held by a single individual or community. Further, all these traditions now found in Paul's letters must have been taken up and used by Paul himself. This on its own indicates a considerable level of agreement between Paul and his tradition. The very fact that he has chosen to use such traditions must indicate that he agreed with the ideas expressed in them enough to reproduce them in his own writings. Thus in the present context, I shall not try to undertake any detailed examination of pre-Pauline Christianity in and of itself, or try to drive too much of a wedge between Paul and any pre-Pauline developments; rather I shall use this material simply as part of the evidence available for Paul himself.[2]

In trying to assess the significance of the person of Jesus for someone like Paul, it is probably somewhat artificial to isolate this from what Paul regards as having been achieved by Jesus' life and death. In terms of technical theological jargon, we cannot easily separate Christology from soteriology. However, reasons of space mean that I have to leave on one side here discussion of what Paul believed Jesus' life and death might have achieved (that is, atonement or soteriology); but we should remember that, for a figure like Paul, Christology may depend on soteriology quite as much as vice versa.

We should also note here that, perhaps surprisingly, neither the issue of Christology nor that of soteriology seem to have been very contentious issues in Paul's churches. Paul probably wrote all his letters to specific churches to deal with specific problems that had arisen.[3] Yet it is striking that rarely if ever was the specific problem of Christology an issue of dispute which he had to address directly.[4] In Romans or Galatians, the issue of the relationship between the Christian movement and the Jewish religion and specific problems within that broad issue (for example should male Christians be circumcised) were the focus of attention. In 1 Corinthians, a variety of ethical issues is addressed, discussing how Christians should relate to each other within the community, and how they should relate to the outside world. In 1 Thessalonians, the main issue is eschatology. And in all these discussions, aspects of Christology and soteriology are brought into Paul's arguments. But these issues are not the prime focus of the debate for the most part. Thus much of what Paul evidently believes about Jesus has to be deduced, at times slightly indirectly.

Nevertheless, it is also verging on a truism to say that, for Paul, the person of Jesus is absolutely central to his life as a Christian. In this Paul is no different from almost every other Christian. As we have already seen in chapter 1, the person of Jesus is of central importance for all Christians: a Christianity without Jesus would be a self-contradiction. Yet how much did Paul know about Jesus?

Such a question is by no means a trivial one. For Paul, the significant events concerning Jesus are supremely the crucifixion and resurrection of Jesus, together with his present status, and the expectation of what Paul believed would come in the future. Paul rarely indicates explicitly that he knows anything about Jesus' life prior to the cross. On a very few occasions he cites Jesus' teaching: in 1 Corinthians 7: 10 he quotes Jesus' teaching on divorce (cf. Mark 10: 11–12 and parallels); in 1 Corinthians 9: 14 he refers to Jesus' teaching that 'those who preach the gospel should live by the gospel' (a rough parallel to the Gospel saying in Matt. 10: 10/Luke 10: 7); in 1 Corinthians 11: 23–5 he reports his tradition of Jesus' sayings over the bread and the cup at the Last Supper (cf. Mark 14: 22–4 and parallels); and in 1 Thessalonians 4: 15 he *may* be citing a saying of Jesus about the future eschatological events.[5]

On other occasions Paul may be echoing, or intending to echo, the teaching of Jesus, but he never explicitly says that he is doing this, and hence it is not clear what he knew in this respect and/or what his readers would have picked up. The closest that he gets to an explicit citation is perhaps Romans 14: 14, where he says 'I am persuaded in the Lord Jesus that nothing is unclean in itself'. This is close in substance to Mark 7: 15; but Paul does not say 'as the Lord said' (as in 1 Cor. 7: 10) and it is not certain if being 'persuaded *in* the Lord Jesus' is intended to be a reference to teaching explicitly given by Jesus during his earthly life. Elsewhere Paul gives a number of (mostly ethical) statements which clearly can be paralleled in sayings attributed to Jesus in the Gospels. Thus for example, 'Bless those who persecute you, bless and do not curse them' (Rom. 12: 14) is close to Jesus' sayings on love of enemies in Matthew 5: 44; 'Do not repay anyone evil for evil' (Rom. 12: 17) is similar to Jesus' saying on non-retaliation in Matthew 5: 39–42; 'pay to all what is due to them – taxes to whom taxes are due, revenue to whom revenue is due, respect to whom respect is due, honour to whom honour is due' (Rom. 13: 7) is close (but not identical) to the teaching of Jesus in Mark 12: 13–17; the command to love one's neighbour as the true summary of the Old Testament Law (Rom. 13: 8–10) is paralleled in the Gospels by Jesus' teaching in Mark 12: 28–34. Yet in all this Paul never explicitly says that he is intending to cite Jesus; nor does he appeal to Jesus' name to give added authority to bolster the instruction concerned. Similarly it is not clear if he expected his readers to pick up these as allusions to Jesus tradition.

Very diverse answers have been given to the problems raised here. Some have argued that Paul could take it as read that his readers would instantly recognise such teachings as those of Jesus and he did not need to spell it out for them every time.[6] However, others have argued that Paul was not intending to quote Jesus at all on these occasions (after all he is never shy about making it clear when he quotes the Old Testament); indeed it may be that some of these sayings were not attributed to Jesus by the time of Paul: rather, they became standard commonplaces in Christian ethical teaching and may then have been subsequently written into the Jesus tradition in the later Gospels.[7]

For myself, I find it odd that Paul should have left so much only implicit if he had really intended to refer to the teaching and authority of Jesus, and if he expected his readers to pick up such references for themselves. Whether the parallels between these Pauline verses and sayings in the Gospels are due to later Christians reading back such statements into the Gospel tradition is not so certain. Perhaps we should think of a pool of ethical traditions on which Paul and Jesus may have drawn. Paul and Jesus were certainly not the only people in the first-century world to encourage non-retaliation and the payment of legal taxes (without ever defining what 'legal' might mean!)

Nevertheless, even on an extreme minimalist view of the extent of Paul's knowledge of Jesus, it is clear that Paul knows some things about Jesus. He knows at least some of Jesus' teaching (cf. above); he knows too that Jesus was born of a human mother ('born of a woman' Gal. 4: 4), and that he was a Jew ('born under the law' Gal. 4: 4). Arguably too he knows of the tradition that Jesus' habit was to address God as Abba, Father: in Gal. 4: 6 (cf. Rom. 8: 15) it is the 'Spirit of his (God's) Son' which God has given to Christians as well, enabling them to address God in the same cry of Abba.

Further, there is a persistent theme running through Paul's letters of the importance of the person of Jesus as an ethical example for the Christian to follow. At least part of the aim of citing the Philippian hymn in Philippians 2: 6–11 seems to be to set up Jesus' person and 'career' as exemplifying the life of humility which the Philippians are to adopt.[8] In 1 Thessalonians 1: 6 Paul extols the Thessalonians for becoming 'imitators of us and of the Lord' in enduring persecution with joy. In 1 Corinthians 11: 1 Paul rounds off his teaching on the question of eating food sacrificed to idols in chapters 8–10 by referring again to himself as an example for the Corinthians to follow. In chapter 9 he has given an extended treatment of himself as an example of one who is prepared to give up his rights for the sake of others, as part of his exhortation to the 'strong' Corinthians to give up their right to eat whatever they like. But now in the concluding verse, the theme of imitation is extended: 'be imitators of me *as I am of Christ'*: he himself is an example to follow precisely in so far as he is an imitator of Jesus himself. Similarly in Philippians 3: 17 he exhorts the Philippians to 'join in imitating' him. The force of the Greek word (*symmimetai*) probably implies being imitators *with* him, that is of Christ. Thus, however, infrequently Paul may actually quote Jesus' teaching, it would seem that Jesus' person is of vital importance as a role model in Paul's ethical teaching.

Nevertheless, one cannot deny that, for Paul generally, the crucial significance of Jesus lies in his cross and resurrection. What then does

Paul think of Jesus? I start with some of the standard christological
titles used by Paul.

Christ

The term *christos* is the most frequent 'title' applied to Jesus by Paul. In
the unquestionably genuine Pauline letters it occurs some 270 times
(as opposed to about 184 uses of *kyrios* (Lord) and only 15 uses of 'Son
of God').[9] Yet in many ways its usage in Paul is very remarkable. As we
have seen in the introductory chapter, the term Messiah is essentially
a title referring to a figure of Jewish eschatological expectation. Moreover,
this figure was thought of as a royal figure, a priestly figure or a
prophetic figure, with the royal idea probably the dominant one.

What is striking in Paul is that virtually all of this background seems
to have disappeared. Thus N. Dahl says:

> In order to understand the sense of the apostle's statements, it is
> not necessary for Paul's readers to know that *Christos* is a term
> pregnant with meaning. Even if one understands 'Christ' only to
> be a surname of Jesus, all the statements of the epistles made
> good sense.[10]

Thus within a (relatively) very short period of time, the term *christos*
seems to have become so firmly attached to Jesus that it has lost almost
all of its original significance and become virtually just another proper
name. Indeed this probably happened prior to Paul himself: in what is
almost certainly a pre-Pauline formulation in 1 Corinthians 15: 3, Paul
quotes an earlier statement of faith about the significance of Jesus'
death in the form 'Christ died for our sins . . .' 'Christ' here has no definite article (and hence does not appear to be a title), and it has even
displaced 'Jesus' as the only name used. Further, unlike the Paul of
Acts, Paul in his letters never uses 'Christ' as a predicate of Jesus: he
never says, or indeed attempts to justify, that 'Jesus is the Christ'.[11]

On the other hand, it is arguable that Paul never loses sight of the
more original titular use of the term. Such usage is not clearly explicit
very often in Paul but Romans 9: 5 ('from them [= Israel] . . . comes the
Messiah') is at least one clear example, and there are others where Paul
uses the definite article ('*the* Christ'), perhaps indicating his awareness
of the titular usage,[12] though this is by no means necessary as a
conclusion.[13]

So too, there are some indications that Paul is aware that, although 'Christ' is verging on being just another name like 'Jesus', the two are not quite comparable. Thus 'Jesus Christ' and 'Christ Jesus' interchange freely, and with no clear indication of any clear preference for one order rather than the other in any particular context. Hence it is not the case that 'Christ' has become the cognomen, so to speak, of Jesus. So too, 'Christ' is never the subject of a sentence with another christological term as predicate. Thus, as Dahl points out, Paul can claim 'Jesus is Lord' (Rom. 10: 9; 1 Cor. 12: 3) or 'Jesus Christ is Lord' (Phil. 2: 11), but never 'Christ is Lord'.[14] Thus Paul does seem to show an implicit awareness that the term Christ is qualitatively different from the name Jesus.

Are there then any characteristic features of Paul's use of the term Christ for Jesus? Does the term evoke specific ideas? Is it used in specific contexts? Given the enormous number of times the term is used by Paul, it is not surprising that it occurs in a wide range of contexts. Moreover, it may be that at times the term has been so firmly attached to Jesus by Paul that little significance in its usage is to be attached to it: if X is predicated of Jesus, and Jesus is the 'Christ', then X can be said of 'Jesus Christ' without any necessary link between X and messiahship. Nevertheless, there are a number of striking constant features in Paul's language about Jesus as the Christ.

One striking group of texts in Paul relates Jesus' identity as the Christ to his death on the cross. Thus Paul talks very regularly of 'Christ crucified' (1 Cor. 1: 23; 2: 2; Gal. 3: 1) or the 'cross of Christ' (1 Cor. 1: 17; Phil. 3: 18). He never talks about the 'crucified Lord' or 'the Lord who was crucified'. The exact link between crucifixion and messiahship is not certain, and Paul certainly never spells it out. At one level such a link would have been absurd to first-century Jews: a Messiah figure, especially a royal Messiah, would be one who would succeed in re-establishing the political fortunes of Israel and establishing himself as the new political ruler as king. That such a figure should have been a failure in political terms, ending up by being executed by the Roman authorities on a Roman cross, would have been the height of absurdity: and indeed perhaps the very fact of the cross could or should have thrown into question any claims of messiahship. Any such claims about a 'crucified Messiah' would then have been an absurd paradox at best, a total self-contradiction at worst.

Nevertheless, it may be that it is just that contradiction or paradox that underlies Paul's language. It is one of the most certain facts about

Jesus' death that he was crucified on the charge of being a messianic pretender (cf. the titulus over the cross). It may have been the claims to have seen Jesus alive after his death that convinced the early Christians that perhaps this charge was in fact profound truth: Jesus was indeed the Messiah.[15] If so then the link between messiahship and the cross, so prominent in Paul, may be a reflection of this primitive belief that the 'charge' on which Jesus was crucified was in fact not a bitter joke or a mocking taunt but reflected God's own positive verdict on who Jesus was.

However, one must also note that such a claim about the messiahship of Jesus must have led to a radical reorientation of what messiahship meant. If *Jesus* was a Messiah figure, then messiahship was no longer to be associated with political kingship and power, but with power-lessness, weakness and death. Perhaps one could refer to the divine power and triumph evident in the resurrection of Jesus; but still the focus on Jesus' cross must have meant a radical reversal of virtually all previous ideas associated with messiahship. And this is probably what is reflected in Paul's admission that the message of 'Christ crucified' is a 'stumbling block for Jews' (1 Cor. 1: 23). Such a claim thus overturns all previous ideas of what a messianic figure might be and fills it with content supplied by the events of Jesus' life and death.

It may be that it is the same idea which is related to the highly distinctive Pauline terminology referring to Christians being 'in Christ'. At times Paul seems to assume that the person of Jesus is some kind of macro-entity, enveloping and encompassing all Christians so that they are 'in' him (cf. Rom. 6: 1–11; 8: 1, etc.). The origin of the idea has been much debated, and we shall consider it further below. However, it may be worth noting here that it is very characteristic of Paul to use the term 'Christ' in such contexts: Christians are 'in *Christ*'.[16] A characteristic context in which the phrase is used relates to the way in which Paul claims that Christians have somehow been joined to the death of Jesus. Thus in Romans 6: 1–11, he claims that by being baptised 'into Christ', Christians have shared in a very real way with Jesus' death: and since this is a 'death to sin', he can claim that all baptised Christians have also 'died to sin' and hence can no longer carry on sinning ('so that grace may abound': cf. 6: 1). So too in Romans 8: 1, there is no con-demnation for those who are 'in Christ Jesus', since Christ has through his death enabled Christians to be set free from the condemnation which would otherwise apply. The details are obscure; but it seems to be the case that being 'in Christ' is clearly connected with sharing in the benefits brought about by Jesus' death on the cross. Thus messiahship and the cross seem to belong inextricably together for Paul.

Son of God

A similar link can be seen between the cross and the idea of Jesus as 'Son of God' in Paul.

We have seen in chapter 1 that the term Son of God was one with a very wide range of meaning in the ancient world, and with no necessary overtones of ideas of divinity. One of the uses of the phrase in Judaism may have been to refer to a Messiah figure, as we have seen. However, Paul gives little indication that he sees a direct link between Jesus' status as a messianic figure and his being Son of God.

Compared with the large number of occurrences of 'Christ' or 'Lord', 'Son of God' occurs relatively infrequently: there are only fifteen occurrences of the term in Paul's letters (cf. above). Nevertheless, this should probably not be seen as a reflection of the relative importance, or lack of importance, of the term for Paul. However, the use of the term in Paul's writings is slightly complicated by the fact that the phrase seems to have been current in the pre-Pauline tradition as well, and Paul's use of the term may represent a slight modification of this pre-Pauline usage.

One example of such pre-Pauline usage may come in 1 Thessalonians 1: 10, which is widely regarded as a pre-Pauline mini-credal summary. Here Paul (or a predecessor) exhorts his readers 'to wait for his Son from heaven, whom he raised from the dead – Jesus, who rescues us from the wrath that is coming'. Jesus *qua* Son seems to be primarily the one who is to come at the parousia. Such a forward-looking reference is, however, not characteristic of other Pauline references to Jesus as Son. 1 Corinthians 15: 28 also looks forward to the End-time and refers to Jesus as Son; but there the 'activity' of Jesus *qua* Son is not to be coming in any salvific role, but finally and definitively submitting himself to the power and authority of God. As we shall see, the idea of submission is far more in line with Paul's other references to Jesus as Son.

Another example of a pre-Pauline usage is probably Romans 1: 3–4, where Paul speaks of 'the gospel concerning his Son, who was descended from David according to the flesh, and was declared to be

Son of God with power according to the spirit of holiness by resurrection from the dead, Jesus Christ our Lord'. Again it is widely agreed that Paul is citing an earlier credal statement here, perhaps to demonstrate his solidarity with the Roman Christian community which he has never visited. Further, it is also widely agreed that Paul may have added to the earlier tradition by glossing it at one or two points. Paul's claim that his gospel was 'concerning his Son', and the assertion that Jesus was declared to be Son of God 'with power' at/by the resurrection may well be Paul's own additions.[17] Both have the effect of making it clear that Jesus can be regarded as Son of God throughout the time period covered by the statement: the whole Gospel is about Jesus *qua* Son; and if Jesus is Son of God *in power* as a result of the resurrection, this leaves open the idea that he was Son of God (perhaps in another mode, for example in weakness) prior to the resurrection.

The pre-Pauline statement may be rather more ambiguous about Jesus' status as Son. Much hinges on the precise meaning of the verb translated as 'declared to be' in the NRSV (Greek *horisthentos*). Does this imply that Jesus was installed into a position or status that he did not have before? Or does it simply imply that Jesus was confirmed in a status which he had had all the time? The most natural interpretation is probably the former, and in any case, the two-fold structure of the statement as a whole suggests some kind of contrast between the two halves.[18]

The pre-Pauline tradition thus seems to have been claiming that Jesus was installed, or made, 'Son of God' at some point. Moreover, the 'point' in time seems to have been the resurrection (cf. the phrase 'by the resurrection from the dead', though the precise force of the preposition translated here as 'by' [Greek *ex*] is not entirely clear.) If so, then it would cohere with one or two other pieces of evidence from the New Testament, suggesting that Jesus' divine sonship was dependent on, and dated from, his resurrection. For example, Acts 13: 33 has 'Paul' citing Psalm 2: 7 ('you are my son, today I have begotten you'), apparently interpreting it as being fulfilled in Jesus' resurrection. Thus it may be that a very primitive Christian view was that Jesus' divine sonship dated from his resurrection and not necessarily from before that. Paul's adaptation of the tradition then serves to modify this idea, claiming that Jesus is God's Son for the whole of his life.

More characteristic of Paul are the passages where Paul asserts a close connection between Jesus as God's Son and the saving event of the cross.[19] This is perhaps already adumbrated in Romans 1: 3 where Paul talks of 'the gospel concerning his Son' (cf. too Rom. 1: 9), since for Paul the 'gospel' is integrally related to Jesus' death on the cross. Thus in Romans 5: 10, Paul claims that 'we were reconciled to God through the death of his Son'; in Galatians 2: 20 he refers to 'the Son of God, who loved me and gave himself for me' (that is in his death on the cross); and in Romans 8: 32 in more strictly theological terms, he speaks of God 'who did not withhold his own Son, but gave him up for all of us'. A slightly wider perspective on the meaning and purpose of Jesus' death is given by Paul just before this in Romans 8: 29: 'For those whom he foreknew he also predestined to be conformed to the image of his Son, in order that he might be the firstborn within a large family.' Jesus' sonship is then also a status or a position which is to be *shared* with others. In this Paul's 'Son' Christology is closely related to what he says about the relationship between Jesus and Adam, as we shall see.

In the debates over the meaning and significance of Paul's references to Jesus as Son of God, much discussion has taken place about two verses where Paul talks about God 'sending his Son' (Gal. 4: 4; Rom. 8: 3). Is this intended to imply that Jesus is thought of as some kind of pre-existent, quasi-divine being, existing in heaven before being sent by God to earth? We must, however, be wary of the dangers of anachronism and of reading statements in the New Testament through the lenses of later Chalcedonian Christian orthodoxy. In fact the language of 'sending' on its own need not necessarily imply that the person sent existed prior to the sending concerned.[20] Thus, in the Old Testament, God is spoken of as having sent a number of human beings, notably prophets, without any ideas of the latter's pre-existence.[21] It is possible that there is some parallel to be drawn between Paul's language in Galatians 4 and Romans 8 and language about the figure of Wisdom: see especially Wisdom 9: 10 ('Send her [Wisdom] forth from the holy heavens, and from the throne of her glory send her'), and Wisdom 9: 17 ('Who has learned your counsel, unless you have given wisdom and sent your holy spirit from on high?'). Here, as in Galatians 4, this sending is linked with the Holy Spirit (cf. Gal. 4: 6: God has sent 'the Spirit of his Son'). And indeed, as we shall see, some kind of link between Wisdom and Jesus is an important facet of Paul's Christology. Nevertheless, it is not so clear that Paul links Wisdom ideas specifically with his Son Christology.[22] In any case it is notable that, in the immediate context of both verses, Paul seems to go out of his way to stress the full identification of Jesus with the human condition: Jesus is 'born of a woman, born under the law' (Gal. 4: 4), and 'in the likeness of sinful flesh' (Rom. 8: 3).[23] The stress is thus on the humanness of Jesus rather than on any idea of him as a pre-existent divine being.

Much more important perhaps is the idea already alluded to briefly in passing in relation to Romans 8: 29: the aim of the 'giving up' of the Son is to enable others to share in the same status of being sons of God.[24] This comes out too in Galatians 4: God has sent his Son so that 'we might receive adoption as sons' (RSV): we are to become as he is. So, too, we have received 'the Spirit of his Son' enabling us to cry Abba, Father (Gal. 4: 6; cf. Rom. 8: 15): by the gift of the Spirit, Christians are in the same relationship to God as Jesus himself in that Christians can address God as their Father in the same words as Jesus did. We have here reflected a fundamental aspect of Paul's soteriology (which is connected inextricably with his Christology): the purpose of God sending his Son was to make others to be like him. Rather than any kind of substitution, or standing-in-the-place-of, Jesus in his death and resurrection somehow becomes the means, the source and origin, whereby a new humanity is created. Rather than Jesus taking the place of others, Jesus is the representative of others in the process of what Morna Hooker has called 'interchange in Christ': 'he became what we are so that we might become what he is'.[25] This suggests that Paul's Son Christology is very closely related to his Adam Christology, to which we now turn.

Adam

In two extended passages Paul explicitly compares Jesus with the figure of Adam (Rom. 5: 12–21; 1 Cor. 15: 21–49). There are too a number of other passages in Paul where many have plausibly seen allusions to the story of Adam in Genesis: see Romans 1: 18–25; 3: 23; 7: 7–11; 8: 19–22, though these are more to do with analyses of the present situation of human beings rather than being explicitly christological.[26] But in Romans 5 and 1 Corinthians 15 Paul makes an explicit comparison between Adam and Christ.

It is not clear what word one should use to describe the precise nature of the comparison. Perhaps it would be best to call it 'typology'.

Certainly it is a comparison that is drawn, not an identity being asserted. Christ is clearly different from the first Adam; and yet there is sufficient similarity between the two figures to make the dissimilarity both meaningful and relevant.

In some ways the passage in Romans 5 is easiest to understand (though many of the details in the section are extremely obscure). Paul is still using (at least in part) the forensic language, that is the language of the law courts (the forum) and ideas of sins committed, guilt and punishment, innocence and reward, which has characterised his argument in Romans up to this point. His claim in Romans 5 is that Adam and Jesus were in similar, if not identical, positions, at least to start with. Both had the potentiality for choosing to obey, or to disobey, God. At this point, however, the paths of the two figures diverge. For whereas Adam was disobedient, Christ was obedient. The results of these two different attitudes and actions were then also correspondingly different. Paul takes up the notion (which can be paralleled in Judaism) that Adam's sinfulness was the origin of death coming in as a punishment for sin (v. 12) to claim that, as a result of Adam's sin, death became a universal phenomenon.[27] It is, however, unlikely that Paul thinks of an 'original sin' as in some later Christian theology, as if people after Adam are somehow guilty of Adam's sin even though they themselves have not sinned. Romans 5: 12 should probably be translated as in the NRSV 'death spread to all *because* all have sinned'. Adam is thus a representative figure, representing the history and experience of the whole human race. Yet then, in a series of contrasts, Paul sets out the claim that Christ's action of obedience, being the opposite of Adam's disobedience, leads to the opposite of what Adam's actions have resulted in: Adam's action led to condemnation, Christ's to justification and acquittal (v. 16); Adam's act led to death reigning, Christ's to Christians reigning in life (v. 17). The metaphors and images change with bewildering speed in this passage but the general model seems clear: the disastrous consequences of sin, condemnation, death and alienation from God resulting from Adam's sin have been reversed by the consequences of Christ's life of obedience which leads to justification, acquittal and life.

The positive, forward-looking side of this comparison and contrast is then developed further by Paul in 1 Corinthians 15: 'as in Adam all die, so in Christ shall all be alive' (v. 22), a claim which Paul proceeds to elaborate further in the rest of 1 Corinthians 15. But now it is clear that, somehow or other, Christ is more than just an isolated single human being. He is the source and origin of a new humanity, so that all who are 'in him' can share in the new life which is his by virtue of his resurrection. His resurrection is the 'first fruits' of the general resurrection that is to come in the future for all (or at least for all Christians: cf. v. 20). And Christ himself is the source of the new life by being the 'life-giving spirit' (v. 45) which enables human beings to obtain the 'spiritual' body which is necessary to enjoy the resurrection life.

We can note at this point the close affinity between the idea of Jesus as the new Adam and Jesus as the Son in that both relate directly to the new potentiality for human beings. But if it is right to correlate the two ideas, then we may perhaps legitimately read some of the ideas associated with Paul's Adam typology into his Son Christology. For Paul, Jesus and Adam are different precisely because of Jesus' obedience in contrast to Adam's disobedience (cf. Rom. 5: 20). Hence for Paul it is supremely as one who is obedient that Jesus is the Son of God. This would tie up closely with 1 Corinthians 15: 28 where the ultimate goal of the Son is to submit in total obedience to the Father.

It may also be appropriate to consider the so-called Philippian 'hymn' (Phil. 2: 6–11) at this point.[28] By almost universal consent, this 'hymn' is pre-Pauline in that it was not originally composed by Paul; the one phrase often suspected as being a Pauline addition, or gloss, to the hymn is the phrase 'even death on the cross' in verse 8. The hymn has often been interpreted as presenting an extremely 'high' Christology, with its claim about Jesus as being 'in the form of God' (v. 6), perhaps too implying that 'equality with God' was a status which he had at one stage and then voluntarily surrendered by 'emptying himself'. This interpretation would thus see Jesus as a fully divine pre-existent being alongside God in heaven prior to his earthly existence.

Such an interpretation has, however, been radically questioned in recent years, notably by J. D. G. Dunn, who has pointed to the close parallel between what is said of Jesus in the first half of the hymn and what is said of Adam in the story of Genesis 1–3.[29] Thus the assertion that Jesus was in the 'form' (Greek *morphē*) of God may be paralleled by the statement that Adam was made in the image (Greek LXX *eikon*) of God (Gen 1: 26).[30] Jesus is then said to have not regarded equality with God to be a *harpagmos* (NRSV 'something to be exploited'). There is a long-standing debate over the exact meaning of the Greek word *harpagmos* here: does it imply here that equality with God was actually enjoyed by Jesus, but not used or clung on to, but surrendered? Or was equality with God something which Jesus did not have and which he refused to try to grasp for himself? The debate about the precise nuance of the Greek word is very fierce, but the issue may not be resolvable on strictly semantic or lexical grounds. The second of the two options above is linguistically possible and again the Adam story may lie in the background: in Genesis 3, Adam is told not to eat the fruit of the tree in the garden, but the serpent tempts Adam by saying that if he does eat 'you will be like God' (Gen. 3: 5). Adam of course does eat in the story of Genesis 3. Thus Jesus' action here in refusing to succumb to the same temptation may show him, as in Romans 5, being in a similar situation to Adam but choosing a different path of obedience rather than disobedience. So too the phrase 'he emptied himself' need not necessarily mean that Jesus somehow divested himself of his divinity (as in later 'kenotic' Christology – in any case such an idea presents formidable problems as soon as one asks for any more precision about what divine attributes Jesus might have given up). The verb can easily have a more general ('metaphorical') sense, meaning that Jesus 'abased' himself.[31] With this general background, it may therefore be that what is being said of Jesus in verses 6–8 is that he is the true Adam in the sense that he lives out the form of existence which Adam was meant to, but failed to do. Where Adam was disobedient, Christ was obedient, that is exactly the same pattern as developed by Paul in Romans 5.

In support of this relatively 'low' view of Jesus as presented in Philippians 2: 6–8 (to use what is probably inappropriate and anachronistic language!), one could also refer to the second half of the hymn. Here it is said that God has 'highly exalted (Greek *hyperupsosen*) him and given him the name that is above every name' (v. 9). The more precise implication of what is said here will be considered shortly. But the force of the Greek verb translated here as 'highly exalted', if taken strictly, implies an exaltation to a position *higher* than Jesus had previously. If verses 6–7 were intended to mean that Jesus was a fully divine being in a pre-existent mode, it is hard to see how he could be raised to a status that is higher than that.

It is thus likely that the Philippian hymn should be seen as another piece of the evidence from Paul's letters for Paul's development of an 'Adam Christology' in the sense of an idea of both similarity and contrast between the two figures of Jesus and Adam. Nevertheless, we have yet to take full cognisance of the second half of the hymn where Jesus is given 'the name that is above every name', a name which all agree is almost certainly that of 'Lord'. It can be argued that a very 'high' view of Jesus would be still consistent with the Adam typology, since (1) in Judaism ideas of Adam's exaltation and glorification can be adduced, and (2) there is a similar development of an exalted status being given to Jesus precisely in his capacity as the second Adam in 1 Corinthians 15: 24–8 after verses 21–3.[32] Still it has to be said that, however 'Adamic' it may be, it is an extremely exalted position which is being ascribed to Jesus here. Yet the question remains: how exalted? I consider first the use of the term Lord (Greek *kyrios*) applied to Jesus both in Philippians 2 and elsewhere in Paul.

Lord

We have already reviewed briefly the very wide range of possible meaning for the term 'Lord' in a first-century context. The term is frequently used of Jesus by Paul (over 200 occurrences), but perhaps its very frequency should warn us against forcing the term into too rigid a mould. As with *christos*, there may be a wide range of meanings and contexts in which the word is used.

The majority of Paul's uses of 'Lord' for Jesus relate to the present or to the future. Rarely does Paul look to the past and speak of Jesus as Lord: as already noted he does not speak of 'the Lord dying' or 'the crucified Lord'.[33] He does, however, frequently refer to Jesus' coming in the future in terms of Jesus as Lord: for example, in 1 Thessalonians 4: 13–18, Jesus is referred to as 'Lord' five times in quick succession; and in 1 Corinthians 16: 22 the Aramaic *Maranatha* invocation is used by Paul to pray for the Lord (= Jesus) to come.

So too Paul frequently refers to matters of present existence in terms of Jesus as Lord. On the rare occasions he cites Jesus' actual sayings, they are uniformly in terms of Jesus as Lord.[34] Perhaps what is in the background is the fairly basic idea of Jesus *qua kyrios* as a master to whom obedience is due: in the present life, Jesus' sayings are the sayings of one who is to be obeyed.[35] A similar idea is clearer (though the Christology is slightly more muddled!) in 1 Corinthians 7: 21–4 where Paul speaks of Christian existence in terms of being a slave or a freed person, but who either way owes obedience to the new master (Lord), that is Jesus. 'Whoever was called in the Lord as a slave is a freed person belonging to the Lord' (v. 22a) (though when Paul reverses this in v. 22b he slightly confusingly talks about being a 'slave of Christ'). Similarly the archetypal Christian confession is 'Jesus is Lord' (1 Cor. 12: 3; Rom. 10: 9), an expression relating primarily to existential commitment in the present: to acknowledge that Jesus 'is' Lord in the present means to accept him as one's master, one's 'boss', to whom unswerving commitment is due.

Yet there is clearly more at times to Paul's use of *kyrios* language applied to Jesus. In 1 Corinthians 8: 5 Paul clearly acknowledges that this same vocabulary is used in the surrounding culture of other 'beings': 'Indeed, even though there may be so-called gods in heaven or on earth – as in fact there are many gods and many lords . . .' What is in mind is almost certainly the cult deities of the Greco-Roman cults who were referred to as 'lords'. Paul's response seems to be not to deny the (ontological) existence of such beings: indeed he regards them as potentially dangerous to Christians who implicitly acknowledge their existence by taking part in their cults.[36] Nevertheless, for Paul, Jesus as Lord is far greater than any other such 'lord', just as God the Father is far greater than any other so-called 'gods' of the ancient world. Thus in terms of relative value and importance (rather perhaps than ontological existence), 'for us there is one God, the Father, from whom are all things and for whom we exist, and one Lord, Jesus Christ, through whom are all things and through whom we exist' (1 Cor. 8: 6). In this very remarkable statement Paul then seems to speak of Jesus as Lord in the same breath as, and alongside, God. Is then Paul attributing divine status to Jesus?

One can perhaps point to a similar phenomenon in the Philippian hymn: at the end of the hymn, as already noted, Jesus is given the name above every name, which everybody agrees is that of 'Lord'. Moreover, this is spelt out here with the claim that 'at the name of Jesus every knee should bend, in heaven and on earth and under the earth, and every tongue should confess that Jesus Christ is Lord, to the glory of God the Father'. There is here a clear allusion to the words of Isaiah 45: 23 ('To me every knee shall bow, every tongue shall swear'), which in Isaiah forms one of the strongest monotheistic statements of the Old Testament where Yahweh demands exclusive worship and praise. Thus here Jesus seems to be taking the place of Yahweh himself: the exclusive position of Yahweh as the one to whom every knee should bow and whom every tongue should confess seems now to be taken

by Jesus as *kyrios*. Are we then to see in the *kyrios* designation a reflection of the divine name itself from the Old Testament: just as God's
name for Greek-speaking Jews was *Kyrios* (cf. above), so now the fact
that Jesus is *kyrios* indicates his divine status for Paul?

The application of Old Testament citations and texts, originally
applied to Yahweh in the Old Testament but now applied to Jesus, can
also be paralleled elsewhere in Paul. Thus in Romans 10: 13, Paul takes
up the words of Joel 3: 5 (LXX 2: 32) ('everyone who calls on the name
of the Lord will be saved'), words which in Joel clearly refer to Yahweh
as Lord and which equally clearly are now applied to Jesus as Lord: the
'Lord' whose name is to be called upon is presumably the Lord Jesus
(cf. v. 9).

A similar very 'high' Christology may be implied in a number of
other features in Paul's letters. Thus Paul regularly places Jesus almost
casually alongside God in his letter openings. Romans 1: 3 is typical:
'Grace to you and peace from God our Father and the Lord Jesus
Christ' (cf. 1 Cor. 1: 3; 2 Cor. 1: 2; Gal. 1: 3; Phil. 1: 2, etc.) Such a usage
is extremely striking: no other Jewish letter starts off with something
like 'grace to you and peace from God the Father and his servant
Moses'! Similarly, in some contexts, Paul can place Jesus alongside
God and God's Spirit apparently almost without thinking: thus the
'grace' of 2 Corinthians 13: 13 ('The grace of the Lord Jesus Christ, the
love of God, and the communion of the Holy Spirit be with all of you')
puts Jesus in such a 'theo'-logical context with little or no apology. And
in 1 Corinthians 12: 4–6, he again places the Spirit, the Lord (almost
certainly Jesus, cf. v. 3) and God in parallel in an almost unreflective
way as displaying the fundamental unity underlying the variety visible
in different gifts of the Spirit and activities which are evident in the
Corinthian Christian community.

A similarly exalted position of Jesus may be indicated by the possibility that Jesus may be the object of worship in Paul. Hurtado in
particular has made much of this aspect of primitive Christianity as
the one distinctive and characteristic feature which differentiates early
Christian claims about Jesus from other Jewish language of 'divine
agency'. Thus in relation to the Pauline corpus, one could refer to the
fact that prayers may be being addressed to Jesus (2 Cor. 12: 2–10),
Jesus is invoked as Lord in the Maranatha prayer of 1 Corinthians
16: 22, Jesus as Lord is the one whose 'name' Christians are to 'call

upon' (cf. Rom. 10: 13; 1 Cor. 1: 2), and in Philippians 2, Jesus is the 'Lord' to whom every knee shall 'bow' (Phil. 2: 10).[37]

However, before one presses this evidence too far, a word of caution may be necessary. For all the exalted things said about Jesus as Lord, it is still the case that Paul seems to be working within a monotheistic framework. Thus, for example, however exalted a status he is claiming for Jesus in 1 Corinthians 8: 6, it is all in the context that there is 'one God': whatever the claim that 'we have one Lord Jesus Christ' might imply, it evidently in no way was thought to prejudice the fundamental claim of monotheistic belief in the uniqueness of God. So too, even in the Philippian hymn, the status of Jesus as the one 'to whom every knee shall bow' is explicitly said to be 'to the glory of God the Father' (Phil. 2: 11). Jesus' Lordship can then for Paul sit quite happily alongside God's Fatherhood and sovereignty. Thus Dunn can assert, very plausibly, that Jesus' Lordship is as much a way of *distinguishing* Jesus from God as it is of identifying Jesus with God.[38] And indeed the way in which Jesus – and Christians – could quite easily live with the idea of two people both being called *kyrios*, but without necessarily confusing them in any way, is shown by the use of Psalm 110: 1 (widely used by early Christians of Jesus): 'the Lord (= God) said to my Lord (= someone else) sit at my right hand . . .' Thus even the exalted language of the Philippian hymn shows that Jesus' status remains ultimately subordinate to God. The same is probably shown too by Paul's statements that Christ belongs to God (1 Cor. 3: 23) in a way parallel to that in which Christians belong to Christ. Similarly God is the head of Christ (1 Cor. 11: 3); and in 1 Corinthians 15: 24–8 the position of Christ as the ruler of 'all' is explicitly interpreted as excluding God from the 'all' and spelling it out that, in the end, Christ will be subject to God himself (v. 28).

So too the application of Old Testament Yahweh-texts to Jesus should not be overpressed. How far New Testament writers were aware of, and explicitly used, the contexts of Old Testament verses they cited is a much-debated issue.[39] It is at least arguable that New Testament use of the Old Testament was far more atomistic, simply taking over the words of scripture and applying them to the new situation. To a certain extent, that is evident in Philippians 2: 10–11 itself, where the words of Isaiah 45: 23 are applied to Jesus in full realisation of the existence and independence, and perhaps ultimate superiority, of God himself (cf. 'to the glory of God the Father'). So too we have seen in the Introduction how, in Judaism, a variety of 'divine agents' could be seen as taking over a number of the functions of God (for example in judgment) without ever being thought to threaten the fundamental monotheistic belief system of Judaism.

Similarly, the idea that Jesus is 'worshipped' in Pauline communities may need more care. Dunn points out that thanksgiving is generally, in Paul, never addressed to Christ but to God through Christ (cf. Rom. 1: 8; 7: 25); the language of 'praying' or 'prayer' (Greek *deomai/deeseis*) is used in relation to God, but not in relation to Jesus (for example Rom. 1: 10; Phil. 1: 4, etc.) – the same applies to the language of cultic or religious 'service' (Greek *latreuo*) in Romans 1: 9; 12: 1; Philippians 3: 3; and that of 'worship' (Greek *proskuneo*) in 1 Corinthians 4: 25.[40] So too in Philippians 2, it is not clear that the worship is to be addressed *to* Jesus rather than to God for what has happened to Jesus. Thus Dunn suggests that one should distinguish between 'worship' and 'veneration' so that, however, exalted a position Paul gives to Jesus, and, however, much it is one of 'veneration', it is perhaps still one step short of outright 'worship'. In this then perhaps Paul as a Jew stays within the boundaries of Jewish monotheistic faith, even granted the very exalted status he ascribes to Jesus.

THE CORPORATE CHRIST[41]

We noted earlier in this chapter the phenomenon of Paul's 'incorporation' language when he talks of Christians being somehow 'in Christ' (cf. p. 48 above). Paul's language is highly distinctive in this respect, though the meaning he attaches to the phrase is not always either clear or consistent. He uses language about being 'in Christ' or 'in the Lord' (though he does not use other descriptors for Jesus in the phrase). Once (but only once) he talks of Christians being 'in God' (1 Thess. 1: 1).[42]

The significance of the language may well vary. At times the phrase is used in a relatively general way. In Romans 9: 1 ('I speak the truth in Christ'), 'in Christ' may mean no more than simply 'as a Christian'. At other times, the proposition 'in' may be instrumental, so that 'in Christ' may mean 'by means of/through Christ'. 1 Corinthian 1: 2 ('sanctified in Christ') may be an example of this; so too 2 Corinthians 5: 19 ('God was in Christ reconciling the world to himself') may *not* be a grandiose statement about the full divinity of Jesus ('God was in Christ') but rather a claim that in/through/by means of Christ, God was reconciling the world to himself.[43]

However, in some instances, Paul's 'in' language seems to demand an almost physical identification of the Christian with Christ so that Christ is the locus *in* which Christians exist. Such a meaning seems to be demanded in the case of verses such as Romans 8: 1 ('there is no condemnation for those who are in Christ Jesus'), 2 Corinthians 5: 17 ('if anyone is in Christ there is a new creation') and Philippians 3: 8–9 ('in order that I might gain Christ and be found in him'). The idea is also clearly implied in Romans 6, as we have seen: Christians have been baptised 'into Christ', and hence the things claimed about Jesus' death (that it is a death to sin) can be predicated of the Christian as well. Similarly, in 1 Corinthians 15, when Paul develops his Adam typology, he says that all those 'in Christ' shall be made alive (v. 22). Christ is not just an individual human being, but some kind of entity whereby what can be said of Christ (e.g. that he has been raised from the dead) can be claimed for those who are 'in Christ' as well.

So too, some of Paul's talk about the church is built on the same idea. In Romans 12, when he wants to impress on his readers the importance of their mutual support for each other, he tells them that they are 'one body in Christ' (v. 5). In 1 Corinthians 12 the diction changes slightly: the community is now said to be 'the body *of* Christ' (v. 27); but the earlier discussion seems to make clear that the genitive is virtually an epexegetic genitive: the body *is* Christ (cf. v. 12: 'just as the body is one and has many members, and all the members of the body, though many, of one body, so it is with Christ'). Christians are each part of a larger macro-entity which somehow 'is' Christ.

Precisely what such language might imply about the person of Jesus is not at all clear. It is certainly not necessarily the case that such language implies that Jesus is thought of as divine.[44] To talk of a human being as being 'in God' in any spatial sense is just as unusual, at least within a Jewish framework of ideas, as to talk of being 'in Christ'.[45]

The language and the ideas concerned were much discussed in earlier Pauline scholarship, with some using the term 'mysticism' to describe what Paul may have had in mind.[46] Such a description is probably unhelpful and misleading: certainly if 'mysticism' implies some kind of suspension of human faculties and any kind of loss of personhood by being absorbed into another, this is all probably alien to Paul. 'Participation' rather than 'mysticism' is probably a more appropriate word used to describe Paul's idea here. Certainly too it is arguable that this 'participation' language is much more central for many aspects of Paul's theology than his forensic language of justification and righteousness which has so often been thought to form the central core of Pauline theology.[47]

The origins of the language and ideas have been much discussed. A derivation from the language of the mystery cults, and/or an alleged 'Gnostic' redeemer myth, have now been largely discounted. Wedderburn has made a strong case for claiming that the language derives from ideas of national solidarity in Judaism and the way in which Jews could identify themselves as a group with their ancestors and (perhaps) with a representative figure of their history (e.g. Abraham).[48] Nevertheless, one has to say that, if this is the origin of Paul's language, the way he has developed it leads to a position far beyond anything in the proposed background. Christ (unlike Abraham or Adam) is an individual figure of the recent past; and for Paul, being 'in Christ' involves not only being with Christ (as one person alongside another) but being somehow joined into a greater whole where what has happened to Jesus can be claimed by Paul either to have happened to the Christian (death to sin) or to be promised in the future (resurrection) by virtue of this union.

Such an idea is extremely alien to our modern culture and difficult for us to envisage.[49] Certainly it is not an aspect of the person of Jesus which we can neatly slot into any preconceived category. Clearly then here Jesus is seen by Paul as occupying a very special role, but it is probably not possible to be more specific in terms of Christology.

WISDOM

One category not considered so far but which clearly is an important one for Paul's Christology is that of Wisdom. We saw in the Introduction how in several texts from Judaism, language about God's Wisdom was developed in such a way as to suggest that Wisdom might be a person in her own right existing alongside God. Whether non-Christian Jews actually made such a conceptual step is perhaps beside the point. What does seem clear is that at various points Paul takes up this language and applies it to Jesus.

The clearest example is probably 1 Corinthians 8: 6 with the claim that Jesus is the Lord 'through whom are all things and through whom we exist'. The closest parallel is probably the language of Wisdom as God's helper and agent in creation (as e.g. in Prov. 8: 22). Hence Paul seems to be ascribing to Jesus a role and a function ascribed to the figure of Wisdom in Judaism. The same seems to be implied in 1 Corinthians 10: 4 in Paul's somewhat enigmatic claim about the rock of the story of the wilderness wanderings of the Israelites: 'The rock was Christ'. All commentators agree that Paul is here presupposing a Jewish exegetical tradition whereby the rock of the Exodus story actually became mobile and followed the Israelites; moreover, the rock which gave the water to the Israelites was identified by some with the figure of Wisdom.[50] The equation made between Jesus and the rock by Paul is thus probably implying an equation between Jesus and the figure of Wisdom.

Paul's language in Romans 10: 6–7 ('the righteousness that comes from faith says, Do not say in your heart, 'Who will ascend into heaven?' (that is, to bring Christ down) or 'Who will descend into the abyss?' (that is, to bring Christ up from the dead)') is probably also relevant here. Paul is alluding to a particular Old Testament passage, namely Deuteronomy 30: 12–13, and the same Old Testament passage is inter-preted of the figure of Wisdom in Baruch 3: 29–30: 'Who has gone up into heaven, and taken her, and brought her down from the clouds? Who has gone over the sea, and found her, and will buy her for pure gold?' Thus again Paul seems to imply an equation of Jesus with the figure of Wisdom. Similarly the language of God 'sending' Jesus in Romans 8: 3 and Galatians 4: 4 is similar to language about Wisdom (Wisd. 9: 10), as already noted (see p. 51 above).

It is hard to deny that some idea of pre-existence is being applied to Jesus here. Dunn has argued powerfully against such an idea, claiming that, just as this Wisdom language was never intended to be anything other than a vivid way of referring to God's wise actions in creating and dealing with the world, so the same idea is implied in Paul's (and other Christian) talk about Jesus using Wisdom language: God's wise plan and action which in the past created and sustained the world is to be seen exemplified in the present in the person of Jesus.[51] It must, however, remain a little doubtful if this really does full justice to Paul's language. Much has been made of the past tense in 1 Corinthians 10: 4: Paul does not say that what the rock represented (i.e. Wisdom) corresponds now in the present to Christ. If so, one might have expected something like 'the rock *is* Christ'. But what Paul says is 'the rock *was*

Christ'. It is thus hard to avoid the conclusion that he really does have an idea of Jesus' real pre-existence, his presence as a person in the Old Testament period. The same is confirmed by a verse in the same context: 1 Corinthians 10: 9 (probably) has 'we must not put Christ to the test, as some of them [= the Old Testament Israelites] did'.[52] Hence, again, Paul seems to presuppose that Jesus was present in the period of the wilderness wanderings.

It would seem, therefore, that Paul did use and exploit Jewish language about God's Wisdom in a new way when applying such language to a person other than God. Undoubtedly Dunn is right in what he affirms positively: God's wise plan *is* to be seen exemplified in the person of Jesus in the present. But Paul seems to have taken this a step further and implicitly claimed that this involved Jesus' existence prior to his birth in some form as well. There is then an implicit very 'high' Christology in Paul alongside the very human picture of Jesus implied in Paul's Adam- and Son-Christology.

JESUS AS GOD?

Does this then mean that Paul thought of Jesus as God? I have earlier tried to show that some pieces of evidence which others have claimed as pointing in this direction (Jesus as *kyrios*, possible worship of Jesus, the use of Old Testament Yahweh-texts applied to Jesus) should be treated with some caution in this respect. However, it remains finally to consider the one text in Paul's letters where Paul *may* refer to Jesus explicitly as God. This is Romans 9: 5, but, as frequently is the case with key verses, the interpretation of the verse is disputed. On this occasion the key issue concerns punctuation. All our old Greek manuscripts come to us without punctuation; hence decisions about how to punctuate the text are those of the modern interpreter. In this case the key issue is whether the final phrase of the verse 'God who is over all blessed for ever' is to be taken as an independent clause (with the verb 'to be' supplied), or whether it is to be taken in apposition to 'the Messiah' which has just come before. The NRSV text appears to take it as the latter and speaks of 'the Messiah, who is over all, God blessed for ever'. The alternative translation is given in the footnote: 'the Messiah. May he who is God over all be blessed for ever'.

In one way it is perhaps easier syntactically to read the text as implying that 'the Messiah' is indeed 'God'. If the final phrase were an independent benediction one might expect the word 'blessed' to come at the start of the clause (cf. 2 Cor. 1: 3). However, one has to say that if this is a reference to Jesus as God, it is unique in the genuine Pauline corpus. That on its own perhaps gives one pause before adopting such an interpretation. So too one may note that there is nothing explicitly about Jesus as such in the verse. Paul is talking about the blessings enjoyed by Israel and seems to be talking in quite general terms about the benefits Israel has enjoyed (the covenant, the law) as well as the things that can be expected to materialise in the future, including the realisation of the promises, and the coming of 'the Messiah'. He therefore seems to be talking about Jewish messianic expectations in general, and not specifically about Jesus. Further, there is really nothing in the background material of Jewish messianic expectations of this time that we know to suggest that Jews thought of the Messiah as 'God'. It would therefore probably be dangerous to build too much on the basis of this single verse. It is probably more likely therefore that the reference to God here is part of a final benediction that is independent of the reference to the Messiah.

CONCLUSION

We have seen that Paul's Christology is very rich and varied. He can speak of Jesus as a very human figure and indeed much of his soteriology demands that Jesus be fully and completely human: as the new Adam, he is the one who for the first time relates to God in the way human beings should do and were created to do. As such, he becomes the source and focus of the new humanity. Yet Paul also clearly makes some very exalted claims about Jesus. He is the Lord, exalted to a unique position of power and authority to God's right hand; he is the embodiment of the divine Wisdom itself, and Jesus perhaps can be spoken of as pre-existent; he is invoked and venerated by other human beings. As Son of God he is supremely obedient to God: he has the power enabling other Christians to be 'sons' (and daughters!) of God. But it is also the case that his sonship is qualitatively different from the sonship of other Christians: others are adopted as sons whereas Jesus is Son almost by right.[53] He is too the 'space' in some sense in which all Christian existence now takes place.

In terms of later christological debates among Christians Paul is perhaps not quite so far down the road to Chalcedon as some have in the past thought. But perhaps that should not surprise us. What is perhaps even more surprising is the enormous amount of christological development that had already taken place by the time of Paul.[54]

NOTES

1. See ch. 3 below for discussion of these writings. Discussion of the authenticity of the Pauline letters can be found in the standard *Introductions* to the New Testament as well as in introductory sections to commentaries.
2. One must, however, bear in mind that the very identification of the material as pre-Pauline is due in part to its being sufficiently *un*like the rest of Paul to be recognisable as such, and hence it will inevitably be, to a certain extent, somewhat 'un-Pauline'.
3. I would argue that this is the case for all the genuine Pauline letters. The only exception among the letters taken here as genuine might be Romans, although I would argue that this too is situation oriented.
4. The one exception might be 2 Cor. 11: 4, where it seems that some kind of christological dispute may lie behind the scenes somewhere.
5. He says 'This we say by a/the word of the Lord', which may be intended as a citation formula introducing a traditional saying of Jesus, though it could just as easily be a claim by Paul himself to be delivering a prophetic oracle. In any case, what follows in 1 Thess. 4 bears little relationship to any saying of Jesus as recorded in our Gospels.
6. Cf. J. D. G. Dunn, 'Jesus tradition in Paul', in B. Chilton and C. A. Evans (eds), *Studying the Historical Jesus: Evaluations of the State of Current Research* (Leiden: Brill, 1994), pp. 155–78. For one of the most optimistic theories of positive links between Paul and the teaching of Jesus, see D. Wenham, *Paul: Follower of Jesus or Founder of Christianity?* (Grand Rapids: Eerdmans, 1995).
7. Cf. N. Walter, 'Paul and the early Christian Jesus-tradition', in A. J. M. Wedderburn (ed.), *Paul and Jesus: Collected Essays* (JSNTSup 37; Sheffield: Sheffield Academic Press, 1989), pp. 51–80. We should not forget that, on conventional dating, the Gospels were written a generation or so after Paul's letters.
8. I am fully aware that this is strongly disputed by some! But see for example L. Hurtado, 'Jesus as lordly example', in P. Richardson and J. C. Hurd (eds), *From Jesus to Paul* (FS F. W. Beare; Waterloo: Wilfrid Laurier University Press, 1984), pp. 113–26.
9. M. Hengel, '"Christos" in Paul', in Hengel, *Between Jesus and Paul* (London: SCM Press, 1983), pp. 65–77, on p. 65.

10. N. A. Dahl, 'The Messiahship of Jesus in Paul', in Dahl, *Jesus the Christ: The Historical Origins of Christological Doctrine* (Minneapolis: Fortress Press, 1991), pp. 15–25, on p. 16.

11. Contrast Luke's presentation of Paul, for example in Acts 18: 5, 28.

12. Cf. 1 Cor. 10: 4; 15: 22; 2 Cor. 5: 10; 11: 2–3; Phil. 1: 15, 17; 3: 7: see Dahl, 'Messiahship', p. 17; J. D. G. Dunn, *The Theology of Paul the Apostle* (Grand Rapids: Eerdmans; Edinburgh: T&T Clark, 1998), p. 198.

13. Cf. Dahl, 'Messiahship', p. 24 n. 11: 'in no case in Paul can *Christos* be translated "Messiah"'.

14. 'Messiahship', p. 16.

15. Cf. the theory of Dahl, 'The crucified Messiah', *Jesus the Christ*, pp. 27–48, discussed below (see p. 212) (though with some doubts expressed there as to whether this will fully explain the origin of the belief that Jesus was a 'messianic' figure). The link between the cross and messiahship in both the Gospels (especially Mark) and Paul is also emphasised by Hengel, '"Christos" in Paul', 76.

16. Being 'in the Lord' does occur sometimes but not quite so frequently: cf. Dunn, *Theology*, pp. 396–7.

17. Cf. W. Kramer, *Christ, Lord, Son of God* (ET London: SCM Press, 1966), p. 110, and others.

18. The second half is rather redundant if it is making no claim at all to be saying anything new about Jesus. This in turn makes it unlikely that 'Son of God' is seen as a 'messianic' description here. If 'Son of David' in the first half of the statement is intended as in any sense messianic, then the contrast inherent in the dual statement indicates that 'Son of God' is saying something additional to 'Son of David'.

19. See M. D. Hooker, *Pauline Pieces* (London: Epworth, 1979), esp. ch. 4.

20. Dunn, *Christology*, p. 38.

21. Cf. Judg. 6: 8; Jer. 7: 25; Ezek. 3: 5–6, etc.

22. See Dunn, *Christology*, pp. 39–40; *Theology*, pp. 277–8.

23. Dunn, *Theology*, pp. 202–3. I am taking here the phrase '*likeness* of sinful flesh' to emphasise the solidarity of Jesus with, rather than his difference from, the rest of the human race. I am aware though that this is much disputed!

24. Paul's language is of course non-inclusive and, to a modern ear, this can sound a little jarring. If, however, we try to make the language about 'sons' more acceptable in a contemporary idiom by using an inclusive word or phrase such as 'children' or 'sons and daughters', we risk obscuring the very close parallel Paul is asserting between the status of Jesus as Son of God and the status of Christians who follow him.

25. See the several essays in M. D. Hooker, *From Adam to Christ: Essays on Paul* (Cambridge: CUP, 1990), pp. 13–69, esp. her 'Interchange in Christ', originally in *JTS* 22 (1971), pp. 349–61.

26. Cf. Dunn, *Theology*, pp. 79–101; Hooker, *From Adam to Christ*, pp. 73–100.
27. Cf. Wisd. 2: 23–4; Sir. 25: 24 (though ascribing the sin to Eve rather than Adam); *4 Ezra* 7: 118; *2 Bar.* 54: 14.
28. The secondary literature on this 'hymn' is now enormous. For a useful survey of past interpretations as well as detailed analysis, see R. P. Martin, *Philippians 2: 5–11 in Recent Interpretation and in the Setting of Early Christian Worship* (Grand Rapids: Eerdmans, rev. edn, 1983); also the collection of essays in R. P. Martin and B. J. Dodd (eds), *Where Christology Began: Essays on Philippians 2* (Louisville: Westminster John Knox Press, 1998), for a range of different interpretations.
29. Dunn, *Christology*, pp. 114–21; also his *Theology*, pp. 281–6 (responding to earlier critiques). Cf. too Hooker, *From Adam to Christ*, pp. 88–100.
30. The Greek words *morphē* and *eikon* may be translation variants of the Hebrew word *tselem* used in Gen. 1: 26.
31. Martin, *Philippians 2:5–11*, pp. 166–9.
32. Dunn, *Theology*, p. 286. For (1), cf. *T. Abr.* A 11; *Life of Adam and Eve* 25.
33. One exception might be 1 Cor. 11: 23–5, where Paul recalls the actions of Jesus at the Last Supper, referring to him as 'the Lord'. But presumably the reason for citing the tradition here is because of its contemporary significance for the *present* life of Paul's Christian communities in their behaviour at the Eucharistic meal.
34. 1 Cor. 7: 10 'I give this command – not I but the *Lord*'; 1 Cor. 9: 14 'the *Lord* commanded'; 1 Cor. 11: 23 'the *Lord* Jesus on the night he was betrayed . . .'; perhaps 1 Thess. 4: 15 'this we say by a word of the *Lord*'.
35. Even if Paul sometimes does not do so (cf. 1 Cor. 9: 15 after 1 Cor. 9: 14)!
36. This seems to be the reason for the strong language used by Paul in 1 Cor. 10: 1–22, in apparent contrast with the seemingly milder language of 1 Cor. 8 and 10: 23–30. In the latter passages he seems to be dealing with the issue of eating food (possibly sacrificed to idols originally) eaten in a secular context; in 10: 1–22 he is dealing with the issue of actually participating in the cults of such deities.
37. Hurtado, *One God, One Lord*, esp. ch. 5 for the Pauline material.
38. Cf. Dunn, *Unity*, p. 53; *Theology*, p. 251–2.
39. In relation to Paul, such a case is argued for strongly by R. B. Hays, *Echoes of Scripture in the Letters of Paul* (New Haven, 1989); for a contrary view, see my 'Paul, scripture and ethics', *NTS* 46 (2000), pp. 403–24.
40. Dunn, *Theology*, pp. 258–60.
41. On this, see especially Moule, *Origin of Christology*, ch. 2; Dunn, *Theology*, ch. 15.
42. 2 Thess. 1: 1 uses the same phrase but this is probably deutero-Pauline, and directly dependent on the usage in 1 Thess. 1: 1.
43. Hence NRSV's translation inverts the more traditional word order: 'in

Christ, God was reconciling the world to himself'. The alternative word order is given in the footnote.

44. Cf. Moule, *Origin*, p. 95: 'Paul was led to conceive of Christ as any theist conceives of God.'

45. Such talk is closer to language associated with Stoic pantheism (as for example Luke's Paul in Acts 17: 28 'in him we live and move and have our being'). Within Judaism, such 'in' language would have to be interpreted as a kind of instrumental 'in' (that is 'through/by means of').

46. Cf. A. Schweitzer, *The Mysticism of Paul the Apostle* (ET London: A. & C. Black, 1931).

47. In contemporary Pauline study, see especially the work of E. P. Sanders, for example his *Paul and Palestinian Judaism* (London: SCM Press, 1975) and other works.

48. A. J. M. Wedderburn, *Baptism and Resurrection* (Tübingen: Mohr-Siebeck, 1987), esp. pp. 342–56. For Wedderburn, this explains the *'with* Christ' language which Paul may then have developed by taking further talk about baptism, which originally was spoken of as *'in(to) the name of* Jesus' (meaning perhaps simply becoming the property of Jesus). This latter category was then abbreviated to be 'in(to) Christ' and ideas of identification then developed.

49. The difficulties are most clearly articulated by Moule, *Origin*, pp. 48–54.

50. E.g. Philo, *Leg. All.* 2.86.

51. Dunn, *Christology*, pp. 176–96; also *Theology*, pp. 266–93.

52. The situation is complicated by the fact that some of our manuscripts read 'the Lord' instead of 'Christ' here, presumably then referring to God rather than Jesus. However, 'Christ' is probably the harder reading and hence (by the normal rules of textual criticism) more likely to be original.

53. Hence perhaps the justification for the practice adopted here of capitalising Son for Paul's references to Jesus: Jesus for Paul is *the* Son of God, whereas other Christians are *adopted* as sons/children (Rom. 8: 15; Gal. 4: 6).

54. The extraordinarily rapid development of Christology, especially in the pre-Pauline period (that is the very earliest years of the new Christian movement), is rightly emphasised by M. Hengel, 'Christology and New Testament chronology', *Between Jesus and Paul*, pp. 30–47.

Chapter 3

THE DEUTERO-PAULINE LETTERS

The New Testament contains thirteen letters which claim to have been written by Paul. Further, there are a number of other texts, not included in the New Testament, which also claim to be letters written by Paul (e.g. *3 Corinthians*, the letter to the Laodiceans). It is now widely agreed that not all of these can be genuine letters of Paul. Paul's activity as a letter writer, and his position as an authority figure within early Christianity (at least for some), evidently led to other people writing 'letters' in his name, purporting to have come from him. The precise extent of this phenomenon of 'pseudonymity' is disputed. Virtually no one today would wish to defend the authenticity of any non-canonical texts (i.e. those outside the New Testament) as genuine letters of Paul. Further, few would doubt that the phenomenon of pseudonymous letters is a feature of *some* parts of the New Testament itself.[1]

The question of how many of the letters in the New Testament attributed to Paul should be regarded as pseudonymous is disputed. Further, the issue of what exactly should be regarded as 'pseudonymity' is not necessarily as black-and-white an issue as it might be in relation to contemporary authors and modern ideas about authorship. It is clear that, strictly speaking, Paul himself actually *wrote* none of the letters ascribed to him: he used a secretary,[2] and a secretary may have had varying degrees of freedom in drafting the ideas given by Paul himself. Thus it has been argued that variations in style, vocabulary, or even possibly finer points of detail in ideas, might be due to varying degrees of freedom exercised by a secretary. Nevertheless, even allowing for this, it seems unlikely that all the New Testament 'Pauline' letters can be regarded as genuine letters of Paul.

Few would doubt that the Pastoral Epistles (1 Timothy, 2 Timothy,

Titus) are pseudonymous: they are written in a quite different style to the genuine Pauline letters, and the ideas expressed are also significantly different. So too Ephesians is very widely regarded as pseudonymous. In addition, Colossians and 2 Thessalonians are regarded by many as being in the same category (though in the case of these two letters there is more scholarly disagreement). There is not enough space to discuss any of the issues in detail here and I must simply state my own view, which is that these six letters (i.e. the three Pastoral epistles, Ephesians, Colossians and 2 Thessalonians) are all pseudonymous.[3] They can therefore be taken as part of a 'deutero-Pauline' corpus of texts. They are letters (whether genuine letters or not is not clear and may vary from one 'letter' to another), evidently written by admirers of Paul and wanting to claim his authority; no doubt too their authors believed they were handing on Paul's ideas, or perhaps interpreting Paul's thoughts, for different situations. However, the decision to take them as pseudonymous means that they are freed to be interpreted independently of Paul. There is thus no pressure to try to force Paul's thought into a mould which must include these letters.[4] Rather, these letters can be treated as independent texts (though of course their very nature as texts claiming to be by Paul invites comparison with Paul's own letters).

This then is probably the most important aspect of any decision about the alleged pseudonymous nature of New Testament texts. Any claim that a letter (or any other text for that matter) is pseudonymous should not be taken as a value judgement about its overall worth. 'Pseudonymous' should not necessarily be equated with 'second rate' or 'worthless'. Whether one should regard the writing of pseudonymous letters as a matter of 'deception' or 'fraud' is debated.[5] Whether people at the time would have been led to regard such a text as of lesser value had they known that it was pseudonymous is one thing. Whether we today should take such an attitude is another. Perhaps though we should be content to leave such value judgements on one side, and allow these texts to speak for themselves.

In relation to the present study, I shall leave 2 Thessalonians out of account. It has considerable interest, especially with regard to eschatology (see 2 Thess. 2) as well as in relation to the question of Christian involvement in everyday work (2 Thess. 3). However, with regard to the more limited question of Christology it has less to contribute. I will therefore focus here on Colossians, Ephesians and the Pastoral Epistles.

COLOSSIANS

Colossians is perhaps one of the richest sources for christological ideas in the deutero-Pauline corpus. Indeed some would say that it provides one of the richest sources in the whole New Testament. Certainly it presents a view of Jesus that is one of the most exalted in the New Testament, at times too going some considerable way beyond anything that Paul himself says in his genuine letters (which is, of course, one of the reasons why Colossians is regarded by many as pseudonymous!).

As already noted, the letter is regarded by many as deutero-Pauline, though, if so, probably one of the earliest of the deutero-Pauline corpus. It is clearly closely related to the unquestionably genuine small letter to Philemon, with very similar (but not identical) lists of greetings in the two letters.[6] It also almost certainly was used by the author of Ephesians.[7] It is usually assumed that, even though the claim to have been written by Paul may be fictitious, the letter is a genuine letter to the church at Colossae.[8] If so, then it may be significant that the city of Colossae was devastated and perhaps destroyed in an earthquake that hit the Lycus valley in c. 60–1 CE and which certainly devastated the nearby city of Laodicea. If then the city of Colossae was still in existence when the letter was written, and if there were still Christians at Laodicea (4: 15 suggests that they are there to 'greet') then the letter must be dated prior to 60. If this letter is pseudonymous, it must then be very early, perhaps even from Paul's own lifetime. Nevertheless, despite an early date, and despite significant continuity with Paul's other letters, Colossians shows considerable development, especially in relation to Christology. Indeed in many respects the whole letter can be regarded as focused primarily on the theme of Christology.

Part of the reason for this may be connected with the purpose for which the letter was written. However, trying to determine what precisely that purpose might have been is not at all easy. Discussion has focused for the most part on the section of the letter in 2: 8–23 where the writer seems to warn his readers against what he sees as dangerous alternatives to the Christian claims he himself wants to put forward. The tone is not as intense or as passionate as some of Paul's debates with opposition groups in his communities; this has led some to cast doubts on whether there is any specific opposition in mind in Colossians at all.[9] On the other hand, the different tone and perhaps less aggressive stance adopted by the author in comparison with Paul may simply be due to the fact that this is not Paul himself writing. Certainly the rather specific warnings and exhortations given here suggest that a specific situation is in mind and a specific danger is being addressed.

There have been innumerable attempts to try to determine what that situation is more precisely.[10] The suggestions have varied widely from Hellenistic mystery cults to Jewish 'gnosticism', from popular Greek philosophy to 'Judaising'tendencies as in Galatians. Particular attention has focused especially here on the phrase *ta stoicheia tou kosmou* (NRSV 'the elemental spirits of the universe'), as well as on the phrase 'worship of angels' in 2: 18 and the use of the verb *embateuon* (NRSV 'entering') in the same verse. Whether, though, one word or phrase can provide the key to illuminate the whole situation is not clear. Further, we must remember all the dangers of 'mirror-reading'a text, assuming that if one author denies X, then an opposition group must have asserted X. We must also bear in mind that this is the language of polemic (even if the polemic is milder than Paul's), and polemical language is not always 'fair': thus the terms used by the writer may not always be the same as those which the 'other side'might have used to describe its own position.

In this section, the writer warns against a 'philosophy' (2: 8) which is 'according to tradition, according to the elemental spirits of the universe and not according to Christ' (v. 8). With this he contrasts the fullness of Christ which spills over into the fullness of the readers as well. He refers to the dying and rising of Christians with/in Christ in baptism in terms of a 'spiritual circumcision' (vv. 11–12) and claims that in the death of Christ the rulers and authorities have been decisively defeated (vv. 13–15).The readers are not to let themselves be judged in relation to food or drink or 'festivals, new moons, or sabbaths' (v. 16), nor to let themselves be disqualified by any insistence on 'self-abasement'or the 'worship of angels' (v. 18). Again referring to the 'elemental spirits of the universe','to' whom (with Christ) the readers have died, the writer asks why they are 'submitting to regulations, Do not handle, do not taste, do not touch' (vv. 21–2).

That some kind of real danger (as the writer sees it) is in mind seems likely, but the details of the language are obscure at critical points. It does seem clear, however, that the situation is one involving Judaism in some shape or form. Thus the references to circumcision (and the claim to have a 'spiritual'circumcision in v. 11), to 'sabbaths'(v. 16) and dietary regulations (v. 16 cf. v. 2 – perhaps Jewish food laws) all seem to indicate this. However, we have become aware in recent study of both the pluriformity of first-century Judaism and also of the extent to which 'Judaism' and 'Hellenism' had interacted with each other (in both Palestine and the Diaspora) to such an extent that a neat division between 'Jewish' and 'Greek/Hellenistic' is no longer possible.

The reference here to the 'worship of angels' (v. 18) is also intriguing though the genitive used here is sadly ambiguous. Are the readers being warned against an activity of worshipping the angels (an objective genitive) or of attempting to participate in the worship (of God) in which the angels are engaged in heaven (a subjective genitive), perhaps via some kind of mystical experience?[11] So too the word *embateuon* used here is uncertain in meaning.[12]

Equally uncertain is the reference to *ta stoicheia tou kosmou* (NRSV 'elemental spirits') in verses 9 and 20. Literally the word *stoicheia* refers to the basic elements (earth, air, fire, water) from which the universe was believed to be composed (cf. Wisd. 7: 17). However, a widespread view was that these substances were thought of as spirits and given the names of deities; and certainly later the word *stoicheia* was used of heavenly powers that were believed to influence the course of human events. It may be that the same is in mind here, as indicated too by the closely related reference to Christ's victory over the powers in verses 11–15. It would seem then that an important factor in the situation of the Colossians was their giving too high a prominence to the heavenly powers (possibly the same as the angels of verse 18, though whether by worshipping them or joining in their worship is not clear – in any case the angels of verse 18 are hardly to be identified *tout court* with the defeated powers of v. 15) and not a high enough position to the person of Christ.

Any more detailed discussion of the position addressed here[13] would probably take us too far afield. What though seems to have been at stake was the position given to Jesus in the overall scheme of things. It is this that the author appears to want to correct, and his main aim is thus to emphasise the innate superiority of the person of Jesus over all other potential rival powers, whether on earth or in heaven (and clearly heavenly powers are often the main focus of attention). Christology is thus absolutely central for the author's purpose in writing.

Although the writer's reason for writing comes to the fore in chapter 2, it is clear that the whole of the letter is written with his overall purpose in mind. Thus the concern to emphasise the unique position of Jesus dominates the first chapter of the letter as well. Nowhere is this clearer than in the passage 1: 15–20, a section specifically devoted to Christology and spelling out the writer's views about Jesus most clearly. It is also a section which presents one of the 'highest' views of Jesus in the whole New Testament. It will therefore form the main part of our discussion of the Christology of Colossians.

Colossians 1: 15–20

The passage is often known as the Colossian 'hymn'. Such a description may be debatable since we know so little about early Christian hymnody. Nevertheless it seems highly likely that the passage represents a pre-formed unit in some kind of quasi-'poetic' form, which has probably been adapted by the writer in the process. The existence of a pre-formed unit is suggested above all by the opening relative clause 'who is . . .' (Greek *hos estin*) which does not relate grammatically very easily to what comes just before. Such an opening relative pronoun does, however, also occur in other sections widely regarded as pre-formed (possibly quasi-liturgical) units (cf. Phil. 2: 6; 1 Tim. 3: 16; Heb. 1: 3). The opening relative pronoun occurs again in verse 18b. Indeed verses 15–18a and verses 18b–20 display a remarkable degree of parallelism with similar words and phrases used in the two parts. Both parts use the 'hanging' relative pronoun 'who is . . .'; both call Jesus the 'firstborn' (Greek *prototokos*); both justify the claim by a statement beginning 'because in him . . .' (Greek *hoti en auto*); both make similar claims about things or events being 'through him' and 'for him'; both mention 'things in heaven and on the earth' (vv. 16, 20). All this suggests that we have here a two-part poetic unit, the two parts formed in deliberate parallelism with each other and echoing each other. The first half of the unit celebrates the role of Jesus in the creation of the world, the second his role in the redemption of the whole created order.

It is, however, widely recognised that the source used by the writer has probably been expanded as it has been taken over. Three elements in particular are widely suspected of being secondary additions.[14] The first is the phrase 'whether thrones or dominions or rulers or powers' (v. 16). This seems to expand the reference to 'all things in heaven and on earth', but (probably) focusing exclusively on heavenly powers. This may well be due to the writer's immediate concerns in the letter to insist on the superiority of Jesus over all other powers, especially other potential heavenly rivals. The second probable addition concerns the reference to 'the church' in verse 18a. The mention of the church strikes a rather odd note here, since up to this point the focus of attention has been the creation as a whole, with no idea of any limitation to a group smaller than the whole human race. Thus it may be that in the original hymn Christ was said to be the head of the 'body', the assumption being that the whole universe was seen as a body, an idea which can be paralleled in Greek and Jewish thought.[15] Finally the reference to making peace 'through the blood of his cross' in verse 20 seems to be slightly alien to the rest of verses 18–20 where the primary ground for the supreme position of Christ seems to be his resurrection.

Whatever we make of the exact history of the tradition prior to its present form in Colossians 1, the Christology of the hymn is quite startling. Jesus is presented in terms which are extremely exalted; and although the section shows some real continuity with earlier Pauline formulations, it goes significantly further at some points in developing its claims about the status of Jesus.

It is now widely agreed that a very significant amount of the language used here seems to be borrowed from the Wisdom tradition of Judaism. Thus what is said about the figure of Wisdom is now applied to the person of Jesus. Jesus is here called the 'image' of the invisible God. Such language could be used of Adam (cf. Gen. 1: 26) and indeed arguably Paul's use of the 'image' terminology is more related to ideas about Adam. However, the reference to being an agent in creation (v. 16) probably rules this out. Rather, Jesus is here being described in terms used of Wisdom.[16] Thus elsewhere Wisdom is the image of God (cf. Wisd. 7: 26; Philo *Leg. All.* 1.43), the means by which the invisible God makes himself known to other human beings.

So, too, the claim that Christ is the 'first born of all creation' recalls the Wisdom tradition as in for example Proverbs 8: 22 ('the Lord created me in the beginning of his ways'). The precise nature of the claim is open to debate: does it imply that Christ was the first created being,[17] or does the word *prototokos* imply rather precedence and superiority over creation? We should not, however, read back later christological controversies into the first century. In any case similar ambiguity surrounds talk of Wisdom who can be seen as both the first created being (cf. Prov. 8: 22) and also God's agent in creation (see below).

The hymn then goes on to state that 'in him all things in heaven and on earth were created . . . all things have been created through him and for him'. The use of prepositions here may not be entirely precise (poetic language is rarely precise!). Nevertheless, what seems clear is that Christ is here being presented as the *agent* of creation,[18] as well as the *goal* of creation.[19] The idea of Wisdom as the agent in creation is attested in texts such as Proverbs 8: 22–31; also Proverbs 3: 9; Psalm 104: 24; Philo, *Fug.* 109. So, too, as we have already seen, Paul himself used such an idea in 1 Corinthians 8: 6 in claiming that Christ was the agent of creation. Where perhaps the writer of Colossians goes further is in claiming that somehow Christ is also the goal of creation ('all things have been created . . . *for* him'). Paul earlier used such language, but always of *God* as the goal of creation (Rom. 11: 36; 1 Cor. 8: 6). Further, it is hard to find a parallel to such language in talk about Wisdom.[20] There seems to be more of an eschatological idea implicit here, perhaps anticipating in part the second half of the hymn, where the role of the risen Christ is to bring/restore the created order to its intended state.

The highly exalted language continues with the claim of verse 17 that Christ is 'before all things', and 'in him all things hold together'. Again, as with verse 15, there is ambiguity in the claim that Christ is 'before' (Greek *pro*) all things: is this a temporal priority or a superiority in status? But certainly an idea of the temporal priority of Wisdom can be easily paralleled (cf. Sir. 1: 4; Prov. 8). So too the idea of God's Wisdom or *logos* as the bonding force which holds all things together can be found for example in Sir. 43: 26 (cf. Philo *QDH* 23; *Fug.* 112).

The final part of this part of the hymn claims Christ as the head of the whole body, though the latter is immediately glossed as meaning 'the church'. The idea of the cosmos as a body was widely used (cf. above) as too was the idea of God as the 'head' of this body. Without the final gloss, this last statement therefore underlines the extraordinarily high place given to Christ as the creator, sustainer and goal of the whole of creation.

The addition of the gloss 'the church' in one way makes the hymn slightly more 'Pauline' in introducing the idea of the church as the body of Christ (cf. Rom.12; 1 Cor. 12). The idea is here considerably developed, however, in that it is no longer apparently the local community but the universal church that is the body of Christ; and the image has changed so that the 'head' is no longer simply one part of the body alongside others (cf. 1 Cor. 12: 21) but Christ as 'head' is the one in supreme authority over the church. However, as we have seen, the movement is

probably not from Paul's idea of the local community as the body of
Christ to an enlarged view, but from a more cosmological idea of the
universe as the body of which Christ is head to the church as such a
body. As such it is probably in part anticipating the viewpoint of the
second half of the hymn which presupposes (though never states) that
the universe is not quite yet in the position it should be but that this
final state will be achieved through the person of Christ, and through
him by means of the church (cf. Col. 1: 24).

The second half of the hymn focuses on Christ as the redeemer,
primarily (at least until v. 20) by virtue of his resurrection (cf. v. 18 'first
born of the dead'). In one way the language is not quite so extraordinary by comparison with the first half of the hymn. The dominant idea
seems to be the exaltation of Jesus in the resurrection to a position of
supreme authority. Further the aim is 'to reconcile all things to himself
[= God]'. The verbal image of reconciliation again takes up an aspect
of Paul's terminology which occurs occasionally in Paul's own letters
(cf. Rom. 5: 10; 2 Cor. 5: 18–20), but is now applied at a cosmic level
('whether on earth or in heaven'). In between comes a claim about
Jesus which is clearly also potentially highly significant: 'because in him
all the fullness of God was pleased to dwell'. Transposed into the static
categories of Greek thought, this might suggest a claim about the
essential divinity of the person of Jesus. In its context in Colossians 1,
and despite the extremely exalted claims made earlier in the hymn, a
slightly different interpretation might be preferable. The 'because' at
the start still seems to relate what is said to the resurrection of Jesus.
Further, the grammar of the Greek suggests that the 'fullness of God'
is the subject of the verb 'was pleased', a verb which normally implies
an element of personal decision and choice. Hence the idea is probably
more that, in Jesus, God in his fullness was pleased to dwell. The language is thus perhaps closer to that of a model of inspiration, with the
idea closely related to that of Jesus as uniquely inspired by God or filled
with God's Spirit.[21] Very similar language is repeated in 2: 9 ('in him
[Christ] the whole fullness of deity dwells bodily'); though we should
note that however 'high' a christological claim is being made here the
very next verse goes on to claim that Christians too are being filled 'in
him'.

It is clear that the Colossian hymn presents the person of Jesus in
extremely exalted terms. The writer of the hymn has clearly used the
Jewish Wisdom tradition and transferred a great deal of what is said

there to the person of Jesus; but he has also expanded it considerably. Thus Jesus is now presented as the agent of creation, existing before the creation of the world and providing the goal of creation. He is too the means whereby the goal is achieved, by virtue of his death on the cross (so the probably later expansion) and supremely by his resurrection.

Quite how all this can be said of a human being living in the recent past is not easy to understand. For those for whom the language of later Christian orthodoxy poses no real problems and who would see Jesus as a fully divine member of a pre-existing eternal Trinity, there might be less of a problem. However, whether the author of the Colossian hymn or the author of Colossians had got quite this far is not so clear. The Wisdom parallels suggest an element of dependence of Jesus on God (though there is nothing like e.g. 1 Cor. 3: 23; 11: 3; 15: 27–8 here), perhaps even as one created by God, albeit before other created beings (cf. the discussion above on the force of 'first born of all creation' in v. 15, or the claim that he was 'before all things' in v. 17). Whether one can claim that what is being asserted here is that God's creative wisdom and power, which in the past led to the creation of the universe, is now most clearly seen in the person of Jesus, active on earth in his ministry and now risen from the dead,[22] may also be doubtful. It is hard to deny that the clear parallelism created by the two *hos estin*'s indicates that the same person is being described in each half of the hymn. And since it is clearly the person of Jesus in the second half, it must also be in the first half. Some real sense of the pre-existence and pre-existent cosmic creative activity of Jesus seems to be asserted here. Jesus is here being put up into the realm of the divine in a way that exceeds much of the rest of the New Testament.

It may also be worth noting that however exalted a role Jesus has in Colossians, there is also a sense in which Christians share in that role. The author is in many ways a truly Pauline writer. He keeps Paul's insistence on the centrality of the cross as the decisive moment of salvation (1: 20, perhaps glossing an earlier version of the hymn: cf. above). He also has the highly distinctive incorporation language of Paul: Christians are 'in Christ' and as such share his destiny as well. As we have already noted, even the very exalted claim that the fullness of the deity dwells in Christ is immediately followed by the statement that 'you are filled in him' (2: 10). The Greek here implies an action already completed and this is in line with the highly distinctive 'realised eschatology' language of the letter as a whole (language which incidentally serves to distinguish the author from Paul himself who is generally rather more circumspect about what has already been achieved in the life of the Christian). The Christian who is 'in' Christ has thereby already been 'circumcised' (by a 'spiritual' circumcision), has died and been buried with Christ in baptism, and indeed *has* now *been* raised with Christ as well (2: 13, cf. 3: 1). Christ then is the 'first born from the dead' (1: 18) not only in terms of a hope for the future but also in terms of a situation which the author claims is a present reality now. The church in the present thus shares in the risen life of Christ (even in part apparently sharing in 'completing what is lacking in his sufferings' 1: 24, though the exact meaning of this is notoriously obscure). It is then at least possible that the claim that the fullness of the deity dwells in Christ 'bodily' (Greek *somatikos*) may be a reference to the church as the body (Greek *soma*) of Christ as being the locus of this divine indwelling. Certainly this exalted view of the church will be continued in the work of one of the first 'readers' of Colossians, namely the author of Ephesians.

In conclusion then we see in Colossians an author dependent in part on a Pauline heritage but taking that heritage considerably further and developing it significantly. Christ is the locus of Christians as in Paul (cf. the 'in Christ' language); but, perhaps under the pressure of the circumstances faced, the picture is considerably enhanced. Drawing heavily on Jewish Wisdom traditions, the author develops the picture of Christ as the pre-existent agent of creation who is also its goal, the cosmic Lord of the whole created order, vastly superior to any other alleged power or authority. It is this vision which undoubtedly contributed to the impetus which led to the later christological claims of the Christian church (though also some of its language caused difficulty, as we have seen). Perhaps its inflated claims can serve as a powerful statement of the claims of the Christian religion to the universality it professes, whatever we may wish to do with it.[23]

EPHESIANS

Whatever doubts there might be about the authorship of Colossians, there is probably more agreement that the so-called 'letter to the Ephesians' is a pseudonymous letter. Its style is very different from Paul's own, and some of the ideas represent a significant shift from Paul's views. Whether it is a genuine 'letter' (addressed to a specific situation), and if so whether that situation is to be associated with the city of Ephesus, are both debated questions.[24] The letter is closest to Colossians among the Pauline corpus; a large number of the words or phrases in Ephesians can be paralleled in Colossians. Yet Ephesians is anything but a slavish copy of Colossians: the author of Ephesians seems to have taken words or phrases from different contexts in Colossians and moulded them into new contexts with at times slight, but subtle, changes in nuance and emphasis.[25]

The exact purpose of the letter (if it is a letter) is not certain. However, what is clear is that the main focus of attention in Ephesians is the church, its nature, its unity, its destiny etc. In some respects then Ephesians represents a significant shift from Colossians where the prime focus of attention is Christology. Any distinction between ecclesiology and Christology may in one sense be a rather artificial one, since the church is what it is for the author of Ephesians (as indeed for all New Testament writers) precisely because of who Christ is and what he has done. Nevertheless there is a subtle shift of emphasis in an 'ecclesiological' direction as one moves from Colossians to Ephesians, as we shall see.

With regard to titles, Ephesians uses the terms 'Lord' and 'Christ', with or without 'Jesus', very freely – one might almost say indiscriminately. Thus 'Lord Jesus Christ', 'Jesus Christ', 'Christ Jesus' and 'Christ' occur without any clear distinction in meaning. Even the use of the definite article with 'Christ' at times (e.g. 1: 10, 12, 20; 2: 5, etc) does not seem to be significant and does not provide any very obvious evidence that the author was aware of the titular use of the term in Jewish messianic expectations.

Ephesians takes over from Colossians the idea of the cosmic role of Christ as the head, and goal, of the universe. Thus 1: 10 speaks of God's plan 'to gather up all things in him [Christ], things in heaven and things on earth'. Similarly 1: 20–2 speaks of God's power at work 'when he raised him from the dead and seated him at his right hand in the heavenly places, far above all rule and authority and power and dominion, and above every name that is named, not only in this age but also in the age to come. And he has put all things under his feet . . .' In a way similar to Paul in 1 Corinthians 15: 24–8, the author is here combining Psalm 110: 1 and Psalm 8: 6 by referring them to Christ; but unlike Paul who refers this to the eschatological future the author of Ephesians relates it to the present status of Christ.[26]

Yet even here, the main focus has shifted slightly from that in Colossians. Even in the very exalted claims of 1: 20–2, Christ is said to have been 'made head over all things *for the church*'. The position of Christ is brought into the discussion in order to bolster what is said about the church. Similarly both Colossians and Ephesians talk about a 'mystery', something hidden for a long time but now revealed. Yet while in Colossians the mystery is identified with Christ himself (Col. 2: 2), in Ephesians the mystery is rather the unity in Christ of all things (Eph. 1: 9–10), or more specifically the unity of Jews and Gentiles in the single glorious church (3: 4, 6).

With this shift of focus away (slightly) from the person of Jesus and on to the church, there is a marked lessening in any stress on the role of Christ in any 'protological' role, that is at the creation or before the creation. The explicit reference to Jesus as God's agent in creation (e.g. Col. 1: 16) is one of the few elements that is *not* taken over by the author of Ephesians from Colossians. Whether Ephesians thinks in terms of Jesus as pre-existent is not entirely clear.[27] The passage in 4: 8–10 (the strange appeal to Ps. 68: 18 and the reference to 'descending' as well as 'ascending') is probably not relevant. The 'descending' in question is most likely not a descent from a pre-existent state in heaven at the incarnation, but rather an allusion to a descent into Hades after the crucifixion.[28]

Less certain is the reference in 1: 4 which says that God 'chose us in him [Christ] before the foundation of the world'. Undoubtedly the main purpose of the verse is to give assurance to the readers of their calling by God as not just a capricious act of the present but as one that goes back to before the creation of the world. What is pre-existent is primarily God's decision to choose 'us'. Yet presumably there is no question at all that 'we' are thought of as pre-existent here. Hence it is uncertain whether the action of 'choosing us in Christ' implies that Christ is thought of as pre-existent either.[29] The precise force of the 'in' here is uncertain (though the writer's usage is not always precise or clear). The 'in Christ' in verse 3 may simply mean 'through' or 'by means of' Christ,[30] and hence the identical phrase in verse 4 may mean the same, and 'by means of' could mean just 'on the basis of what Christ was to do'. But in any case, as we have already noted, the primary stress here is not really christological as such but more 'ecclesiological', that is focusing on Christians as chosen by God.

Ephesians shares with Colossians, and indeed with the other Pauline letters, the idea of the church as the 'body' of Christ, and the unity of all Christians 'in' Christ. Yet it is noticeable that there seems to be a slight shift of emphasis as one moves from Colossians to Ephesians away from the very strong 'incorporation' language one gets in both Colossians and in the genuine Pauline letters.[31] The phrase 'in Christ' occurs very frequently in Ephesians, yet as often as not it seems to lack the strong idea of incorporation which is present in the earlier letters of the Pauline corpus. We have already noted that the phrase 'in Christ' in 1: 3 may represent an instrumental use of the preposition *en* ('by means of Christ') rather than the incorporation idea (though it is true to say that the incorporation idea may occur at some other places, e.g. 1: 11). We may also note one of two small changes between Colossians and Ephesians where the incorporation language tends to be weakened or to disappear. Thus Colossians 3: 18 states that wives should be subject to their husbands 'as is fitting *in* the Lord', which may mean something like 'as is fitting for people who are in [= incorporated in] the Lord'. The parallel in Ephesians 5: 22 states that wives should be subject to their husbands '*as to* the Lord'. Any incorporation idea disappears and 'the Lord' is the supreme dominant figure whom all should obey. So, too, it may be significant that, in Ephesians, the situation of being 'in Christ' is sometimes as much a matter of future hope as of present reality: thus, for example, 4: 15 states: 'we *are to* grow up [in the future] in every way into him who is the head, *into* Christ' (i.e. we are presumably not yet 'in' Christ). In line with this general trend there is, too, in Ephesians more of an element of separation between Christ and the church than in Colossians. The emphasis is very much on the fact that Christ is *head over* the church, quite as much as on any unity between Christ and Christians.

The same idea recurs in other images of the church which occur in Ephesians. For example, in 2: 20–2 the author uses the image of the church as a building, or specifically a temple. The idea is already present in Paul (see 1 Cor. 3: 16–17), though the author of Ephesians does not use the motif to stress the 'holiness' of the church, or the fact that it is the locus of God's in-dwelling Spirit, as Paul does. It is, though, perhaps significant that in the imagery of Ephesians, Christ is *not* the temple itself, but one stone (the all-important 'cornerstone') alongside other stones. Similarly in the passage in 5: 22–33, developing the command to wives to be subject to their husbands, the author talks of the relationship between Christ and the church as similar to that of a marriage bond. But the emphasis is more on Christ and the church as two separate entities (despite the reference to husband and wife becoming 'one flesh' in 5: 31) rather than on their innate unity.

Ephesians thus shows us probably a further development within the deutero-Pauline corpus, moving on from Colossians and in some respects slightly further away from the genuine Paul in terms of Christology. In his zeal to promote his ideas about the glorious status of the church, its origin, its destiny and its place in the world, the author makes some subtle shifts in terms of Christology and about the relationship between Christ and the church. In many respects Ephesians is of course more modern than Paul, not only because of its later date: Paul's ideas about incorporation are notoriously difficult to grasp for the modern mind; so, too, the vivid futurist eschatology of Paul (and of all early Christianity) inevitably had to be modified in the light of the course of on-going history; and the much greater stress on realised eschatology which we see in Ephesians is clearly part of that process. Ephesians thus presents us with a Paul in part adapted to make sense in a new age, a process which is incumbent on all who would seek to relate the New Testament to their contemporary scene. Such a process of adaptation is even more evident in the Pastoral Epistles, to which we now turn briefly.

THE PASTORAL EPISTLES

The so-called Pastoral Epistles – 1 Timothy, 2 Timothy and Titus – are almost universally regarded as pseudonymous. They are written in a style, and with a vocabulary, which is similar across all three 'letters' but which is very different from the other letters of the Pauline corpus. They are usually taken as a unit and considered as a single entity (as indeed I shall do here) though it may be worth noting that there are one or two differences between the letters, not least in the area of Christology. Whether they are genuine 'letters' or not is unclear. Almost certainly the 'addressees' (Timothy and Titus) are as pseudonymous as the claim to be written by Paul; but whether the author (if indeed it is right to think of a single author) was addressing a single, real community in writing these texts is less certain. That there seems to be a danger in mind is reasonably clear,[32] but the precise details are obscure.

Whatever the concrete 'danger' or 'opposition' that is in mind, it is clear that the Pastorals are aiming to present 'Paul' in a new situation, adapting him to a new age and a new environment. It is possible too that part of the purpose of the letters is to defend Paul against other criticisms by showing (in letters purporting to be his) that he is 'sound', 'orthodox' and not one whose teaching gives offence to broader society.[33] Certainly we know that in the late first century and into the second century, Paul became a controversial figure, a fact which can probably be deduced in part from a text like 2 Pet. 3: 16 (indicating that, in debates between 'orthodox' and 'heretics', Paul was appealed to by both sides); we also know from other texts (e.g. the *Pseudo-Clementine Recognitions*) that Paul's reputation was attacked. Anyway, for whatever reason, the Pastorals present us with a Paul who is 'safe', 'sound' and who presents an ethos and a lifestyle which would be broadly accepted within the wider Greco-Roman world, namely one of sobriety and devout piety, basically providing no threat to the *status quo*.

The author of the Pastorals clearly knows some of Paul's language, but that language is often used in such a way that many of the depths of Paul's own thought are lost. This certainly applies in the area of Christology no less than in other areas of 'theology'. Thus, for example, the author clearly knows – and uses – Paul's characteristic language of 'in Christ'. The phrase occurs quite frequently in the Pastorals. However, almost without exception the writer speaks of abstract entities, rather than people, being 'in Christ'.[34] He refers to 'the faith and love that are in Christ Jesus' (1 Tim. 1: 14; 2 Tim. 1: 14), 'the grace that is in Christ Jesus' (2 Tim. 2: 1), 'the salvation that is in Christ Jesus' (2 Tim. 2: 10), but rarely if ever of Christians being 'in Christ'.[35] For the most part Jesus is seen as an example, exhibiting all the moral virtues that the Christian is to have or to strive for. Perhaps the closest the Pastorals get to Paul's idea of the incorporation of the Christian in Christ is in the summary statement quoted in 2 Timothy 2: 11–13: 'if we have died with him, we will also live with him; if we endure, we will also reign with him', though the union of the Christian with Christ here is simply that of one individual alongside another and in any case seems to be a matter of future hope rather than present reality (as in Paul).

As far as christological 'titles' are concerned, 'Christ' seems to be just a proper name and the word appears to have lost all its original significance in Jewish messianic expectations (though in this the Pastorals are not so unlike Paul himself, as we have seen). Indeed, in one passage the writer goes out of his way to stress that 'Christ Jesus' is above all a 'man' (1 Tim. 2: 5) and almost nothing more. Any special claim about Jesus here relates to his being a 'mediator' between God and human beings, but this is apparently unrelated to the appellation 'Christ'.

Jesus is often called 'Lord' (*kyrios*) (cf. 1 Tim. 1: 2, 12; 6: 3, 14), a term which is also frequently applied to God in the Pastorals. Sometimes too it is difficult to tell whether *kyrios* refers to God or to Jesus.[36] It is perhaps worth just noting that references to Jesus as Lord come strongly in 1 Timothy, become more ambiguous in 2 Timothy and seem to die away in Titus (where there is no clear reference to Jesus as 'Lord').

By contrast, the other main christological 'title' often referred to in discussions of the Christology of the Pastorals – Jesus as 'saviour' (Greek *sōtēr*) – shows an opposite tendency: from no clear references in 1 Timothy, there is one in 2 Timothy (1: 10) and then three in Titus (1: 4; 2: 13; 3: 6). The word is used as well six times of God. The term almost certainly reflects the influence of the growing 'ruler cult' in the wider Greco-Roman world towards the end of the first century CE. In this the emperor was widely acknowledged as a 'saviour', bringing 'salvation' to the world by his achievements.[37] Thus the language of the Pastorals, describing Jesus as the 'saviour' figure, is almost certainly intended to be a Christian response to such claims, asserting that the 'true' 'saviour' is to be identified with the person of Jesus and not with any emperor or other ruler.[38]

The same idea probably underlies the distinctive terminology of the Pastorals in referring to the 'epiphany' (Greek *epiphaneia*, often translated 'manifestation' or 'coming'). This was also a word widely used in relation to the arrival or appearance of important dignitaries and of the emperor. An inscription at Ephesus speaks of Julius Caesar as 'the god made manifest, offspring of Ares and Aphrodite, a common saviour of human life'.[39] In the Pastorals, the 'epiphany' language is used mostly to refer to the future coming of Jesus (cf. 1 Tim. 6: 14; 2 Tim. 4: 1, 8; Tit. 2: 13), once apparently of his first coming (2 Tim. 1: 10). Thus the language of the Pastorals seems to be deliberately trying to 'up-stage' the language and claims associated with the emperor in the contemporary situation in which the author is writing.

For the most part the epiphany language of the Pastorals seems to indicate that the author is working with a relatively simple two-stage schema whereby Jesus has been born on earth and has died, but has now been exalted to heaven from where he will 'appear' again at the end of time. Thus in very brief form 2 Timothy 2: 8 speaks of 'Jesus

Christ, raised from the dead, a descendant of David'. This is one of several epigrammatic quasi-credal statements with which the Pastorals are peppered. Here the focus is very similar to that of the mini-credal summary used by Paul in Romans 1: 3–4 (indeed the author of 2 Timothy may be dependent on this): Jesus is the one who is born (the reference to Jesus as a descendant of David is unique in the Pastorals here) and is now raised from the dead.

This is expanded slightly further in the formulaic-type summary in 1 Timothy 3: 16: 'revealed in flesh, vindicated in spirit, seen by angels, proclaimed among Gentiles, believed in throughout the world, taken up in glory'. There is here a reference to Jesus' first coming, though what precisely is in mind is not clear. The stress is primarily on the subsequent 'career' of Jesus as exalted: 'vindicated in spirit' is presumably a reference to the resurrection, and the rest of the statement is about the post-resurrection situation. Whether there is any idea of pre-existence implied in the first phrase ('revealed in flesh') is not certain. The phrase itself need not imply that Jesus existed somewhere else before being 'revealed'.[40] 2 Timothy 1: 9, which talks of 'grace given to us in Christ Jesus before the ages began', has been thought by some to imply some idea of pre-existence. However, again the issue is not clear cut. The verse is similar to Ephesians 1: 4 and raises exactly the same exegetical difficulties. The prime stress is on the act of divine election which is said to have taken place before the creation of the world. But, as in Ephesians, presumably there is no question of 'us' being pre-existent in this verse. So too then it must be doubtful if the 'in Christ Jesus' reference here implies that Jesus is thought of as pre-existent either.

No discussion of the Christology of the Pastorals, or indeed of the New Testament, should ignore one verse which has generated great debate in relation to Christology. This is Titus 2: 13 which can be read as implying that Jesus is in some sense 'God'. Thus the NRSV translates the verse as 'we wait for the blessed hope and manifestation of our great God and Saviour Jesus Christ'. If this is the correct translation, it would be one of the rare instances in the New Testament where Jesus is explicitly called 'God'. However, the translation is not certain. It is possible to translate the verse as speaking of 'the great God and our Saviour Jesus Christ', that is distinguishing God from Jesus (so NRSV footnote). The Greek has no definite article with 'Saviour' and this gives support to those who would defend the reading making this a single reference to Jesus alone as both 'God' and 'saviour'. At the same time, the article with 'Saviour' is missing elsewhere and hence the argument from the syntax here may not be decisive.[41] Overall it seems unlikely (and would be slightly anomalous) if the author were here ascribing divinity to Jesus. Elsewhere Jesus is a 'mediator' between God and humanity (1 Tim. 2: 5) and the stress is explicitly here on the fact that Jesus, in contrast to God, is a *man*. Jesus has been raised from the dead (presumably by God) and will appear at the end of time. Clearly Jesus is seen in an exalted role, and in a role (or roles) which enable him to be placed alongside God in, for example, the opening greetings of the letters, though always here (and elsewhere) clearly distinguished from God (cf. 1 Tim. 1: 2; 2 Tim. 1: 2; Tit. 1: 4). Overall therefore it would seem more likely that Titus 2: 13 should be read as referring to God and Jesus as two separate persons.[42]

Determining precisely what the Christology of the Pastorals was is not easy in part because of the way in which the author cites so many formulaic summaries which appear to be pre-formed: hence one cannot always be certain how much is due to an earlier tradition and how much to the author (or indeed if it is right to try to drive any wedge between the two at all!). Nevertheless, for the most part, the Pastorals seem to show us an attempt to rewrite Paul's ideas so that they relate to the contemporary world and be heard by others in ways that are both sensible (in terms of the current ideas) and also not too offensive. Jesus is thus now the Christian answer to claims about the emperor in the Greco-Roman world, with the Christian way offering the true 'salvation' for the believer.

NOTES

1. Outside the Pauline corpus, it is very unlikely that both the letters attributed to Peter are genuine letters of the apostle Peter himself. The two are so different, stylistically and in other ways, that at the very most one might possibly be a genuine letter of Peter. The prime candidate for this is 1 Peter (though even here there are serious problems with such a theory), and 2 Peter is almost universally accepted as a pseudonymous letter. See the commentaries and standard *Introductions*.
2. Cf. Rom. 16: 22; the only exception might be odd sections of letters, cf. Gal. 6: 11.
3. For detailed arguments, see the standard *Introductions*, as well as Introductions to commentaries on the individual books. The decision taken here about authenticity is certainly a widely held one.

4. See my *Reading the New Testament*, pp. 57–8.

5. Cf. L. R. Donelson, *Pseudepigraphy and Ethical Argument in the Pastoral Epistles* (Tübingen: Mohr-Siebeck, 1986); D. G. Meade, *Pseudonymity and Canon* (Tübingen: Mohr-Siebeck, 1986).

6. Compare Phlm. 23 with Col. 4: 10–13.

7. This is the standard critical view today, though it is disputed by some.

8. This is of course not self-evident: a pseudonymous letter may have both a fictitious author and a fictitious addressee.

9. See M. D. Hooker, 'Were there false teachers at Colossae?', in B. Lindars and S. S. Smalley (eds), *Christ and Spirit in the New Testament* (FS C. F. D. Moule; Cambridge: CUP, 1973), pp. 315–31, repr. in *From Adam to Christ*, pp. 121–38.

10. See the surveys in J. D. G. Dunn, *The Epistles to the Colossians and to Philemon* (Grand Rapids: Eerdmans, 1996), pp. 23–35; J. M. G. Barclay, *Colossians and Philemon* (Sheffield: Sheffield Academic Press, 1997), ch. 3.

11. As in e.g. the *Songs of the Sabbath Sacrifice* at Qumran (4Q400–7).

12. This word was the lynchpin of M. Dibelius's view that what was in mind here was participation in pagan mystery cults.

13. To call it a 'heresy' or an 'error' may be too strong or loaded a description.

14. See A. J. M. Wedderburn, in A. J. M. Wedderburn and A. T. Lincoln, *The Theology of the Later Pauline Letters* (Cambridge: CUP, 1993), pp. 14–16.

15. See E. Lohse, *Colossians and Philemon* (Philadelphia: Fortress Press, 1971), pp. 51–4; Dunn, *Colossians*, pp. 94–5. Cf. Plato, *Tim.* 31–2; Philo, *QDH* 155; *de somn.* 1.128.

16. Cf. Dunn, *Christology*, pp. 187–94; also his *Colossians*, ad loc.

17. As indeed Arius later claimed: cf. E. Schweizer, *The Letter to the Colossians* (London: SPCK, 1982), pp. 250–2.

18. 'In' (Greek *en*) could well be instrumental, 'by means of', and hence virtually the same as *dia* 'through'.

19. 'All things have been created ... *for* (Greek *eis*) him'.

20. Schweizer, *Colossians*, p. 70; Dunn, *Colossians*, p. 92.

21. Cf. Dunn, *Colossians*, pp. 103–4.

22. Cf. Dunn, *Christology*, p. 194.

23. See Barclay, *Colossians*, ch. 5.

24. The words 'in Ephesus' in the opening greeting in 1: 2 are missing from a number of important manuscripts; also the document has a curiously impersonal air to it, with virtually no personal greetings at the end (only 6: 21–2 which represent an almost verbatim repetition of Col. 4: 7–8).

25. As noted earlier, the relationship is very widely – though not universally – assumed to go from Colossians to Ephesians, rather than vice versa.

26. It is quite characteristic of Ephesians to collapse the future eschatological hope into claims about the present reality.

27. Sometimes claims that such an idea is presupposed in Ephesians have to appeal to the evidence of Colossians for support!

28. Cf. the reference to the 'lowest parts of the earth' which is slightly odd if 'of the earth' is simply a genitive of apposition: see Dunn, *Christology*, pp. 186–7, and, for an alternative view, see e.g. A. T. Lincoln, *Ephesians* (Dallas: Word, 1990), pp. 244–7, who gives a full discussion.

29. So Dunn, *Christology*, p. 235, and, for a different view, e.g. Lincoln, *Ephesians*, pp. 23–4.

30. See J. L. Houlden, *Paul's Letters from Prison* (Harmondsworth: Penguin, 1970), ad loc.

31. Cf. J. A. Allan, 'The 'In Christ' Formula in Ephesians', *NTS*, 5 (1958), pp. 54–62.

32. Cf. the warnings about dangerous teachings in e.g. 1 Tim. 4: 1–3; 6: 20; 2 Tim. 2: 14–18; Tit. 1: 10–16.

33. See C. K. Barrett, *The Pastoral Epistles* (Oxford: OUP, 1963), pp. 17–19; also his 'Pauline Controversies in the Post-Pauline Period', *NTS* 20 (1974), pp. 229–45.

34. Cf. J. A. Allan, 'The 'In Christ' Formula in the Pastoral Epistles', *NTS* 10 (1963), pp. 115–21.

35. The closest is perhaps 2 Tim. 3: 12: 'all who live a good life in Christ Jesus'.

36. For example, in 2 Tim. 1: 18, 'May the Lord grant that he will find mercy from the Lord on that day', are the two 'Lord's' the same? Is one – or both – Jesus? Or do they refer to God?

37. Cf. F. M. Young, *The Theology of the Pastoral Epistles* (Cambridge: CUP, 1994), p. 64.

38. This is also one of the features shared between the Pastoral Epistles and the Lukan writings: cf. pp. 139–40 below.

39. Young, *Theology*, p. 64; M. Davies, *The Pastoral Epistles* (Sheffield: Sheffield Academic Press, 1996), p. 44.

40. The issue is similar to the problem of interpreting Paul's talk of God's 'sending' his son in Rom. 8: 3; Gal. 4: 4.

41. Cf. 1 Tim. 1: 1; 4: 10. See Davies, *Pastoral Epistles*, p. 47.

42. So M. Dibelius – H. Conzelmann, *The Pastoral Epistles* (Philadelphia: Fortress Press, 1972), p. 143; Young, *Theology*, p. 53. Davies also points out that the stress on the humanity of Jesus elsewhere as well as on the fact of his death and on the 'immortal' nature of God (cf. 1 Tim. 1: 17) would surely demand some explanation if Jesus is thought of as 'God'; the fact that this is not supplied may then be significant (*Pastoral Epistles*, pp. 47–8).

Chapter 4

HEBREWS

The so-called 'Letter to the Hebrews' is one of the most difficult texts of the New Testament to understand, and almost every aspect of the text is controversial and debated. Yet for our purposes – the study of New Testament Christology – it is one of the richest sources to be mined. Although in the past it has been associated with Paul,[1] it is now universally recognised as the work of a different author who may, however, have some tenuous connection with the circle of people associated with Paul.[2] The author is thus an unnamed, probably other-wise unknown Christian who nevertheless has provided us with a highly distinctive, and highly developed, presentation of the significance of the person and work of Jesus.

The aim and purpose of the text is not clear. It is usually termed a 'letter', or an 'epistle'; but although it finishes with an (albeit rather brief) set of personal greetings typical of other letters of the time (13: 23–4), its opening has none of the conventional features of a letter (e.g. 'A to B, greetings'): rather it moves straight into a claim about God and his new manner of communicating with human beings past and present (1: 1–2). The body of the text is taken up with what might be called a doctrinal treatise on the person and work of Jesus, though interspersed at various points are a number of exhortations to the readers to draw the necessary implications from what has been said. On the basis of these exhortations, most commentators have assumed that Hebrews is a genuine letter, that is a personal communication to a specific group of people in a specific situation, and that the doctrinal exposition is primarily designed to address that situation.

However, trying to pin down the details of that situation, or the group addressed, is not at all easy. Most assume that those addressed are Jewish: the argument is mostly on the basis of a discussion of the Jewish tradition (its Scriptures, its cult and its institutions) and of their continued validity. Further, it would seem that one aspect of the situation which the author is concerned to address is a danger (as he sees it) of the readers lapsing back into the practice of the Jewish religion which they had evidently given up when they became Christians. There are continual dire warnings of the dangers of apostacy (6: 4–6; 10: 26–31; 12: 15–17); and the whole tenor of the argument of Hebrews, which aims to show the superiority of the Christian dispensation over against that of Judaism and especially the Jewish cult, suggests that the Christian group addressed here is being attracted back to the claims of the Jewish cultic system. Whether we can be more precise than this is uncertain. It may be that the existence of persecution (cf. 10: 32–4) led some to think that (re-?)joining the Jewish community might give greater protection. However, it must be said that much of the doctrinal part of the letter would then be somewhat unrelated to such a situation. It would seem more likely that the Christian readers felt themselves positively attracted to a Jewish cult. Again, though, it is difficult to be more specific. Lindars has suggested that a sense of guilt and remorse for post-baptismal sin might have led Christians to lay too little value on what had been achieved by Jesus and to seek to return to the Jewish cult to make up for what was perceived as a deficiency.[3] This is possible and would fit some of the evidence though we cannot say more. All we can say is that the author sees it as a pressing concern to show that the Christian claims about what has been achieved through the Christ event far outpass anything that could be achieved through the Jewish cultic system, and this is the major thrust of all that the author says in relation to Jesus.[4]

If though the situation of the readers is not clear, the same applies in relation to the author. With regard to the (perhaps less important) issues of his identity and geographical situation, we can only speculate. More important perhaps is the question of the background of thought presupposed by the author of Hebrews. In particular, there is the question of how far the author is imbued with ideas of more Greek philosophical thought and a Platonic-like dualism, with a contrast drawn between the heavenly realm of ideas and ideals and the earthly realm of imperfect shadows and copies of the heavenly ideals. It is certainly the case that some of the language of Hebrews can be read in this way. Thus when the author claims that the earthly sanctuary is a sketch or shadow of the heavenly one and quotes Exodus 25: 40 'see that you make everything according to the *pattern* that was shown you on the mountain' (Heb. 8: 5), or claims that the law is 'a *shadow* of the good things to come and not the true form of these realities' (10: 1), such language can easily be taken as reflecting a Platonic-type dualistic way of thinking, not far removed from that of a figure like Philo of Alexandria.[5]

At the same time, one must also say that this is by no means the whole story. Even one of the verses cited above indicates as much: Hebrews 10: 1 says that the law is 'a shadow of the good things *to come*'. Hebrews has just as much of an idea of a temporal dualism as of any Platonic-type special dualism.[6] Thus, right at the start, the author contrasts what has happened previously by way of God communicating with human beings with what has happened 'in these last days' (1: 2). Any contrast is not (or anyway not just) a static contrast between earthly and heavenly in the present; it is between the eschatological new/future and the old past. In line with this too, the use of Scripture in Hebrews is characteristically different from the allegorical use of Scripture by someone like Philo.[7] Scripture in Hebrews does not lose its literal sense. It is not taken as referring to some other reality co-existing in the present. Rather its referent is accepted, but as often as not it is interpreted in relation to a future reality. For example, the use of Psalm 95 in Hebrews 4 is used to point to the sabbath rest for the people of God that is still to come in the future. Part of the complexity of Hebrews arises from the claim that part of the hoped-for eschatological future has already happened in the life and death of Jesus (though of course in this respect Hebrews is no different from the rest of the New Testament). Thus life in the presence of God in heaven is part of the eschatological hope for Christians, but has already been attained by Jesus who has passed into the heavens already, so that heaven and earth co-exist in a set-up that could be regarded as similar to that of a Platonic-type dualism. Nevertheless, despite any superficial similarity, it seems that Hebrews still retains the eschatological temporal dualism that is so characteristic of Jewish and Christian thought in the rest of the New Testament.

What then of the Christology of Hebrews? In one sense one could say that the Christology of Hebrews presents one facet of the confusion regarding the author's thought world as a whole. As with several other New Testament writers we have considered, a number of rather different christological ideas seem to lie side by side with each other in a way that seems confusing to later interpreters but apparently caused no embarrassment to the original author.

Nowhere is this more evident perhaps than in the opening verses of the letter, Hebrews 1: 1–4, comprising a single, long, sonorous but rhetorically impressive sentence. At first sight (and indeed at second sight as well!) it is full of christological significance. It is not, however, at least initially, primarily about the person of Jesus but about *God*: it sets up a contrast between the way God has communicated with human beings in the past (through prophets) and the way God has 'in these last days' chosen to speak to human beings in the present – through his Son. The schema here is clearly that of a temporal dualism with the idea, so prominent in early Christianity, of an eschatological future anticipated in the present in the Christ event. This Son, the author claims, has been 'appointed heir of all things', where again the primary reference seems to be eschatological: looking to the future, the writer claims that the Son will (at the end of time) inherit all things.

At this point, however, the point of reference switches violently. This Son, it is said, is the one 'through whom he created the worlds. He is the reflection of God's glory, and the exact imprint of God's very being, and he sustains all things by his powerful word' (vv. 2b–3). The language is extremely close to language used of Wisdom in some Hellenistic Jewish texts, as well as to some of the language used by Philo. Thus the same Greek word translated 'reflection' above in Hebrews 1: 2 (Greek *apaugasma*) appears in the description of Wisdom in Wisdom 7: 25–6: 'She is a breath of the power of God, and a pure emanation of the glory of the Almighty . . . she is a reflection (Greek *apaugasma*) of eternal light, a spotless mirror of the working of God.' So too the reference to the Son as God's agent in creation (Heb. 1: 2b) recalls the idea of Wisdom as exercising this role (cf. Prov. 8: 22). What then we seem to have here is another example of a so-called Wisdom Christology, where what is said about Wisdom in Jewish tradition is now said of Jesus.

It is hard to deny that some kind of pre-existence is being attributed to Jesus here. Some have attempted to deny this, suggesting that perhaps what may be in mind is some kind of 'ideal' pre-existence whereby God's creative power (his 'word' [cf. Ps. 33: 6] or his 'wisdom') can be spoken of in personified terms as his 'first born' (hence as his Son) which can then later be seen as definitively expressed in the person of Jesus.[8] Nevertheless it is hard to escape the force of the structure of the sentence in verse 2 with two consecutive relative clauses: the Son is the one 'whom he has appointed heir' *and* 'through whom he also created the worlds'. The first must refer to the person of Jesus; hence it is hard to deny that the second does as well.

The claim that Jesus is someone whose existence reaches back continuously into the past is an idea that recurs elsewhere. In 7: 3 the author plays on the description of the figure of Melchizedek in Genesis 14, claiming too (as we shall see) a close similarity between Jesus and Melchizedek. As part of the comparison, the author refers to the 'fact' that Melchizedek is 'without father or mother' (playing on the lack of mention of any parents of Melchizedek in Gen. 14); hence, the claim is that the same must apply to Jesus. Jesus is therefore eternal in relation to the past as well as the future. The unchanging nature of Christ as the same '*yesterday*, today and for ever' is asserted in 13: 8. Thus the idea of Jesus as pre-existent is one that the author does at times assert.

Nevertheless it is also probably the case that such an idea is not central for Hebrews. The Wisdom Christology as such does not recur elsewhere in the letter. What is striking about this author's writing is the way in which, alongside this language of Jesus as an eternally pre-existent being, there is language which one could perhaps describe (probably anachronistically) as 'adoptionist'. Jesus has *become* what he is by virtue of an act of appointment by God during his life, or as a consequence of his death and resurrection.[9] This is already intimated in the clause which precedes the claim about the Son as God's agent in creation: in 1: 2b it is said that God has 'appointed' the Son to be the heir of all things. This idea recurs prominently throughout the epistle: Jesus has *become* superior to the angels (1: 4); he has been begotten by God to become his Son (1: 5; 5: 5, both citing Ps. 2: 7 – in the latter case it is clear that this is on the basis of his death); he has been anointed by God above his fellows (Heb. 1: 9); he has been crowned with glory and honour *because* of his suffering and death (2: 9), he has been made perfect through his suffering (2: 10), he has been appointed by God and reckoned to be more worthy than Moses (3: 2–3), he learnt obedience through suffering and has thus been made perfect (5: 7–8), etc. Further, the whole thrust of the argument of the letter as a whole is not really to look backwards to what happened in the period before Jesus' own lifetime. Rather, it is to suggest (1) that with the coming of Jesus a new situation has been created (cf. 1: 1), and (2) that this situation is one whose consequences reach into the indefinite *future*. The results of

Jesus' death have an effect that will not cease. Hence the readers should not be looking for ways in which to make up for alleged 'defects' in the *post*-Jesus situation (e.g. by lapsing back into the Jewish cult). If there is a stress to be placed in 13: 8, it is probably not on the claim that Jesus is the same yesterday as well as today, but on the assertion that Jesus is the same yesterday, today *and for ever*. The Wisdom Christology of 1: 2b–3 remains something of an 'erratic block' within Hebrews and perhaps the more 'adoptionist' language can be seen as more typical of the writer's thought as a whole.

After the opening statement, the author gives a long list of Old Testament quotations applied to Jesus which have enormous christological potential. The main thrust of the section is to show that Jesus is superior to the angels. Quite why this should be deemed necessary is not clear. It is possible that the author sees a danger of angel worship among his readers, though if so this is never explicit. It is possible too that the author is trying to guard against a Christology which sees Jesus as an angel, though this too is never explicit. More likely perhaps is what is implied in 2: 2: the angels are the mediators of the law (cf. Gal. 3: 19, etc.). Hence if Jesus is shown to be far greater than the angels, then the new regime mediated by Jesus must be vastly superior to the regime mediated by the angels, that is for the author of Hebrews, the Jewish cult.[10]

In the course of the argument, there are a number of striking details. Much of the language could be regarded as 'messianic', and indeed the sonship language itself seems to be in part borrowed from the language of Jewish royal ideology so that, for example, the verse from the royal psalm, Psalm 2: 7 ('You are my Son, today I have begotten you') is cited in Hebrews 1: 5 to claim that Jesus is God's Son. Other Old Testament quotations here have, however, potentially more christological significance. Thus in 1: 8, Psalm 45: 6 is quoted with, apparently, Jesus addressed directly as God himself: 'Your throne, *O God*, is for ever and ever'. And in Hebrews 1: 10, verses from Psalm 102: 25–7, originally predicated of God, are here referred to Jesus. According to some this shows an idea of full divinity being ascribed to Jesus.[11]

One should, however, perhaps be a little cautious. The quotation of Psalm 45 is an exact repetition of the words of the psalm which are there addressed to the king. There is presumably no idea of ascribing divinity to the Israelite king in such language when used in the Old Testament, and hence one should be wary of assuming that such an idea is present in Hebrews 1. In any case the dominant thought seems to be not so much that the Son can be called 'God'; rather it is that the throne of the Son is 'for ever and ever' and that, as he has loved righteousness and hated wickedness, God has anointed him above his fellows. His position is above that of the angels because, due to his ethical stance, he has been appointed *by God* to a position on a 'throne' which will be for ever. The dominant theme is the (future) permanence of the position of the Son on the throne he has been given by God. The Son is thus wholly dependent here on God and anything implied in the address of the Son as 'God' as well must be seen in this light. So too in 1: 10–12, Psalm 102 is indeed cited, but clearly here (re-)interpreted as an address *by* God *to* the Son. The note about creative activity picks up of course what is said in Hebrews 1: 3; but the main thrust seems to come at the end with the claim that the position and status of the Son will not change in the future (cf. v. 12b 'you are the same and your years will never end').

The end of the catena introduces an Old Testament citation that will be of crucial significance later in the argument: in 1: 13 the author cites Psalm 110: 1 'Sit at my right hand until I make your enemies a footstool for your feet'. The verse was very widely used in early Christianity, though it is the unique contribution of the author of Hebrews to pick up on another verse from Psalm 110, namely 110: 4: 'You are a priest forever after the order of Melchizedek'. It is quite typical of the author of Hebrews to 'flag up' as it were things that will be considerably developed later by a brief allusion at an earlier point in the discussion.

Whatever the precise nature of the exalted status given to Jesus, the next section of the letter in chapter 2 makes it very clear that Jesus is above all seen as a human figure. The author takes up the verses from Psalm 8: 5–7 'What is man that you are mindful of him or the son of man that you visit him . . .' (v. 5 RSV). 'Son of man' here is clearly just another way of referring to generic 'man' and in itself has no christological significance. However, the author then carries on with the quotation with the claim that 'man' has been made a little lower than the angels but has now been 'crowned with glory and honour'. The author then makes the point that this manifestly does not apply to all human beings. However, he claims that such a statement can be seen to be true of Jesus. By virtue of his suffering and death, he has now been crowned with glory and honour.

Further, it is then made clear that this exalted position of Jesus is one that is to be shared by other human beings in the future. Jesus' role is not to have such a glorious position in splendid isolation but to 'bring *many* children to glory' (Heb. 2: 10). In this respect Jesus is called the 'pioneer' (Greek *archegos*) of their salvation (2: 10), a word which recurs again in 12: 2. A similar idea comes in 6: 20 where Jesus is called a 'forerunner'. So too it is stressed very strongly that Jesus is like others in every respect, and only and precisely insofar as he is similar to others is he in a position to be able to help others. The model with which the author of Hebrews is working is clearly one where Jesus is one who enables others to share in the position and status which he himself occupies. This is clearly similar in some ways to Paul's Adam Christology, though without any idea of Jesus as any kind of corporate personality or of Adam as a corporate figure. Further, 'Adam' as such is not mentioned in Hebrews. Whether then it is right to call this an 'Adam Christology' as such is uncertain,[12] but the similarities between Paul and Hebrews here at a deep level are striking.

Again, though, at the very end of the section the writer 'flags up' what will be a key element in the later discussion: Jesus' similarity to others is to enable him to be a 'merciful and faithful *high priest*' (2: 17) and it is this idea of Jesus as high priest which is so distinctive and so characteristic of this letter.

The notion of Jesus as a high priest is developed by the author of Hebrews in the body of the letter, above all in chapters 7–10. The general aim is clearly to show the superiority of both the person of Jesus as priest and also the results of his priestly activity in relation to priests and priestly activity in the Jewish cult.

One way this is done is by fastening on the Old Testament verse Psalm 110: 4 'You are a priest for ever after the order of Melchizedek'. As we have already noted, the first verse of Psalm 110 ('The Lord said to my Lord, sit at my right hand') was very widely used in early Christianity. It seems to have been a peculiar and distinctive feature of Hebrews to have latched on to this other verse of Psalm 110 and to have developed the idea of Jesus as a priestly figure. But it is as a particular kind of priest, namely a priest 'after the order of Melchizedek'. This is adumbrated earlier in Hebrews 5: 6, 10 but then developed in detail in chapter 7.

The mysterious figure of Melchizedek appears in the Old Testament outside Psalm 110 only in the brief and enigmatic story of Gen. 14: 18–20.

He appears out of the blue as a king whom Abraham meets after his rescue of Lot. Little is made of the story in Genesis itself, though it is clear that the enigmatic figure of Melchizedek led to speculation by other Jewish groups about this figure, notably in the so-called Melchizedek scroll from Qumran (11QMelch = 11Q13) where Melchizedek seems to take the role of God's agent as judge in the heavenly court.[13] The development in Hebrews is, however, quite different. The author fastens on many details (and silences) in the brief account of Genesis in order to try to show the innate superiority of Melchizedek over Abraham and hence, derivatively, the superiority of the priesthood of Jesus, the priest after the order of Melchizedek, over the Levitical priesthood.

We have already seen how the author of Hebrews plays on the fact that no mention is made of Melchizedek's parents to claim that he must have been 'without father or mother' (a slightly bizarre argument from silence!) and in this respect he is like the Son who is also eternal. The author then seizes on the details in the story in Genesis where Abraham paid tithes to Melchizedek and Melchizedek blessed him. This he claims shows the innate inferiority of Abraham to Melchizedek, and hence derivatively of the Levitical priesthood which derived from Abraham (since Levi was a descendant of Abraham). Indeed the writer claims that Levi himself paid tithes to Melchizedek 'because he was still in the loins of his ancestor when Melchizedek met him' (Heb. 7: 10). As well as emphasising the superiority of the Melchizedek-type priesthood over the Levitical priesthood, the writer emphasises the radical difference and discontinuity between the two systems. Jesus, the priest of the Melchizedek line, is of a different tribe (Judah) from the Aaronic priests (cf. vv. 13–14). Further, the Levitical priesthood needs a succession of different priests since they all die, whereas the priesthood of Jesus continues forever (vv. 23–4).

The argument of chapter 7 is then taken up in chapter 8 with the claim that 'we [do indeed] have such a high priest' (8: 1) in the person of Jesus. And the author then proceeds to spell out what exactly has been achieved and is being achieved by Jesus as the Melchizedek-type high priest. This he does by reference to the theme of sacrifice and also intercession.

In relation to sacrifice, the author develops two ideas. In chapter 8, Jesus is first presented as the inaugurator of a new covenant. The author cites in full the famous prophecy of a new covenant, in Jeremiah 31, in Hebrews 8: 8–12 and claims that the very name of the covenant as 'the *new* covenant' must render the old covenant obsolete (v. 13).

But then the author proceeds to draw out yet further analogies and comparisons, this time with the institution of the great sacrifice on the Day of Atonement (chs 9–10). Perhaps because the problem he is facing is one of worry about continuing sin and the efficacy of forgiveness/atonement available, the author makes a startling move in identifying Jesus not only as the high priest but also as the sacrifice itself. Jesus then as the high priest offers *himself* as the definitive and final atonement sacrifice. Again the author claims that there are both similarities and differences. Jesus is both an atonement sacrifice, like that of the Jewish cult, and also far greater than anything present in that cult. The author focuses especially on the physical arrangements of the Temple, especially the separation of the Holy of Holies, the place thought to be where the presence of God himself dwelt. This was only ever entered once a year by the high priest on the Day of Atonement. The author deduces from this that, under the old dispensation, access to God is not available. Further, the atonement rites offered by the high priest never succeed in removing the barrier of sin but deal only with ceremonial defilement (9: 10). All this is, according to Hebrews, far outpassed by the action of Jesus as high priest who has offered himself as a sacrifice and in doing so has passed into the heavenly sanctuary (9: 12).[14] It is here that some of the more Platonic-type elements emerge in the discussion. The author seems to think of the heavenly sanctuary existing alongside the earthly one, the latter being a pale imitation of the former. Hence the claim that in his death, and passing from a life on this earth to a life in heaven, Jesus has made the transition past the veil which covers the entrance to the Holy of Holies and entered the true heavenly sanctuary. This may then be in part due to the author's being influenced by a Platonic-like dualism; it may though also be the inevitable consequence of trying to press Christian claims about Jesus into a verbal image that can scarcely take them without some strain!

The author now reverts to the idea of the new covenant to show that the effects of Jesus' sacrifice are permanent. Thus 'whereas an atonement sacrifice deals with past sins, a covenant sacrifice inaugurates a permanent arrangement for the future'.[15] This is the main point of the ensuing discussion in 9: 15–28. Further, the non-repeated nature of Jesus' death shows that the arrangement is permanent and does not have to be repeated (cf. also 10: 1–12).

Finally, we may note the way in which the author of Hebrews thinks of Jesus as now in heaven, having made his once-for-all sacrifice of himself, interceding to God on behalf of others (7: 25). Thus the activity of Jesus continues on in the present and into the indefinite future as the one who continually pleads the cause of other human beings before God. Hence there is no need to resort to any other means for access to God. Any such attempt would be a denial of the person of Jesus and all that he has achieved, a danger which then earns the harshest warnings from the author (cf. 6: 4–6, etc.).

The argument of Hebrews is involved and not always easy to follow. Clearly it presupposes ideas and categories of thought that are somewhat alien to many modern people. The whole idea of the sacrificial cult, for example, is assumed here as self-evidently valid without any question, even though for many today such ideas are alien if not repugnant. Nevertheless, within its own frame of reference, it is a powerful argument, developing ideas about Jesus and his work that are quite different from those of Paul and of other New Testament writers. If nothing else, Hebrews shows the variety and complexity of New Testament Christology. But Hebrews also shows us the variety and complexity which can exist within a single writer. As we have seen, the author of Hebrews can speak of Jesus in all but divine terms, he can have Jesus addressed as 'God' at one point, and he can evidently think in terms of Jesus as pre-existent. But alongside this, he can present Jesus as a supremely human figure, one who was – and must be – similar in every respect to other human beings if he is to be their true helper.

NOTES

1. It is, for example, taken as Pauline in the old Authorised Version. So too it is placed among the other Pauline letters in one of the earliest manuscripts we have of the epistles, namely P[46] (the so-called Chester-Beatty papyrus).
2. Heb. 13: 23 refers to 'our brother Timothy', suggesting perhaps the author has some connection with the members of Paul's entourage.
3. B. Lindars, *The Theology of the Letter to the Hebrews* (Cambridge: CUP, 1991), pp. 4–15.
4. We should, however, note here that the issue seems to be primarily one about the value of the Jewish *cultic* system. Unlike the position in, say,

Pauline churches, the issue of the Jewish law as an ethical requirement is not really raised at all. Indeed, the author of Hebrews (like Paul) assumes as self-evident that Jewish Scripture has lost none of its validity as scriptural witness and hence can be mined and used continuously.

5. Any direct influence of Philo on Hebrews is, however, unlikely: see R. Williamson, *Philo and the Epistle to the Hebrews* (Leiden: Brill, 1970).

6. See C. K. Barrett, 'The eschatology of the Epistle to the Hebrews', in W. D. Davies and D. Daube (eds), *The Background of the New Testament and its Eschatology* (FS C. H. Dodd; Cambridge: CUP, 1956), pp. 365–93.

7. On the use of Scripture in general in Hebrews, see G. Hughes, *Hebrews and Hermeneutics* (SNTSMS 36; Cambridge: CUP, 1979).

8. Cf. Dunn, *Christology*, pp. 52–5; Lindars, *Theology*, p. 33; cf. also G. B. Caird, 'Son by appointment', in W. C. Weinrich (ed.), *The New Testament Age* (2 vols; FS B. Reicke; Macon: Mercer University Press, 1984), vol. 1, pp. 73–81.

9. See Dunn, *Christology*, p. 52; *Unity*, p. 259.

10. The law as ethical command does not seem to be an issue in the context of the writing of Hebrews: cf. n. 4 above.

11. Cf. e.g. Ben Witherington, *The Many Faces of the Christ: The Christologies of the New Testament and Beyond* (New York: Crossroad, 1998), pp. 215–16.

12. Dunn, *Christology*, pp. 109–11, treats this explicitly in his chapter on Jesus as the 'Last Adam', though cf. the reservations expressed by Lindars, *Theology*, p. 39: there is no reference to Adam as such.

13. He is even apparently called 'God' at one point: cf. 11QMelch [=11Q13] 2: 10. See p. 28 above.

14. The author is probably referring to the Holy of Holies, though rather confusingly speaks here of the 'Holy Place', i.e. the temple itself. Perhaps the author is thinking of heaven as a single-chamber temple: see the discussion in Lindars, *Theology*, p. 91.

15. Lindars, *Theology*, p. 95.

Part 2

THE SYNOPTIC GOSPELS

Chapter 5

INTRODUCTION TO THE GOSPELS

When we turn from the New Testament epistles to the Gospels, we are clearly turning to a very different kind of literature, a different *genre*. Instead of letters dealing with doctrinal and ethical issues in Christian communities after the time of Jesus, we have texts that purport to be giving information in story form about the life of Jesus himself. At first sight it is tempting to take these texts at face value for what they appear to be: exact transcripts of things that Jesus actually said and did, and reliable sources of information about Jesus himself.

For a variety of reasons, such an option is not one which we can easily take today. For a start, the very fact that there are four Gospels makes for difficulty in this respect: the four Gospels are by no means identical and the picture of Jesus which each one gives is at times very different from that given in each of the other Gospels. Thus, as we have already noted in the introductory chapter, the Gospels may tell us as much about the views of their authors as they do about the events they are purportedly describing.

In relation to the Fourth Gospel, such a view has been accepted as critical orthodoxy for a long time. The picture of Jesus in John is in many respects very different from the picture in the other three, so-called 'synoptic', Gospels. Further, most would agree that, in general terms, the synoptic picture is more likely to reflect the realities of Jesus' own time, and the Johannine account represents an (at times) extensive rewriting of the Jesus tradition by a later Christian profoundly influenced by his own ideas and circumstances.[1] However, it is now recognised that what applies to the Fourth Gospel applies equally to all the Gospels: the synoptic Gospels, quite as much as John, have been influenced by the ideas and the circumstances of their authors. Thus in reading *all* the Gospels, we have to be aware of the fact that we are reading accounts of Jesus' life as mediated by later Christians and hence we may learn as much, if not more, about the latter as about Jesus himself in studying the Gospel texts.

The situation regarding the synoptic Gospels is rendered easier in one way (though more complex in another) by the fact that the three Gospels are very similar to each other. The very word 'synoptic' used to describe these Gospels refers to the fact that they can be placed along-side each other and compared with each other, often story by story and at times word by word.[2] Thus it is almost universally agreed today that the three synoptic Gospels are in some kind of *literary* relationship with each other. The similarities between them are so extensive and wide ranging that it seems most likely that one evangelist has used one of the other synoptic Gospels as a source, or that the evangelists have used common source material. The most widely held view today is the so-called Two Source Theory. This postulates that Mark's Gospel was the earliest to be written and was used by Matthew and Luke as a source; further, Matthew and Luke also had access to a further source, or body of source material, now lost and today known as 'Q'. There is not enough space here to defend this theory, and full treatments can be found elsewhere.[3] I shall therefore assume it in the rest of this study.

One's solution to the Synoptic Problem might have considerable effect on one's assessment of the work of the evangelists in writing their Gospels. Certainly in earlier scholarship, a so-called 'redaction-critical' approach to the Gospels, which (broadly speaking) attempted to iden-tify the particular ideas and characteristics of the evangelists, was often explicitly based on a particular solution to the source-critical question of the relationship between the Gospels. Thus, in seeking to isolate, say, Matthew's or Luke's ideas, attention was focused on the ways in which Matthew or Luke had changed (or 'redacted') their presumed source Mark. The differences between Matthew/Luke and Mark were then the prime source of evidence for determining Matthew's/Luke's ideas.

Such an approach has however been called into question in recent years.[4] Such a method does make any 'results' of redaction criticism potentially heavily dependent on one's solution to the Synoptic Problem; and it has become clear in recent times that probably no one can ever claim to have finally and definitively solved the Synoptic Problem for ever. But more important is the fact that focusing on the changes which an evangelist made to his tradition may well give a misleading, if not distorted, picture of the Gospel writer's concerns. For such changes constitute only part of the evidence of the Gospel. Just as potentially important are instances where the evangelist has agreed with his source material and hence taken a positive decision to reproduce that material without any significant change. By focusing only on changes one is in danger of missing, or discounting, such material completely. Thus in recent times, there has been a trend to take more seriously the evidence of the Gospel text considered as a whole as providing the primary evidence for determining the particular concerns of an evangelist. Thus, in seeking to identify the particular christological ideas of, say, Matthew, we should consider not only Matthew's changes to Mark (or to Q if we could identify the Q wording in any instance with a degree of certainty); we should also consider the Gospel taken as a whole, perhaps bracketing off the question of where Matthew's text has come from and what sources he has used to construct his present text. It would probably be wrong to play one of the above approaches off against the other. Rather, both have a legitimate role to play in any search for the distinctive views of the Gospel writers. Thus in what follows, I shall seek to use insights of both approaches, the so-called 'diachronic' *and* 'synchronic', in seeking to determine the Christologies of the evangelists.

A further problem in relation to the Gospels has already been alluded to in the first chapter. None of the Gospel writers ever addresses his readers directly. (Mark 13: 14 or John 21: 24–5 are perhaps the nearest one gets.) Rather, each of the evangelists tells a story, and, insofar as 'ideas' are being promoted through the story, the ideas are articulated by characters in the story. What we have is therefore a 'narrative Christology'. But how far can the ideas and views attributed to characters in the story be regarded as those of the evangelist himself? Or how far is the evangelist recording (or trying to record) the views of people in the past?

Clearly there is no single answer which will cover all cases. The evangelists differ among themselves; and the various characters in their stories differ. The question may be particularly pressing in the case of Luke, who may be more conscious of the pastness of the past, as we shall see. It is also clear that, even within the 'story worlds' of the evangelists' stories, characters differ from each other and some are more 'reliable' than others.[5] The views of a Judas, or of a high priest, or a Pharisaic opponent of Jesus, are presumably not shared by the evangelist telling the story. In contrast, without strong evidence to the contrary, it would seem reasonable to assume that the views of Jesus himself, or of God (on the rare occasions these are made explicit), are regarded positively by the evangelist.

With these preliminaries in mind, we may turn to be Gospels themselves. I start with what I am assuming here to be the earliest Gospel, namely the Gospel of Mark.

NOTES

1. On this, see ch. 9 below.
2. The Greek word *syn* means 'with', 'optic' refers to viewing – hence 'synoptic' implies being able to be seen together.
3. The classic treatment in the English-speaking world is probably still B. H. Streeter, *The Four Gospels* (London: Macmillan, 1924). See too Kümmel, *Introduction*, pp. 38–80. A useful collection of essays is provided by A. Bellinzoni (ed.), *The Two Source Hypothesis: A Critical Appraisal* (Macon: Mercer University Press, 1985). One of the main competitors to the Two Source Theory is the revived 'Griesbach hypothesis' (according to which Matthew comes first, Luke second, and Mark is dependent on both Matthew and Luke): see W. R. Farmer, *The Synoptic Problem* (Dillsboro: Western North Carolina Press, ²1976). On this see my *The Revival of the Griesbach Hypothesis* (SNTSMS 44; Cambridge: CUP, 1983). For more on the theory of the existence of Q, see ch. 12 below.
4. Cf. my *Reading*, pp. 120–3.
5. The word 'reliable' is something of a technical term in literary studies to refer to a character whose viewpoint is that of the author and which is being commended to the reader through the story.

Chapter 6

MARK

The person of Jesus is absolutely central for Mark. Such a statement may sound bland, even trite to the point of being ridiculous. As we have already said, the person of Jesus was central for all early Christians. And to say that Jesus occupies centre stage in Mark's story hardly distinguishes Mark from the other evangelists: in all the Gospels, Jesus is the central figure of the narrative. Yet it is perhaps the case that, even more than in the Gospels of Matthew and Luke, the question of who Jesus is provides the central focus of Mark's narrative. The opening verse identifies who the narrative is all about ('The gospel of Jesus Christ, the Son of God' 1: 1); John the Baptist in Mark speaks only about Jesus in his preaching (1: 7–8);[1] the voice from heaven at Jesus' baptism speaks only to identify who Jesus is ('You are my Son, the Beloved' 1: 11). And this continues throughout the story as told by Mark. A key point in the narrative is the confession of Peter at Caesarea Philippi where Peter makes his assertion about Jesus' identity ('You are the Christ' 8: 29). At Jesus' trial before the Sanhedrin, a key issue is clearly the question of who Jesus is (14: 61–2); and finally, when Jesus dies, the centurion at the foot of the cross identifies and confesses Jesus as the Son of God (15: 39). Coupled with this is a prominent theme running through the whole of Mark's Gospel concerning *secrecy*. On several occasions, Jesus seeks to hide his identity and keep it secret (cf. 1: 39; 3: 11–12; 8: 30; 9: 9, etc.) The question then of who Jesus is – and perhaps who is allowed (or can) know who he is – is an absolutely central one for Mark.[2]

We must also bear in mind all that has been said in the introductory chapter about the nature of the Gospels as narratives, and about the fact that Mark does not write a doctrinal treatise on Christology.

Christology is of vital importance for Mark, but he presents what he wants to say in the form of a story. Mark's Christology is thus very much a 'narrative Christology'. Yet we should not lose sight of the fact that, in the telling of his narrative, key christological terms or 'titles' play an important role. Part of Mark's aim is clearly to ascribe such terms or titles to Jesus; part too of his aim may have been to give a particular emphasis or 'twist' to some of these titles, via the narrative. It may therefore be appropriate to try to approach the question of Mark's Christology via his use of key christological titles, whilst bearing in mind all the caveats we mentioned earlier about over-reliance on the use of titles in analysing New Testament Christology.

Lord

The term Lord (*kyrios*) seems to play a rather insignificant role in Mark. This is perhaps surprising, given that Mark (very probably) comes from a Hellenistic Christian milieu, and in many respects shows himself strikingly similar to Paul and Pauline Christianity. Yet *kyrios* does not seem to have been a very important term christologically for Mark. It occurs in Mark 5: 19 at the end of the story of the Gerasene demoniac ('Tell them how much the Lord has done for you'); but it is not clear if the reference here is to Jesus or to God. In Jesus' instructions to the two disciples to fetch the colt on which he will ride into Jerusalem, they are told to tell anyone who asks that 'The Lord needs it' (11: 3); but it is uncertain how significant christologically this is: the words could simply mean 'our master needs it'. Finally, there is the debate in 12: 35–8 between Jesus and the scribes about whether the Messiah can be the Son of David. Jesus, appealing to Psalm 110, claims that the Messiah must be David's 'Lord' and hence cannot be his son. Again the significance is not at all clear. The argument seems to be something of a verbal swordplay; and it is in any case not explicitly related to Jesus himself but has the form of a rather abstract discussion about 'the Messiah' in general.

These are the only instances where Mark uses *kyrios* in a potentially christological way and hence it seems that the term was not of great interest or significance for him.

Messiah

There is more uncertainty about the significance of the term Messiah/Christ for Mark. In terms of numbers of occurrences, the word *christos* is relatively rare in the Gospel, occurring only seven times (1: 1; 8: 29; 9: 41; 12: 35; 13: 21; 14: 61; 15: 32). How significant the term is, and what meaning Mark attaches to the term, is not always clear. For example in 9: 41 ('whoever gives you a cup of water to drink because you bear the name of Christ') the term seems to have lost all its original significance as a title and has become just a proper name. The same may also apply in the title verse in 1: 1 ('The gospel of Jesus Christ'). In 13: 21 the word refers to false messiahs; in 15: 32 it is part of the mockery of Jesus by the crowds while he hangs on the cross; and 12: 35 is part of the somewhat abstract debate between Jesus and the scribes which we have already considered briefly (cf. above).

The term does occur significantly in Peter's confession (8: 29) and in the question put to Jesus about his identity by the high priest at the Sanhedrin trial (14: 61). Further, whatever its precise significance, the word does occur in the title verse 1: 1, part of the function of which is evidently to announce to the reader right at the start who Jesus is and what categories he is to be seen in.

Yet there must remain some doubt about just how significant this is as a christological category. It is clearly one that Mark does not regard negatively.[3] Yet one wonders if it expresses the most important aspect of Jesus' person for Mark. This may be indicated by two pieces of evidence. First, in the two main occurrences where Jesus is called the Christ (and in both, implicitly or explicitly, accepts the term), Jesus is immediately portrayed as going on to refer to his role as Son of Man (8: 31; 14: 62). Perhaps then, for Mark, talk of Jesus as a Messiah figure has to be qualified by reference to Jesus as a Son of Man figure.

Second, the way the story of Peter's confession is told in Mark's narrative may be revealing. The story is placed by Mark immediately after the story of the healing of the blind man at Bethsaida (8: 22–6). It is widely agreed that the two stories are deliberately juxtaposed by Mark: the healing of the blind man serves as a kind of 'acted parable' for Peter's confession, so that the man coming to 'sight' illustrates Peter's coming to the 'insight' of who Jesus is. The healing story is, however, notable for the fact that the man only comes to full sight gradually. He is healed in two stages, and after the first stage, can only see in a confused way. It may be then that Mark wishes to imply that Peter only comes to a true insight of who Jesus is gradually, and at this point in the narrative, with his confession of Jesus as Messiah, has only reached an intermediate stage.[4] This is suggested too by the immediate sequel to the story in Mark: here Jesus speaks of his role (as Son of Man) as one who must suffer rejection, violence and death (8: 31), a role which Peter vehemently disputes (v. 32) and which in turn evokes a stern rebuke by Jesus ('Get behind me, Satan!' v. 33). It seems that, for all Peter's correct insight in his confession, he has failed to grasp one of the most important facets of Jesus' mission. Thus for Mark, although messiahship is an important factor in the picture of who Jesus is, it may not express all that there is to say, perhaps not even the most important thing about Jesus. As already hinted at, some of this may be indicated by the use of the term Son of Man.

Son of Man

In terms of numbers of occurrences the term Son of Man is clearly of great importance for Mark, occurring as it does some fourteen times. Apart from two occurrences in chapter 2 which seem to refer to Jesus' activity in his earthly ministry (2: 10, 28), the phrase comes exclusively in the second half of the Gospel. Here it is used in two related contexts. First, it is used by Jesus to relate to his destiny of having to undergo suffering and death (cf. the three passion predictions in 8: 31; 9: 31; 10: 33, all of which are in terms of Jesus in his role as Son of Man; also similarly 9: 13; 10: 45; 14: 21, etc.). Then secondly it is used to refer to Jesus in his role at the parousia, 'coming' as the one vindicated by God and now active in dispensing judgement (8: 38; 13: 26; 14: 62).

It is quite clear that, for Mark at least, the last part of this overall picture is seen in terms of the vision of Daniel 7. Mark 14: 62 and 13: 26 clearly allude to the Danielic passage (cf. the language of the Son of Man 'coming' on/with the 'clouds of heaven'). Hence Jesus *qua* Son of Man is clearly identified with the figure who is described in Daniel 7: 13 as 'one like a son of man'.

Although it is disputed, a strong case can be made for the other main pole of Mark's language about Jesus as Son of Man being also Danielic, namely the idea of Jesus as the one who is to suffer. In Daniel 7, the 'one like a son of man' acts as some kind of representative of the 'saints of the Most High'. In Daniel's vision these correspond to the Jews suffering persecution under Antiochus Epiphanes because of loyalty to their Jewish faith and practice. Thus although the 'son of man' figure of Daniel 7 is not explicitly said to be a suffering figure, nevertheless the context in which the chapter was written suggests strongly that the scene of vindication and triumph which it paints is one of triumph out of suffering. Thus built into the Danielic picture may be the twin idea of both suffering *and* subsequent vindication. It is just this which is reflected in Mark's picture of Jesus: Jesus *qua* Son of Man fulfils the Danielic role by being one whose destiny is to suffer but who is promised vindication after that suffering in the heavenly court.[5]

Both these features are clearly of great significance for Mark. The idea that Jesus is one who must suffer is one that dominates the Gospel. The whole narrative is structured to show in story form the gradual build-up in hostility to Jesus by others, and also the failure of the disciples to support him, so that in the end Jesus is isolated from everyone and dies alone and almost in despair (cf. the cry of dereliction in 15: 34). Yet beyond that despair there is hope and a promise of vindication by God, so that Jesus will come again at the end of time in triumph (13: 26; 14: 62).

It may be worth noting too at this point that the two Son of Man sayings in the early part of the Gospel (2: 10, 28) may also fit this pattern.[6] Both occur in a series of five controversies (2: 1–3: 6) which illustrate the start of the build-up of the hostility to Jesus shown by the Jewish authorities, a hostility which will end in his death (cf. the death plot in 3: 6). A number of features in these stories act as pointers to the reader to the fate in store for Jesus.[7] The references to Jesus as Son of Man may perform the same function, acting as hints to the reader of what is to come: the one who can forgive sins (2: 10) and who also is Lord of the Sabbath (2: 28) is the one who is arousing hostility and opposition and who will therefore have to go the way of the 'Son of Man' figure, the way that leads to the cross.

Seen in this light the Son of Man sayings in Mark show a remarkable coherence and homogeneity; they also clearly highlight key features of what is important about Jesus for Mark. Yet does Son of Man express the most profound truth about Jesus for Mark? Arguably not.[8] As in all the Gospels, no character apart from Jesus uses the term. It is thus never used in any kind of confessional setting: no one ever says 'you are the Son of Man'. Nor is there any secrecy attached to the term. Quite what the significance of secrecy is in Mark is debated; but one important aspect seems to be that it provides a means by which Jesus' true identity is only revealed when it is clear that it will not be misunderstood. Yet no secrecy attaches to the term Son of Man. No one is ever warned not to make Jesus' identity as Son of Man known to others. Finally we may note that on just two occasions in Mark, God himself speaks. In the stories of the baptism and the transfiguration, a voice from heaven says that Jesus is 'my son' (1: 11; 9: 7), implying that Jesus is to be seen as Son *of God*.[9] It is then perhaps 'Son of God' that expresses a yet more profound truth about who Jesus is, and it is to this that we must now turn.

Son of God

Although not frequent in the Gospel, the term Son of God applied to Jesus occurs at key points in Mark's narrative. It (probably) occurs in the title verse 1: 1,[10] whose function is in part to define for the readers the terms of the story to come:[11] the narrative is about the one who is the Son of God – indeed, as we shall see, the narrative to a certain extent defines what divine sonship means. The application of the 'title' to Jesus is given the backing of the authority of God himself in the words of the voice from heaven at the baptism and the transfiguration.[12] The demons recognise that Jesus is the Son of God, but their knowledge is put under a ban of secrecy (3: 11–12). Only at the Sanhedrin trial does Jesus himself acknowledge the term openly (14: 61–2). Then, in what is a climactic scene in Mark's narrative, at the moment when Jesus dies on the cross, the centurion confesses Jesus to have been the Son of God (15: 39). Despite then its relatively infrequent occurrence in the Gospel, it seems clear that Son of God is of vital significance for Mark as the term most adequately describing who Jesus is. But what does the phrase imply or mean?

We have seen in chapter 1 that the term had a very wide range of possible meanings in the ancient world. One possible meaning is reflected in the use of the phrase in Judaism to refer to a righteous sufferer, a person persecuted for his faith and his commitment (Wisd. 2–5). A background such as this would certainly explain some of the Markan references, especially the verses in the passion narrative. But it remains doubtful how far this will explain the fact that Jesus *qua* exorcist is seen as Son of God (cf. Mark 3: 11–12), or the heavy invest-ment in the term made in 1: 1; 1: 11; 9: 7.

Another possibility is that the term is used messianically: Jesus *qua* Son of God is seen as the Messiah.[13] A lot of the Markan evidence would appear to support this. The question of the high priest at the

Sanhedrin trial ('Are you the Christ, the son of the Blessed [i.e. God]?') places Christ/Messiah and Son of God in parallel as if they were synonymous. So too the opening title verse does almost the same.[14] If at the same time a Messiah is conceived in terms of a royal figure, this would all tie in with the very strong stress that emerges in the later part of Mark's passion narrative (especially ch. 15) where it is implied repeatedly that Jesus is a 'king'.[15] So, too, right at the start of Mark's passion narrative, Jesus is 'anointed' (14: 3–9). There is then a powerful strain in Mark's passion narrative emphasising that Jesus is a *royal* figure: it is as the messianic king that he goes to his death, even though the very narrative itself, by virtue of the fact that it is recounting a violent and shameful death, implies an almost complete reversal of previous ideas of what royalty and messiahship involved. It may be then that Jesus' divine sonship is seen by Mark exclusively in these royal, messianic terms.

Yet it may be that Son of God for Mark expresses more as well. We have already seen that the word 'Messiah' itself is relatively rare in Mark and does not receive an enormous emphasis. Further, as we saw, the story in 8: 26–30 may imply that Peter's confession of Jesus as *christos* is somewhat inadequate. It *may* be that it is simply the *idea* of messiahship that is inadequate, and to a certain extent this must be the case, since Mark clearly does not regard the term *christos* itself as an improper one to apply to Jesus. Yet it may also be that Mark regards (an)other term(s) as more adequate to capture the essence of who Jesus is. In one way, Son of Man may be exercising this role.[16] But it may also be that Son of God, whilst in one way capable of being taken as (simply) a messianic, royal term, also carries further overtones of meaning for Mark. It may then be these that are important for Mark and hence lead to the term being used on its own, without an explicit reference to messiahship, in such key contexts as 1: 11, 9: 7 and 15: 39.

The scene at the crucifixion may provide the key. Here the centurion's confession (15: 39) is in response to the actual death of Jesus (v. 37); but that moment of death is immediately followed by the note about the veil of the Temple being torn in two (v. 38). This note about the veil is clearly meant to have great symbolic meaning for Mark, as in some way indicating the theological consequences and significance of Jesus' death. The problem is to know what that significance is, and in particular to know which veil is in mind. Two possibilities are often noted. One is that the veil is the barrier separating Jews from Gentiles – hence its removal means the universalisation of the Gospel to encompass all people. However, it may be that what is in mind is the veil inside the Holy of Holies in the Temple. This is the veil that symbolically hides and separates God from all human beings. If then it is this veil that is symbolically destroyed in the death of Jesus, then Mark's narrative becomes an extraordinarily powerful piece of theological writing. For the narrative implies that, in the death of Jesus, the barrier preventing human beings from seeing God has been removed. God is now seen – but is seen precisely in the figure of the dead Jesus hanging on a cross. It is then this that seems to be reflected in the centurion's confession of Jesus as Son of God.[17]

Jesus *qua* Son of God is the one who enables God himself to be seen. (In this then Mark is perhaps closer to much later Christian claims about Jesus' divine sonship than others.) But the context is also vitally important. For not only does the centurion's confession say something about Jesus: it may also say something about *God*. The narrative seems to be emphasising starkly that God is to be seen in this figure of powerlessness, weakness and death. This too is what Mark's narrative has been leading up to as a climax. It is the moment when Jesus' true identity is seen in its clearest light and hence shows what it means to be '*Son* of God'. But it also shows something of the God who lies behind the whole story, who defines and accepts Jesus as his Son, and who reveals himself – on the cross. The very first line of Mark's Gospel defines the terms of the story that is to come: Jesus *is* the Son of God. But what sonship means, *and* what 'God' means, is determined by the story itself. It is thus very much the case that Mark offers a *narrative* Christology. The story is vital and indispensable for his message. It is almost as if Mark is aware that christological terms can be multivalent. Hence he writes his story to show what he regards as the true significance of words that can be spoken. Jesus is the Christ, the Son of God. But the nature of kingship, sonship and of divinity, are all given a stark new meaning by Mark's story, especially by his account of Jesus' death on the cross. Mark's Jesus is perhaps closest to the 'crucified God' of some modern theologians.[18]

NOTES

1. In this then Mark differs from Q where John the Baptist gives his own eschatological preaching and warnings: cf. Luke 3: 7–9 par.

2. On the theme of secrecy in Mark, see my Introduction and the other essays in Tuckett (ed.), *The Messianic Secret* (London: SPCK, 1983); also H. Räisänen, *The Messianic Secret in Mark's Gospel* (ET Edinburgh: T&T Clark, 1991).

3. This has been denied by some who have argued that Mark is uniformly negative about the disciples in the story: cf. e.g. T. J. Weeden, *Mark – Traditions in Conflict* (Philadelphia: Fortress Press, 1971), who thinks that Mark is conducting something of a vendetta against the disciples in the story and, through them, against an opposition group in his own church. However, the structure of the pericope here suggests that Mark thinks that Peter's confession is not entirely wrong: the words of Peter are clearly contrasted with the views of the 'people' mentioned in vv. 27–8. Clearly they are *in*adequate – hence the implication is that Peter's viewpoint is better. Whether it is entirely right is another matter: see below.

4. Cf. E. S. Johnson, 'Mark 8: 22–26. The Blind Man from Bethsaida', *NTS* 25 (1979), pp. 370–83.

5. For a similar view, cf. M. D. Hooker, *The Son of Man in Mark* (London: SPCK, 1967). See further, pp. 216–19 below (in relation to Jesus himself).

6. For what follows, cf. my 'The present Son of Man', *JSNT*, 14 (1982), pp. 58–81.

7. E.g., in 2: 7 Jesus is accused of 'blasphemy', anticipating the charge on which he will be condemned to death in 14: 64. In 2: 20, the prediction is made that the time will come when 'the bridegroom will be taken away', almost certainly another allusion to Jesus' death.

8. For what follows, cf. J. D. Kingsbury, *The Christology of Mark's Gospel* (Philadelphia: Fortress Press, 1983), esp. pp. 157–66 (although I am less persuaded by Kingsbury's own interpretation of the significance of Son of Man for Mark).

9. Kingsbury rightly stresses the importance of the fact that here it is *God* himself speaking, and hence presumably expressing a 'point of view' which Mark would regard as unquestionably valid and important. This must then tell against some who have argued that Mark wishes to 'correct' a 'Son of God' Christology by his 'Son of Man' Christology: cf. Weeden, *Mark*; also N. Perrin, 'The Christology of Mark: A study in Methodology', *JR* 51 (1971), pp. 173–87, repr. in W. R. Telford (ed.), *The Interpretation of Mark* (London: SPCK, 1985), pp. 95–108.

10. The words 'Son of God' are missing from some MSS of Mark, but the importance of the term in the rest of Mark suggests that they should probably be read here as well.

11. This probably applies to the whole of the prologue of the Gospel in 1: 1–13 (or perhaps 1: 1–15): see F. J. Matera, 'The prologue as the

interpretative key to Mark's gospel', *JSNT* 34 (1988), pp. 3–20; and what applies to the prologue applies to the initial 'title' verse even more.

12. Hence any theories that Mark disapproved of the term, or wanted to correct it, e.g. via Son of Man, are very implausible. Cf. n. 9 above.

13. Cf. D. H. Juel, 'The origin of Mark's Christology', in Charlesworth (ed.), *The Messiah*, pp. 449–60.

14. Though 'Christ' in 1: 1 has no definite article and is virtually a proper name: cf. above.

15. Cf. 15: 2, 9, 12, 18, 26, 32. Some of these are said in apparent mockery, but Mark's passion narrative is shot through with a powerful use of irony and hence these mockings are probably intended by Mark to express a profound truth about Jesus.

16. As we have already noted, talk of Jesus' messiahship in 8: 30 and in 14: 61 is immediately qualified by Mark's Jesus talking of himself as Son of Man.

17. Cf. H. L. Chronis, 'The torn veil: Cultus and Christology in Mark 15: 37–39', *JBL* 101 (1982), pp. 97–114.

18. Cf. especially J. Moltmann, *The Crucified God* (ET London: SCM Press, 1974), whose debt to the Markan passion narrative is clear.

Chapter 7

MATTHEW

—⊃⊂—

All the general observations we have already made – about the potentially misleading picture which can emerge by focusing on christological titles alone, and about the importance of taking seriously the genre of the Gospels as stories, not doctrinal treatises – apply even more when we turn to the Gospel of Matthew and seek to identify Matthew's Christology. We must also be alive to the possibility that a neat, coherent Christology may not emerge from the Gospel. Matthew is famous (or infamous!) among the evangelists for presenting elements that appear at times to be in considerable tension with each other on key issues such as Jesus' attitude to the Jewish Law, or Jesus' attitude to Gentiles.[1] There is no space here to enter into these debates, but their very existence should alert us to the fact that the Christology which emerges from Matthew's Gospel may present at least a rather variegated picture.

With Matthew we must also be aware of the evangelist's indebtedness to his sources. Matthew is almost certainly using Mark as a source, and, as we have seen, Mark's Gospel focuses on the christological question of who Jesus is in a major way. Many of the texts that are key parts of the evidence for Mark's Christology thus reappear in Matthew. We cannot discount the significance such texts might have in Matthew simply because they are taken over from Mark. Matthew has made a conscious decision to include them and hence they contribute to the overall picture of Matthew's Christology.[2] But we may also note some places where Matthew changes Mark in rewriting the Markan account, and some of these changes may tell us a lot about Matthew's own concerns. Our approach here will therefore be both synchronic and diachronic, looking at Matthew's story as a whole *and* at the way he has (at times) adapted his sources.

I start with some of the christological titles used by Matthew, but we must bear in mind that these may only give us part of the whole picture.

Son of God

Few would question the importance of the category Son of God as being of crucial significance for Matthew's Christology. Within modern Matthean scholarship, no one has done more to emphasize this than J. D. Kingsbury who, in a range of studies and using a number of different approaches to the text, has shown how the term plays a key role in Matthew's presentation of the Gospel story.[3]

Several of the key texts are taken over by Matthew from Mark (though, as already noted, this need not detract from their importance for Matthew as well as for Mark!). Thus, like Mark, Matthew has God himself state that Jesus is his Son at the baptism (Matt. 3: 17) and the transfiguration (Matt. 17: 5). So too Matthew has the declaration of Jesus' divine sonship at the Sanhedrin trial (26: 63) and by the centurion at the foot of the cross (27: 54). Like Mark, he has Jesus implicitly refer to himself as the Son in the parable of the wicked husbandmen (Matt. 21: 33–46, cf. Mark 12: 1–12), though Matthew then reinforces this (again implicitly) by the parable which Matthew places immediately after: here Matthew has the (Q) parable of the Great Supper (22: 1–10, cf. Luke 14: 16–24), and, in Matthew, the meal is a marriage feast by a king for his 'son' (probably intended to refer to God and Jesus respectively). In Luke the supper is an ordinary meal made by an ordinary man, and it is very likely that Matthew's reference to the king and his son here is due to MattR. Thus Matthew has significantly enhanced the Markan allusion to Jesus as God's Son.

Similar enhancement occurs elsewhere. Matthew adds to Mark an account of Jesus' birth and the events surrounding it. Here Jesus is presented as born of a virgin who conceives 'by the Holy Spirit' (1: 18), by implication then being 'Son of God'. The term itself is then used explicitly in 2: 15 where Matthew sees the return of Jesus from Egypt as the fulfilment of the prophecy from Hosea 'Out of Egypt have I called my son' (Hos. 11: 1). Later in the Gospel, Matthew changes Mark on occasions to mention Jesus' divine sonship. At the end of the

story of the walking on the water, Matthew replaces Mark's characteristic note about the disciples' failure to understand (Mark 6: 52) by
saying that the disciples 'worshipped' Jesus, openly confessing 'Truly
you are the Son of God' (Matt. 14: 33). In the story of Peter's confession, Matthew expands Peter's words as they appear in Mark from 'You
are the Christ' (Mark 8: 29) to 'You are the Christ, the Son of the living
God' (Matt. 16: 16). He then follows this with the famous blessing on
Peter (Matt. 16: 17–19): hence the reaction of Jesus to Peter's confession
is now unambiguously positive.[4] At the account of Jesus' crucifixion,
Matthew also expands Mark on two occasions so that the mockers
now explicitly refer to Jesus' claim to be the Son of God (Matt. 27: 40,
43). Matthew shares with Luke the Q saying Matthew 11: 25–7 (cf. Luke
10: 20–1) where Jesus as the Son is in a unique position in relation to
God; and finally Matthew alone has the risen Jesus command the
disciples to go out and baptise 'in the name of the Father, the Son and
the Holy Spirit' (Matt. 28: 19), placing the Son alongside God himself
and the Spirit in a trinitarian-type formula that looks far more in line
with later Christian orthodoxy than most of the rest of the New
Testament. In view of all this evidence there can be little doubt that Son
of God is a christological term of very great importance for Matthew.

Its precise significance is another matter. In some respects Matthew
presents a significantly different viewpoint from that of Mark, even in
relation to the texts they share in common. For example, the centurion's
confession at the foot of the cross is presented rather differently. In
Mark, as we saw, the centurion's confession is in direct response to
Jesus' death: Jesus dies, the veil of the temple is torn in two, and the
centurion makes his confession. Matthew, however, interposes
between the verse about the temple veil and the centurion's confession
the note about the earth being split open, tombs being opened and the
bodies of the dead being seen alive by many (27: 51b–3). The centurion's
confession is thus not so much a response to the death of Jesus itself,
but rather to a great divine miracle of (general) resurrection. Certainly
some of the starkness of Mark's account is lost in Matthew's re-telling.

Jesus' divine sonship for Matthew may have a number of facets. In
one way, Jesus *qua* Son of God is the one who is supremely obedient
to God the Father. The extra redactional references to Jesus as Son of
God in Matthew 27: 40 and 43 in the mockery at the cross strongly echo
the language of Wisdom 2 about the righteous sufferer (especially Wisd.
2: 18), so that Jesus as God's Son is seen as the suffering, righteous

person. At the baptism, Matthew prefaces the story of the baptism itself with an extra conversation between John the Baptist and Jesus, where John questions whether it is right that he baptise Jesus rather than vice versa, but is told by Jesus to go ahead so that they will 'fulfil all righteousness' (Matt. 3: 15): for Matthew 'righteousness' is clearly a key word and refers to the right behaviour, the obedience, which human beings owe to God.[5] If Jesus here then 'fulfils all righteousness' in being baptised, he is above all being obedient to the will of God. God's declaration that Jesus is his Son at the baptism itself then confirms this. This is also shown by the Q Temptation story which immediately follows the baptism in Matthew. Here Jesus is explicitly tested by the Devil as Son of God: 'If you are the Son of God . . .' (Matt. 4: 3, 6). Each time it is a temptation to put God to the test; but each time Jesus shows himself obedient to God's word (cf. especially 4: 4).

Yet there is clearly more to Jesus as Son of God for Matthew than this. At the account of the Transfiguration, God declares Jesus to be his Son, and then immediately tells the disciples 'Listen to him!' (17: 5). Matthew here echoes Deuteronomy 18: 15 and the prediction of a prophet like Moses. As we shall see, Matthew invests some energy in presenting Jesus as a Mosaic-type figure (see below). But in any case, the picture here is not so much of a figure showing obedience as of a person to whom obedience is now demanded. Jesus is not so much the obedient, subservient one, but the authoritative teacher who must himself be obeyed. So, too, in 11: 25–7, Jesus as the Son is the uniquely privileged recipient of divine revelation. And in 28: 19, Jesus as the Son takes his place in a quasi-divine trio alongside God the Father himself and the Holy Spirit. It may be then that, to a certain extent, the term Son of God can cover more than one aspect of Jesus' person.

As already noted, Kingsbury has maintained that Son of God is a key christological term for Matthew and few would disagree with him on that. He has, however, also claimed that Son of God is in effect the one and only important christological category for Matthew, and that all other christological terms are subservient to this one. In this respect Kingsbury has not commanded quite so much support. Many would in fact claim that several other christological terms, as well as other features of Matthew's story which may not use explicit christological categories or titles, may also make an important contribution to Matthew's overall picture of who Jesus is.

In support of this we may note that the term Son of God actually appears explicitly only once in the birth narratives, and then almost in passing (2: 15). If it is implied in the story of the virgin birth, it is only implicit: and indeed the story of the virgin birth itself is only noted almost in passing (1: 18: cf. below). So, too, the opening verse in Matthew 1: 1, which seems to function in a way similar to Mark 1: 1 in defining the key terms of the story to come and identifying the central character of Jesus, does not refer to Jesus as Son of God: Matthew 1: 1 speaks of the book of the 'genesis' of 'Jesus Christ, Son of David, Son of Abraham'. At the very least, this suggests that other terms and categories may have an important role to play in filling out the picture of who Jesus is for Matthew. We shall therefore turn our attention to some of these other terms and categories now.

Lord

It has often been noted that there are a number of occasions in Matthew where Jesus is addressed as 'Lord' (*kyrios*). Matthew takes over some of the occurrences in Mark we have already considered (though there is no parallel to Mark 5: 19); but he also has a number of additional instances where people address Jesus directly in the vocative as *kyrie* 'Lord' (or 'master'; cf. 7: 22; 8: 2, 6, 8, 21, 25; 9: 28; 14: 28, 30; 15: 22, etc.). Further, Matthew appears to restrict the use of the term either to those who are the recipients of Jesus' miraculous powers (e.g. the leper in 8: 2, the centurion in 8: 6), or the disciples and other followers of Jesus (e.g. Peter in 14: 28, 30). The vocabulary of the little scene in Matthew 26: 21–5 is characteristic and revealing. Here at the account of the Last Supper, Matthew takes over from Mark the little story of the disciples' questioning of Jesus about who will betray him; but Matthew alone adds the explicit question of Judas (v. 25). Matthew's wording here may be significant: the disciples ask 'Is it I, Lord?' (v. 22); Judas, the betrayer, is made to ask 'Is it I, *rabbi*?' (v. 25). Only the true followers of Jesus are apparently allowed by Matthew to address Jesus as *kyrios*.

The precise significance of the term is not entirely clear. We have seen on several occasions that *kyrios* is notoriously wide-ranging in its potential meaning; and certainly the vocative *kyrie* need be no more than a polite form of address, as can be seen from Matthew's Gospel itself (cf. the use of *kyrie* meaning simply 'master!' in parables such as in Matt. 13: 27; 21: 30). G. Bornkamm's often quoted claim that 'the title and address of Jesus as *kyrios* in Matthew have throughout the character of a *divine* Name of Majesty'[6] probably goes further than the evidence on its own will allow. Certainly the uses of the term by the disciples need ('only') imply that Jesus is the true 'master' for those who acknowledge him as such. Nevertheless the use of the term is a significant part of Matthew's Christology. It is, though, also noticeable that the word is sometimes linked with the term 'Son of David' (cf. 15: 22; 20: 30, 31) by those appealing to Jesus for help, and it is to this that we now turn.

Son of David

The idea that Jesus is a/the Son of David (and also, as such, probably the Christ/Messiah) is also very important for Matthew. Matthew signals this right at the start by referring to Jesus in the opening verse of the Gospel as Son of David (1: 1); and the birth narratives which follow make this a key feature. Thus the genealogy (1: 1–16) is divided (by Matthew: cf. v. 17) into three groups of fourteen generations, with David explicitly mentioned as 'king' at a key turning point (1: 6).[7] Moreover, the pericope which follows in 1: 18–25, often called the story of the 'virgin birth', has probably much more to do with the idea of Jesus as Son of *David*, rather than Son of God. Matthew traces Jesus' genealogy back through Joseph rather than Mary, which then creates a slight embarrassment if Joseph was not in fact Jesus' father. Hence the story of 1: 18–25, with its focus on Joseph and his obedience to the angel in taking Mary into his house, seems designed to show Jesus as being fully adopted into the true Davidic line and hence a true Son of David, almost despite the circumstances of his birth.[8] The importance of the theme for Matthew is shown by the very next story in the Gospel, the coming of the Magi (2: 1–12): here the wise men are looking for 'the king of the Jews' (v. 2) which sends Herod into turmoil, asking where 'the Christ' should be born (v. 4), giving rise to the citation of Micah 5: 2 in v. 6 with its clear Davidic allusion that the coming ruler 'will shepherd my people Israel'.

A number of references to Jesus as Son of David occur in the rest of the Gospel. It is notable, however, that many occur in the context of Jesus' healing miracles: those in need of healing address Jesus as Son of David (cf. 9: 27; 12: 33; 15: 32; 20: 30–1). Quite what the significance of this is in Matthew's story is not clear. There is no firm evidence that a messianic figure, a Davidic successor, would be thought of as a miracle worker. The closest one might get is perhaps a few odd references to Solomon, David's son, as an exorcist.[9] But the parallel between this and Matthew is by no means exact (the Matthean references are not in the context of exorcisms) and the references in the Jewish texts are rather obscure.

It may be that, by emphasising this aspect of Jesus' activity under the rubric 'Son of David', Matthew is self-consciously seeking to alter other conceptions of what Davidic messiahship is all about, changing the categories from political leadership to one of obedient, merciful healing and saving activity.[10] So, too, it is notable that the Son of David references in Matthew are in contexts which highlight the opposition between Jesus and the Jewish religious authorities.[11] Thus for Matthew, Jesus fulfils the hopes for a Davidic king in a surprising and unexpected way, a way which leads to opposition and rejection by the Jewish leaders.

Son of Man

Matthew also takes over the references to Jesus as Son of Man from both Mark and Q. Moreover, Matthew seems happy to adopt all the categories of the Son of Man sayings from his sources, including references to Jesus' present activity, his suffering and his future vindication.

It is, however, the latter group of passages that Matthew redacts and expands significantly, so that for Matthew Jesus *qua* Son of Man is placed in an even more exalted position than in Mark. For example, Mark 8: 38 speaks of the Son of Man 'coming in the glory of his father and with the holy angels'. Matthew 16: 27 says that the angels are '*his* angels', and he adds that the Son of Man will dispense judgement itself: 'then he will repay each person according to their works' (echoing Ps. 61: 13). So, too, in the next verse, Matthew changes Mark's note that some standing by Jesus will not taste death 'until they see the Kingdom of God come with power' to 'until they see the Son of Man coming in his kingdom' (Matt. 16: 28/Mark 9: 1). The Son of Man himself how has his own 'kingdom'.

Other references to Jesus as Son of Man in Matthew are in line with this exalted picture of Jesus. In the interpretation of the parable of the Tares (Matt. 13: 36–43: the interpretation may owe a lot to MattR), the Son of Man sows the good seed and also exercises the process of judgement itself, sending out 'his' angels to gather the equivalent of the tares (interpreted as 'all causes of sin and all evil-doers' v. 41 NRSV) to destroy them in judgement. Similarly in the parable of the sheep and the goats, which in Matthew forms the climax of Jesus' teaching activity (Matt. 25: 31–46), the story opens with the scene: 'When the Son of Man comes in his glory, and all the angels with him, then he will sit on the throne of his glory . . .', followed by the scene of judgement itself.

Son of Man ideas may also be present in the final appearance of the risen Jesus in Matthew, where Jesus says 'All authority on heaven and on earth has been given to me' (28: 17), words which echo the scene in Daniel 7: 13 when authority is given to the figure who is 'one like a son of man'. However, this must remain slightly uncertain, since Matthew does not use the actual expression 'Son of Man' here.

Matthew has thus highlighted especially the activity of Jesus *qua* Son of Man as the judge in the final judgement and given him an extremely exalted role, similar to that of God himself, and certainly going beyond the picture in Daniel 7 which seems to be primarily in terms of the Son of Man figure as one who receives a favourable judgement in the heavenly court. The enhanced role of the Son of Man figure in Matthew is closer to the role of the Son of Man figure in *1 Enoch* and *may* show a common background of thought between these two texts.[12] But in any case, it seems that 'Son of Man' is an important terms for Matthew, enhancing significantly the role of Jesus beyond the Markan picture.

We have already seen noted on a number of occasions that a focus on christological titles alone is inadequate for assessing a writer's Christology. In the case of Matthew, a number of categories and factors are also clearly christologically significant, even though they do not use explicit christological 'titles'. I consider three briefly here.

Moses

It is clear that in some important respects, Matthew sees Jesus as a new Moses-type figure.[13] Jesus' teaching is evidently of vital significance for Matthew: Matthew arranges his Gospel around five great blocks of Jesus' teaching (Matt. 5–7, 10, 13, 18, 24–5); and the importance of Jesus' teaching in general is emphasised by the final command of the risen Jesus to the disciples to make further disciples 'teaching them to obey everything that I have commanded you' (28: 20). The number five has been seen by many as possibly significant, with the five blocks of teaching corresponding (at least in general terms) to the five books of the Mosaic Law, the Pentateuch.[14]

Certainly, too, there are some significant parallels between Jesus and Moses in other parts of Matthew. In the birth stories, the account of the slaughter of the innocents, the flight into Egypt and the return from Egypt, all echo aspects of the story about Moses in Exodus. Matthew's extra note in the account of the Transfiguration that Jesus' 'face shone like the sun' (Matt. 17: 2) echoes the story of Exodus 34 of Moses' face shining.[15] As we noted earlier, the command of the divine voice from heaven at the Transfiguration that the disciples should 'listen to him [= Jesus]' (17: 5) probably alludes to Deuteronomy 18: 15, the prediction of the coming of a 'prophet like Moses'. And the fact that Jesus' first great teaching discourse, the 'Sermon on the Mount', is on a mountain (5: 1)[16] is probably intended to echo Moses' experience on Mount Sinai in going up to receive from God the Decalogue (and other laws) to bring them back to the children of Israel to give to them as their instructions for living.[17]

Coupled with this too is probably the very strong element in Matthew seeking to show that Jesus' teaching is in a line of continuity, not discontinuity, with the Old Testament Law. This is perhaps clearest in 5: 17, a verse which occupies a key position in the Sermon on the Mount as a programmatic statement of Jesus' teaching that is to follow: 'Do not think that I have come to destroy the Law and prophets, I have not come to destroy but to fulfil'.[18] So, too, there are many instances where Matthew tries to portray Jesus' teaching as less of a threat to the Jewish Law than it appears in Mark.[19] Jesus is the fulfilment of the Old Testament for Matthew, a theme shown supremely in the famous formula quotations in Matthew, and, as part of this, Matthew portrays Jesus as a new Moses figure, 'fulfilling' (though without abrogating) the first Moses – and all this despite the fact that the name 'Moses' as such is never applied to Jesus!

Wisdom

Jesus is also for Matthew in some sense the embodiment of divine wisdom.[20] Again Matthew rarely uses the term explicitly of Jesus. But, in 11: 19, he may well have changed the Q saying 'Wisdom is justified by her children' (cf. Luke 7: 35) to 'Wisdom is justified by her works', echoing the reference to 'the works of the Christ' at the start of this section in 11: 2. Thus the works of divine Wisdom are the works of Jesus. In Matthew 23: 34, Matthew has probably changed another Q saying which in Q referred to something said by (personified) Wisdom: 'The Wisdom of God said 'I will send you prophets . . .'" (cf. Luke 11: 49); in Matthew this becomes 'Therefore *I* say to you, *I* will send you prophets . . .' A saying of Wisdom in the past has become a saying of Jesus himself in the present.

So, too, the extra sayings in Matthew 11: 28–30 which Matthew has appended to the Q sayings in 11: 25–7 (cf. Luke 10: 21–2) have echoes with what is said of Wisdom in Sirach 51, especially Sirach 51: 23–6. Thus, for example, the invitation 'Come to me' (Matt. 11: 28) is close to Wisdom's invitation 'Draw near to me' (Sir. 51: 23); and the reference to Jesus' easy 'yoke' (Matt. 11: 30) is similar to the reference to Wisdom's 'yoke' in Sirach 51: 26.

It is, however, not clear how important such ideas are for Matthew. Matthew only once refers to divine Wisdom explicitly (Matt. 11: 19), and indeed Matthew's readers would presumably never have picked up Matthew's redactional change to Q at Matthew 23: 34: we can only identify it with the aid of a synopsis. So too, even in Matthew 11: 28–30 where the Wisdom motifs are perhaps strongest, Matthew never explicitly mentions the figure of Wisdom; indeed, in a number of respects, Matthew's portrayal of Jesus here is *not* explained by categories of Wisdom at all: above all the reference to Jesus as the one who is 'meek and lowly of heart' is not derivable from Sirach 51 or other Wisdom texts.[21] Certainly, too, there is no indication that Matthew thought that Jesus might be a pre-existent being like Wisdom (cf. Prov. 8: 22). At most then it seems that Matthew's redaction (especially of Q) shows a tendency to enhance the picture of Jesus so that Jesus is now identified with the figure of Wisdom,[22] and so is part of the general picture whereby the Matthean Jesus 'fulfils' another strand of Jewish thought. However, this by no means exhausts Matthew's picture of Jesus which has many sides to it.

Servant

The idea of Jesus as 'meek and lowly of heart', which we noted above as not easily derivable from Wisdom ideas, is also an important theme from Matthew. It is also connected with Matthew's beliefs about Jesus as the fulfilment of other Old Testament texts. Thus in the story of Jesus' triumphal entry into Jerusalem on a donkey, Matthew adds to Mark the explicit note that this fulfils the prophecy of Zechariah 9: 9 of the 'king' coming as one who is '*meek* and riding upon an ass . . .' (Matt. 21: 5).

Probably related as well are the two formula quotations given by Matthew of the prophecies of the suffering servant figure of Deutero-Isaiah. Modern scholarship has isolated four passages in Deutero-Isaiah which seem to refer to a single 'servant' figure, the most famous of which is probably the suffering servant chapter of Isaiah 53. References to Jesus as the suffering servant are, however, perhaps surprisingly, relatively rare in the New Testament. Matthew does though have two formula quotations from the servant songs: in 8: 17 he cites Isaiah 53: 4, and in 12: 18–21 he cites the whole of the first servant song (Isa. 42: 1–4). Yet the precise nature of the way he sees these texts 'fulfilled' by Jesus is at first sight a little surprising. In 8: 17 the verse from the famous suffering servant chapter is applied to Jesus' miracles, not his passion ('he bore our diseases' is taken as implying simply that he removed them, not that he bore them vicariously himself). In Matthew 12: 18–21, Isaiah 42 is applied to Jesus' wish for privacy and secrecy (cf. 12: 16). The emphasis thus seems to be on Jesus' meekness and lowliness here.[23]

All these aspects show part of the importance of the theme of fulfilment for Matthew: the Jesus story is the fulfilment of many aspects of the Old Testament and a wide variety of texts. For Matthew this is important to show that Jesus, and Christianity, are in a line of firm continuity with the Jewish past (cf. 5: 17 which is clearly programmatic for Matthew). Yet continuity does not necessarily imply identity. Continuity must imply an element of difference as well as sameness. Thus, for Matthew, in Jesus something *greater* than Solomon or Jonah is here (12: 41, 42), something *greater* than the temple is here (12: 6). Perhaps something of this is shown by the references to Jesus being 'with' his people, which is the final category we shall consider in this discussion of Matthew.

Jesus with his people

A vitally important theme of Jesus 'being with' his people unites the beginning, middle and end of Matthew's Gospel. In the very first chapter, the name of Jesus is said to be 'Immanuel' (in fulfilment of Isa. 7: 14), which is explicitly translated as 'God with us' (Matt. 1: 23). This is echoed at the very end of the Gospel where the final words of the risen Jesus to his disciples are 'I am with you always, to the close of the age' (28: 20). And in the middle of the Gospel, Jesus declares that 'Where two or three are gathered in my name, I am there among them' (18: 20), a saying which clearly refers to the post-Easter situation. The Jesus of Matthew thus promises his followers that he will be with them throughout their time on earth, and moreover the presence of Jesus will mean the presence of God (cf. 1: 23).[24] This is not necessarily the same as Chalcedonian orthodoxy, and is probably thinking in much more dynamic terms than the static terms of later Christian theologising. Nevertheless it is claiming for Jesus a uniquely exalted status, as indicated too by the trinitarian baptismal formula in 28: 19, where Jesus is placed alongside God and the Spirit. Jesus is then the place where God acts and where God is present, and there is a significant overlap between Jesus' actions and those of God.[25]

Matthew's Christology is thus extremely rich and varied. He clearly uses several key terms (or 'titles') as important descriptors of who Jesus is. Yet he also works with these terms creatively, at times adapting their meaning and significance to bring out what he sees as key aspects of the role of Jesus. He also works with a number of other categories and concepts which are not covered by 'titles' to enhance his picture of Jesus. As with Mark, we have a 'narrative Christology' quite as much as any based on titles alone, and Matthew makes his points from the story *qua* story.[26]

NOTES

1. Cf. e.g. the well-known problems of trying to reconcile e.g. Matt. 5.17–20 with the antitheses of Matt. 5.21–48 (on the validity of the Law), or Matt. 15: 3 with Matt. 23: 2 (on the validity of the scribal oral tradition), or Matt. 10: 5–6 with Matt. 28: 19 (on the attitude to Gentiles and the Gentile mission).
2. Cf. p. 107 above.
3. Cf. e.g. J. D. Kingsbury, *Matthew: Structure, Christology, Kingdom* (Philadelphia: Fortress Press, 1976), chs 2–3; *Matthew* (Philadelphia: Fortress Press, 1977), esp. ch. 2; 'The figure of Jesus in Matthew's story: A literary-critical probe', *JSNT* 21 (1984), pp. 3–36; *Matthew as Story* (Philadelphia:

Fortress Press, 1986), as well as numerous articles.

4. Cf. above p. 111 for the possibility that, in Mark, Peter's confession may be viewed as slightly inadequate.

5. Cf. 5: 20; 6: 33, etc. This is universally recognised in Matthean scholarship: cf. B. Przybylski, *Righteousness in Matthew and his World of Thought* (SNTSMS 41; Cambridge: CUP, 1980). Matthew's use of the word 'righteousness' may thus be very different from that of Paul.

6. G. Bornkamm, G. Barth, H. J. Held, *Tradition and Interpretation in Matthew* (ET London: SCM Press, 1963), pp. 42–3. (My italics).

7. The division is somewhat artificial since the last group only comprises thirteen names!

8. See K. Stendahl, 'Quis et unde? An analysis of Matthew 1–2', in G. N. Stanton (ed.), *The Interpretation of Matthew* (London: SPCK, 1983), pp. 56–66 (originally published 1960). As noted above, the virgin birth itself is noted almost only in passing in 1: 25.

9. Cf. Josephus, *Ant.* 8.45–9; *Pseudo-Philo* 60.3; *T. Sol.* See D. C. Duling, 'Solomon, exorcism, and Son of David', *HTR* 68 (1975), pp. 235–52; 'The therapeutic Son of David: An element in Matthew's christological perspective', *NTS* 24 (1978), pp. 392–409.

10. D. Verseput, 'The role and meaning of the 'Son of God' title in Matthew's Gospel', *NTS* 33 (1987), pp. 532–56.

11. See G. N. Stanton, *A Gospel for a New People: Studies in Matthew* (Edinburgh: T&T Clark, 1992), pp. 180–5.

12. Cf. pp. 25–6 above for the ways in which the Danielic picture was probably developing in the first century. Matthew and *1 Enoch* are also notable in both using the phrase 'throne of his glory' in relation to the Son of Man (Matt. 25: 31; *1 Enoch* 62: 3), which is certainly not very common diction.

13. The most detailed case for this in recent years has been made by D. C. Allison, *The New Moses: A Matthean Typology* (Minneapolis: Fortress Press, 1993).

14. Quite how far the parallel can be taken is, however, uncertain. It is not easy to relate each specific Matthean discourse to each of the books of the Pentateuch in turn: e.g. the first discourse (the Sermon on the Mount) is more closely related to the second book of the Pentateuch (Exodus: Matthew's Jesus going up the mountain to deliver a substantial body of ethical teaching is more closely related to Moses going up the mountain in Exod. 20 to receive, and then pass on, the Decalogue.) So, too, the teaching discourses do not exhaust either Matthew's Gospel as a whole, or indeed the full extent of Jesus' teaching in Matthew (cf. Matt. 23!).

15. The specific detail of Moses' face shining 'like the sun' is found in later

interpretations of the Moses story: cf. Philo, *Vit. Mos.* 1.70; also *Pseudo-Philo* 12.1.

16. The fact that the Sermon takes place on a 'mountain' may well be due to MattR: in Luke's parallel in Luke 6, it is a sermon on a 'plain'.

17. For other possible examples of a Moses typology in Matthew, see Allison, *New Moses* (though some of his examples seem a little more forced than others).

18. There are many issues of detail in trying to interpret this verse, not least of which is how precisely to understand the meaning of the word 'fulfil' here. Nevertheless, the general thrust of the saying is clear: Jesus' teaching is *not* to be seen as destructive of the old Mosaic Law but as in a line of continuity with it.

19. There is no space to go into any detail here, though cf. Matthew's re-telling of Mark's stories of the Sabbath controversies (Matt. 12: 1–14/ Mark 2: 23–3: 6), the dispute on purity (Matt. 15: 1–20/Mark 7: 1–23), the teaching on divorce (Matt. 19: 1–12/Mark 10: 1–12) or on the great commandment (Matt. 22: 34–40/Mark 12: 28–34). See G. Barth, 'Matthew's understanding of the Law', in Bornkamm, Barth and Held, *Tradition and Interpretation in Matthew*, pp. 58–164; also R. Mohrlang, *Matthew and Paul: A Comparison of Ethical Perspectives* (SNTSMS 48; Cambridge: CUP, 1984), pp. 7–26.

20. On this, see M. J. Suggs, *Wisdom, Christology and Law in Matthew's Gospel* (Cambridge, MA: Harvard University Press, 1970).

21. Cf. Stanton, *Gospel for a New People*, pp. 366–71.

22. In Q Jesus may be seen as one of Wisdom's prophetic messengers: see pp. 195–6 below.

23. See D. Hill, 'Son and Servant: An essay on Matthean Christology', *JSNT*, 6 (1980), pp. 2–16. For an attempt to see much greater significance in the quotation of Isa. 42 in Matt. 12, see R. Beaton, 'Messiah and justice: A key to Mathew's use of Isaiah 42.1–4', *JSNT* 75 (1999), pp. 5–23.

24. Cf. U. Luz, *The Theology of the Gospel of Matthew* (Cambridge: CUP, 1995), pp. 30–4.

25. Cf. also above on the way in which Jesus *qua* Son of Man takes on the role of judge at the final judgement.

26. Cf. Luz, *Theology, passim*.

Chapter 8

LUKE-ACTS

When we turn to Luke's Gospel to try to discover what Luke may have thought about Jesus, we are immediately faced with an additional complicating factor. By almost universal consent today, Luke's Gospel is the first half of a *two*-volume work comprising Luke's Gospel and the book of Acts. Luke, and apparently Luke alone of the evangelists, saw fit to continue his story on after the time of Jesus' earthly life into an account of the early history of the Christian church. Thus in order to assess Luke's ideas, on Christology or on any other matter, we have to take into account not only the evidence of Luke's Gospel but also the evidence provided by Acts.

On the one hand, this is a great bonus, providing as it does a much wider range of material to be able to use as evidence. On the other hand, it makes things a great deal more complicated since it is clear that, on many issues, Luke's Gospel and Acts seem to present rather different viewpoints. It then becomes all the more difficult to determine what Luke's own view might be. Thus, to take an example not so directly related to the question of Christology, Luke's Gospel is well known for its stress on the blessings on the poor (cf. Luke 6: 20), attacks on the rich (cf. Luke 6: 24; 12: 16–21; 16: 19–31) and the theme of the necessity of any would-be follower of Jesus to give up *all* his/her possessions (see especially Luke 14: 33; cf. also 5: 21, etc.). Yet in Acts, at least after the first five chapters, such demands seem to be forgotten. Reasonable well-to-do people are converted to the Christian faith and yet are apparently not expected to give up all their possessions; so, too, as the Pauline mission goes to the many cities of the Empire, implicitly with considerable financial backing, none of the evangelistic appeals to the various audiences mentions the demand to sell possessions. It appears that Luke is very much aware of the historical nature of the story he tells. Some things belong to a past era and do not necessarily apply to his own present. There are thus differences between different phases of the story which Luke tells and Luke makes little or no attempt to gloss over them. All this makes it rather harder to determine what Luke's own viewpoint might be. If we can identify a strong motif or theme in part of the Lukan writings, does this tell us what Luke himself believed, or simply only what Luke thought other people in the story believed at that stage in the narrative?

This has considerable effect on the question of Luke's Christology.[1] For example, it has been argued strongly by some that there is a clear distinction visible between Luke's use of the term *kyrios* applied to Jesus in the Gospel as compared with the usage in Acts.[2] In Acts the usage is ubiquitous, reflecting Luke's own views and those of the post-Easter community. In the Gospel, however, the term is hardly ever used by human characters in the story, apart from the vocative *kyrie* which is much less significant christologically. (The angels refer to Jesus as *kyrios* in Luke 2: 11, and the narrator frequently uses the term. But these are not human characters in the story: only Elizabeth in 1: 43 is the exception.) For some this is a clear indication that Luke does not read back post-Easter ideas and terminology into his pre-Easter story.

It is, however, not certain that the evidence will bear this amount of weight.[3] Thus although it is true that characters in the story only use the vocative *kyrie*, some instances are in close proximity in Luke's story to a reference to Jesus as 'the Lord'. Thus Zacchaeus says 'to *the Lord*, 'Look, half my possessions, *Lord*, I give to the poor" (Luke 19: 8; cf. too 12: 41–2). The one addressed as 'Lord', with *kyrie* in the vocative, is '*the* Lord' (*ho kyrios*). Nevertheless, if the references to Jesus as Lord do not quite fit the alleged pattern, it may well be that other Christological categories do.

We may note here, for example, Luke's use of the term 'Son of Man'.[4] Luke retains virtually all the Son of Man sayings by Jesus from his sources Mark and Q. There are, too, a number of Son of Man sayings in Luke's Gospel that are peculiar to Luke, and it is at least arguable that Luke has created most, if not all, of these. Luke thus shows no inhibitions at all about having Jesus use the phrase Son of Man to refer to himself in the Gospel story. However, in Acts the term disappears almost completely. There is one occurrence, and one only, where anyone uses the term and this is the vision of the dying Stephen (Acts 7: 56).

Apart from this no one uses the term, even in places where it might be considered highly appropriate (e.g. Acts 17: 31). Luke thus seems to be aware of the fact that Son of Man was a phrase used extensively by Jesus but not by later Christians. It is thus appropriate to use it in the Gospel story but not in Acts.

A similar picture emerges in some of the texts associated with a 'Wisdom Christology' in Q. As we shall see, Q appears to have had a distinctive christological viewpoint whereby Jesus is one of a long line of prophetic messengers of personified Wisdom, all of whom suffered violence and death (cf. Luke 7: 35; 11: 49–51; 13: 34–5). The prime evidence of this idea in Q is provided by the Q verses as they appear in Luke.[5] Yet Luke shows no interest in developing such ideas outside these Q texts. Nowhere else in Luke-Acts is there any mention of Wisdom as a personified being in her own right, let alone as the agent who sends out the prophets all of whom are to suffer. Luke thus seems happy to repeat the idea as it appears in his source material, but he does not develop it further.

Examples like this suggest that Luke is very much a 'historian', aware of the temporal difference between his own day and the time of the events he is describing in his story. Moreover, he may be someone who has considerable respect for his source material. All this means that we have to approach the material in Luke-Acts with considerable sensitivity if we wish to discover what Luke's own ideas were, and we certainly cannot simply repeat what appear to be strong motifs in Luke-Acts, especially if they occur in only parts of the story.

The other factor which must be borne in mind is that, like Mark and Matthew, Luke writes a story. He does not write a doctrinal treatise. Any Lukan Christology is thus in the form of a narrative Christology, and the characteristic features of Luke's presentation of Jesus come via the medium of the story. In this of course Luke is no different from Mark and Matthew. However, Luke may be slightly different from the other two evangelists in laying slightly less store by the various christological titles. Certainly it would seem that the meaning of the christological titles may have been significantly influenced by the Jesus event. Indeed one influential Lukan scholar has gone so far as to argue that Luke has little or no idea of what the individual titles might have meant originally and Luke uses them indiscriminately.[6] This probably goes too far and Luke certainly seems sensitive to the fact that certain christological categories are more appropriate for some periods in his story than others.[7]

Still it may be fair to say that, for Luke, key events are just as important for determining the significance of Jesus as any specific titles.

One of the key events in this respect is the exaltation/ascension of Jesus.[8] Several details in the Gospel point forward to Jesus' coming exaltation. In 9: 31, his death is described as an *exodos* (NRSV 'departure'), probably hinting at (among other things) his coming departure from the earth which for Luke is his ascension/exaltation. In 9: 51, his journey to Jerusalem is described in sonorous terms as the time for him to be 'taken up' (Greek *analempsis*), again almost certainly hinting at the ascension. The ascension story itself is pivotal for Luke. Indeed so important is it for Luke, with at least two important aspects, that Luke tells it twice (Luke 24: 50–3; Acts 1: 9–11). It represents the climax of Jesus' earthly life and so forms a fitting end to the narrative of the Gospel. But the ascension of Jesus is also the necessary presupposition for the gift of the Spirit on the new Christian church, and the empowering of Christians to spread the Gospel throughout the world. It is thus appropriate too that the story of the ascension forms the start of the book of Acts.[9] Generally too, as is well known, Luke tends to play down some of the significance of the return of Jesus at the end of time, with more stress placed on the present lordship of Jesus.[10] For example, Luke's redaction of Jesus' saying to the high priest at the Sanhedrin trial (Luke 22: 69, cf. Mark 14: 62) omits all reference to Jesus' coming again, and the focus is entirely on the present position of Jesus at the right hand of God: 'From now on the Son of Man will be seated at the right hand of the power of God.' It is this too that forms the thrust of the speeches in Acts where the stress is on how God has exalted Jesus to his present position of glory.

An important theme with christological significance is also provided by Luke's references to the Holy Spirit. Luke-Acts is well known for its great stress on the activity of the Spirit, especially in Acts where the whole mission of the church as Luke recounts it takes place under the constant guidance of the Spirit. Yet the revival of the activity of the Spirit is not confined to Acts and is presaged in the Gospel narrative. In the birth stories, all the major actors are guided by the Spirit; at the start of Jesus' own ministry, Jesus himself is baptised with the Spirit, and in what is clearly for Luke a programmatic scene in the synagogue in Nazareth (Luke 4: 16–30), Jesus announces the fulfilment of the text from Isaiah 61: 1 in his own person, saying that the Spirit of the Lord is upon him and has anointed him (Luke 4: 18–19). Then at the end of the story in the Gospel, Jesus announces that he himself will send the promised gift of his Father (in context clearly the Holy Spirit) on to his disciples (24: 49). Jesus is thus for Luke one who is himself anointed by the Spirit and who then dispenses the Spirit.[11]

Luke is also famous for presenting, perhaps more than any other New Testament writer, the picture of the human Jesus. Jesus in Luke is above all the one who has compassion, especially for the poor, the outcasts of society and sinners. Luke's concern for the poor has already been noted above (cf. Luke 1: 52–3; 4: 18; 6: 20; 7: 22), as well as the stress that comes in the Gospel on the necessity of giving up one's possessions (cf. 14: 33; 18: 22) and the attacks on the rich (6: 24; 12: 16–21; 16: 19–31). Luke too presents in the most positive terms of all the evangelists the relationship between Jesus and tax collectors, people generally despised by other Jews because of their dishonesty and their collaboration with the Romans. Thus as well as the story of Levi (5: 27–30), Luke – and Luke alone – has the story of Jesus meeting Zacchaeus (19: 1–10) as well as the parable of the Pharisee and the tax collector (18: 9–14), with its surprising twist at the end that it is the tax collector, and not the pious Pharisee, who is justified before God. In 3: 12 and 7: 29, tax collectors are presented as responding positively to John the Baptist. Jesus' concern for sinners is reflected in stories like Luke 7: 36–50 (peculiar to Luke in this form) and parables like the Prodigal Son (15: 11–32, again only in Luke). And Jesus too displays concern for the interests of women (cf. the widow of Nain's son in Luke 7: 11–17, Mary and Martha in 10: 38–42, the crippled woman in 13: 10–17 and Jesus' meeting with the weeping women on the via dolorosa in 23: 27–31, all of which are in Luke's Gospel only). The picture of the human Jesus, the compassionate Jesus, the one who is the friend and champion of those whom society has downgraded, has always found its strongest base in the Gospel story as Luke presents it.

What though of the more traditional christological titles and categories used by Luke? How far do these contribute to Luke's Christology? As already noted, we must be conscious of Luke's historical sensitivity in writing his story and of the fact that he may have thought that some terms and categories were more characteristic of earlier Christians and/or earlier periods than of his own. This may apply in the case of the idea of Jesus as a prophetic figure which I consider first.

Prophet

Luke's Gospel has a number of details suggesting that Jesus was, or at least was regarded as, a prophet. Jesus announces the fulfilment of the prophecy of Isaiah 61: 1 in Nazareth in his own anointing by the Spirit, and arguably the Spirit here is the Spirit of prophecy. Jesus then later explicitly compares his mission with that of the prophets Elijah and Elisha in going outside the limits of their own country and people (Luke 4: 25–7). When Jesus restores the widow of Nain's son to life, the crowd say 'a great prophet has risen among us' (7: 16). When Jesus is anointed by the sinful woman in the house of Simon the Pharisee, Simon says to himself 'if this man were a prophet, he would have known who and what kind of woman this is' (7: 39). In 13: 33 Jesus himself expresses his coming fate in Jerusalem in prophetic terms: 'it is impossible for a prophet to be killed outside Jerusalem'. And on the road to Emmaus, the two disciples refer to their (apparently disappointed) hopes about Jesus as 'a prophet mighty in word and deed before God and all the people' (24: 19). In the speeches in Acts, Jesus is twice alluded to as the 'prophet like Moses' of Deuteronomy 18: 15 (Acts 3: 23; 7: 37). Some indeed have argued that the category of the 'prophet like Moses' provides an important over-arching key to Luke's presentation in Luke-Acts, especially the so-called 'Travel Narrative' (Luke 9: 51–18: 14) which occupies a key position in the structure of the Gospel as a whole.[12]

On the one hand, we cannot be certain if this idea is central for Luke himself. Apart from the two references in Acts, the idea of Jesus as a prophetic figure does not feature prominently elsewhere in the preaching of the early Christians as recorded in Acts. Moreover, many of the references to Jesus as a prophet in the Gospel are evidently the views of others (cf. 7: 16, 39; 24: 19). And in chapter 24, there may be an element of correction implicit in the story: when Jesus himself starts to talk to the two men about himself, it is in terms of his being the 'Christ' (v. 26) and the necessity of the Christ to suffer. It may of course be that there is no contrast implied and that precisely as the 'Christ' figure, Jesus is a prophetic figure. We have seen earlier that a 'messianic' figure, as one who is 'anointed', could be a prophetic figure as well as a royal or priestly one. Perhaps then for Luke, Jesus as the Christ is the one 'anointed' (with the Spirit: cf. too Acts 4: 26–7) and this implies that he is a prophet. On the other hand, much of Luke's presentation of

Jesus as a Christ figure suggests rather that he is a royal, Davidic figure (see below). It thus seems unlikely that *christos* and prophet are seen by Luke as synonymous (though of course both do describe Jesus for Luke). Perhaps then we should see the description of Jesus as a prophet in Luke as another part of Luke's historical awareness and sensitivity. Luke is aware that Jesus was seen by others as a prophet, and indeed Luke has Jesus himself at times use the prophetic category to refer to himself (cf. 4: 24; 13: 33). Yet perhaps for Luke this is not the most important category to express the deepest truth about Jesus.

Son of Man

We have already noted in passing Luke's use of the term Son of Man.[13] Luke generally seems to keep all the Son of Man sayings from his sources Mark and Q. And indeed it is Luke who may preserve some of the Q Son of Man sayings more accurately than Matthew.[14] In addition, Luke has a number of Son of Man sayings which are peculiar to his Gospel (17: 22; 18: 8; 19: 10; 21: 36; 22: 48; 24: 7). Yet, for the most part, these sayings do not say anything new about Jesus' role *qua* Son of Man beyond what is there in the sources.[15] Moreover, as we have seen already, Luke does not carry the term over into the preaching of Christians in Acts. It seems then as if Luke is again aware of the fact that the term was prominent in an earlier period. The term is characteristic of the tradition of Jesus' own preaching prior to Easter, but Luke may be aware that its usage then ceased. Hence he leaves it in his Gospel but does not develop it in the story in Acts.

The Bringer of Salvation

More characteristically Lukan may be language which Luke uses associated with 'saving' and 'salvation'. Luke frequently refers to the 'salvation' that the Jesus event is bringing (cf. Luke 1: 69, 71, 77; 2: 30; 3: 6; 19: 9; Acts 4: 12; 13: 26, 47; 16: 17; 27: 34; 28: 28) and also often refers to the fact that as a result of Jesus people are 'saved'.[16] On three occasions Jesus is called a 'saviour' (Luke 2: 11; Acts 5: 31; 13: 23). Such language became very common in later Christian history. It is, however, not so frequent in the New Testament, though it does occur quite frequently in the Pastoral Epistles and may, as we have seen, reflect language used about the Emperor in the Emperor cult which developed towards the end of the first century. The Emperor was seen as a 'saviour' figure bringing 'salvation' to the people of the Empire; so then Christian claims about Jesus as a saviour figure could act as a kind of counter-claim to assert the 'true' nature of the salvation available through Jesus.[17]

Lord and Christ

Of all the christological titles or categories, two are clearly of great importance to Luke: Jesus as Lord (*kyrios*) and Jesus as Christ (*christos*). It is indeed the explicit justification of the use of these two terms for Jesus which governs the programmatic speech of Peter in Acts 2: the whole of the speech is, in one sense, an attempt to provide a detailed justification for the claim that God has made Jesus to be 'Lord' and 'Christ' (2: 36). Indeed this structure to the speech, and the importance which the speech clearly has within the book of Acts as a whole, must clearly throw into question any claim that Luke is totally uninterested in christological titles; certainly the way that Luke's Peter clearly seeks to justify the use of these two terms suggests that Luke does see the terms as having some significance.

Both terms are justified on the basis of an argument from scripture and an appeal to the resurrection/exaltation of Jesus. In relation to 'Lord', Luke's Peter appeals to the words of Psalm 110: 1 ('the Lord said to my Lord, sit at my right hand'). The argument is that, as Jesus is now at God's right hand in glory, the words of the Psalm must apply to him. Hence he can appropriately be designated the 'Lord' of Psalm 110: 1. Similarly Psalm 16: 8–11 is cited (in Acts 2: 25–8), with the reference to God saying to David 'you will not abandon my soul to Hades, or let your Holy One see corruption'. Clearly this did not apply to David himself but must be a reference to the Davidic Messiah to come. Since Jesus has been raised from the dead, his story fits the words of the Psalm and hence he must be the promised Messiah. Thus he can appropriately be designated 'Messiah' as well. Hence the conclusion in verse 36 to the double argument and the appeal to scripture: 'God has made him both Lord and Christ'.

The idea that, in the events of Jesus' life and death, scripture has been fulfilled is an important feature of the Lukan writings. The motif of the fulfilment of scripture is often thought to be highly characteristic of Matthew's Gospel, and indeed it is. But it is no less characteristic of

Luke. The programmatic scene at Nazareth has Jesus read Isaiah 61 and claim 'Today this scripture has been fulfilled' (Luke 4: 21). And in the highly important series of stories of resurrection appearances in Luke 24 a constant theme is the claim that everything has happened in accordance with what has been predicted in scripture (cf. 24: 27, 46). So, too, in Acts the events are shown to fulfil scripture: the gift of the Holy Spirit fulfils the prophecy of Joel 2: 28–31 (Acts 2: 17–21), the Gentile mission is given the backing of scripture from Amos 9: 11–12 by James (Acts 15: 16–17), etc.

Lord

In terms of Christology then, the speech of Acts 2 makes it clear that the important christological terms applied to Jesus derive from scripture. As 'Lord', Jesus is primarily the one who fulfils the scripture of Psalm 110 by virtue of his resurrection/exaltation. Again we see the crucial significance for Luke of Jesus' exaltation as well as the stress on scripture. And for the rest of the story Luke uses the term *kyrios* for Jesus very freely. Moreover, Luke uses the term throughout the Gospel and Acts, suggesting that Jesus is *kyrios* throughout his ministry.[18]

We have already seen on several occasions that the word *kyrios* itself is capable of a very wide range of meanings. Thus *kyrios* can be (just) a term of polite respect, or a reference to a human master; it can also be used by Jews to refer to God himself. Despite the claims of some recently, it is unlikely that Luke intends any great claims to divinity by his use of the term *kyrios* for Jesus.[19] The fact that *kyrios* is used of God as well is clearly known by Luke who can refer to God as Lord quite freely. Indeed at times it is not always quite clear whether Luke is thinking of Jesus or of God when he refers to the 'Lord'.[20] But Luke does not necessarily confuse the two ontologically, so to speak. Luke, like Greek-speaking Jews using Psalm 110: 1, knows full well that that verse is about two distinct people, both of whom can be, and are, referred to as *kyrios*.[21] Rather, it is Jesus' unique status as the one who has been exalted in/by the resurrection who, via Psalm 110, can be called *kyrios*. And, for Luke, the resurrection is supremely the action of God on Jesus: God is the one who has raised Jesus from the dead (cf. Acts 2: 32; 4: 10; 5: 30; 10: 40; 13: 30, 37).

Christ

Luke's use of *christos* is perhaps even more important to him than the use of *kyrios*.[22] The justification in Acts 2 of the use of the *christos* title via the idea of Davidic messiahship as developed from Psalm 16 indicates that, for Luke, Jesus *qua christos* is a Davidic, royal figure.[23] Certainly the idea of Jesus as a royal Davidic figure comes prominently elsewhere in Luke. It is present in the birth narratives, a section where several of the key Lukan themes are announced and adumbrated (cf. Luke 1: 67–8; 2: 11; 2: 26); it is present in Peter's confession (9: 20); and in the account of the triumphal entry into Jerusalem, Luke changes Mark's version of the cry of the crowds from 'Blessed is the one who comes in the name of the Lord' (Mark 11: 9) to 'Blessed is the *king* who comes in the name of the Lord' (Luke 19: 38). The idea is strongly developed in the programmatic speech of Peter in Acts 2, as we have seen; it is then reinforced in Acts 4: 26 where the royal messianic Psalm 2 is applied to Jesus. And the speech by Paul at Pisidian Antioch in Acts 13 reiterates much of the argument, with a similar appeal to Psalm 16, as has appeared in Peter's speech in Acts 2 with Jesus as the recipient of the promises made to David.

Luke, however, goes one stage further and clearly states that it is in his capacity as the *christos* that Jesus has suffered. Thus the risen Jesus in Luke 24 explains to the disciples on the road to Emmaus that the sufferings of the Messiah are all foretold in the Old Testament (24: 26–7), and this motif is repeated in Acts (Acts 3: 18; 17: 3; 26: 23). It is in fact not easy to find much about a 'messianic' figure explicitly in the Old Testament anywhere; but there is certainly nothing about a suffering messianic figure.[24] The claim that 'the Messiah must suffer' seems to be a Lukan innovation, at least insofar as it makes the explicit claim that suffering is predicated of 'the Messiah' in Jewish scripture.[25]

Further, it is noticeable that by the time Luke gets to the second half of Acts (and hence presumably closer in time to his own day), it is the notion of Jesus as the Messiah that seems to be the one and only christological idea that recurs. Thus, in Thessalonica in Acts 17, Paul goes to the synagogue trying to explain to the Jews there that 'it was necessary for the Messiah to suffer' and that Jesus is the Messiah (v. 3). In Corinth Paul argues that 'the Messiah is Jesus' (18: 5) as does Apollos (18: 28). Similarly, in front of Agrippa, Paul refers to Jesus as the Messiah who must suffer (26: 23).

In contrast, it is striking that in using this Christ language of Jesus so much, Luke has effectively deleted almost all the ideas and expectations associated with the term in Jewish thought.[26] Jesus is a royal figure for

Luke, but his throne is in heaven, not on earth. The expectation that Jesus might restore a 'kingdom' in this-worldly terms to Israel is quietly but firmly silenced: the two men on the road to Emmaus say that they had been hoping that Jesus would 'redeem' (or rescue) Israel (Luke 24: 21); but Jesus in his response implicitly rejects such hopes, pointing instead to his role of suffering as the role ordained by scripture for the 'Messiah'. So too at the start of Acts, the question of the disciples 'is this the time when you will restore the kingdom to Israel?' (Acts 1: 6) is brushed aside by the risen Jesus, apparently as irrelevant and unimportant compared with the gift of the Holy Spirit and task of mission of the church (1: 7–8). Jesus is thus a Davidic king who is quite unlike any Davidic king of the past or any Davidic figure who might have been expected. His throne is in heaven, not on earth, and the 'peace' he brings is also in heaven (Luke 19: 38).

One wonders then how much the actual idea of messiahship itself is important for Luke. Luke does indeed take over the term Messiah and develops it strongly so that, as we have seen, by the end of Acts it is the dominant christological category. Yet the ideas associated with the term in Jewish tradition all seem to have been radically altered and transformed as Luke adapts them and applies them to Jesus. Certainly it seems unlikely that Luke could have had any meaningful conversation with a non-Christian about the possible messiahship of Jesus: such a conversation would be a non-starter since the two parties would be on such different wavelengths. What is perhaps more likely is that for Luke the messiahship of Jesus works as part of a strategy of 'legitimation', serving to link the Christian claims with Judaism and thus to provide antiquity – and hence respectability – for the new Christian movement.[27] On its own, the idea of Jesus' messiahship may be of less interest to Luke himself christologically. Luke's own Christology may to a certain extent be rather more hidden from us as Luke distances himself from the story he tells.[28]

Two other features of Luke's Christology should also be mentioned here. First, the Lukan Jesus is a figure who is very much subordinate to God. Although we are considering here Christology, Luke may not fit quite so easily into the subject of the discussion at this point simply because he is as much interested in Jesus from the point of view of 'theo'-logy, that is the idea of God.[29] For Luke, Jesus is subordinate to God.[30] Thus it is God consistently who raises Jesus from the dead (Acts

2: 32–3; 3: 15; 4: 10; 5: 31, and see above). God declares Jesus to be his son (Luke 3: 22; 9: 35) and also works miracles through Jesus (cf. Acts 2: 22): if Jesus performs miracles it is because God is with him (Acts 10: 38; cf. Luke 11: 20: Jesus exorcises 'by the finger *of God*'). God has made Jesus Lord and Christ (Acts 2: 36); Jesus is supremely a *man* chosen by God to do God's will (Acts 2: 22; 17: 31). This is not to deny in any way the position of preeminence Jesus has in relation to the world, for example in bestowing the Spirit on other men and women (Acts 2: 33); but it it is only by virtue of his subordination to God that he can do so.

The second point to note here is that Luke presents Jesus as for the most part *absent* in the post-Easter period. As we have noted several times already, the exaltation of Jesus is vitally important for Luke. Yet for Luke it seems to be an exaltation *to* heaven. The ascension story in Acts seems to signal a final *removal* of Jesus from this earth. As such, at least in Acts, it marks the end of the (forty-day) period when the risen Jesus is seen by others. After the ascension, Jesus is scarcely ever encountered directly by characters in the story.[31] Jesus remains in heaven, and if there is any mediation between the heavenly world of God and the world of everyday events, the principal 'actor' is the Holy Spirit, not the risen Jesus. Luke is thus rather different from both Paul and Matthew in this respect, both of whom appear to have a firm belief in the continuing abiding presence of the risen Jesus in the church.[32] Luke has more an idea of an 'absentee' Christology.[33] In this respect (if not in many others!) Luke is remarkably close to John who also seems to think in terms of Jesus as primarily absent, being replaced in the post-Easter situation by the presence of the Paraclete (John 14–16).

Luke thus presents us with an account that leaves more than a few loose ends. Luke's clear intention to be a historian means that he distances himself somewhat from the story he writes. Insofar as Luke does allow his own ideas to be visible, he seems to be very concerned to show Jesus as the 'Messiah' of the Jewish expectation, but the meaning of the term has been heavily influenced by the Jesus event itself. It is *Jesus*, as the man chosen by God and now raised by God from the dead to be with Him in heaven, who provides the hermeneutical key which interprets individual words or 'titles' such as 'Messiah'. In this, Luke is of course no different from many other New Testament writers, and in particular he is very close (again) to John, whom we shall consider next.

NOTES

1. I have tried to deal with this in more detail in my 'The Christology of Luke-Acts', in J. Verheyden (ed.), *The Unity of Luke-Acts* (BETL 142; Leuven: Leuven University Press & Peeters, 1999), pp. 133–64.
2. C. F. D. Moule, 'The Christology of Acts', in L. E. Keck and J. L. Martyn (eds), *Studies in Luke-Acts* (London: SPCK, 1968), pp. 159–85, esp. 160–2; repr. in Moule, *Forgiveness and Reconciliation: Biblical and Theological Essays* (London: SPCK, 1998), pp. 51–80, esp. 52–4.
3. Cf. E. Franklin, *Christ the Lord: A Study in the Purpose and Theology of Luke-Acts* (London: SPCK, 1975), esp. p. 52.
4. On this, see my 'The Lukan Son of Man', in Tuckett (ed.), *Luke's Literary Achievement* (JSNTSup 116; Sheffield: Sheffield Academic Press, 1995), pp. 198–217.
5. Matthew, as we have seen, regularly 'upgrades' the Christology to identify Jesus with the figure of Wisdom.
6. Cf. H. Conzelmann, *The Theology of St Luke* (ET London: Faber & Faber, 1960), pp. 170–1.
7. Cf. above on Luke's use of the term Son of Man, or the category of Wisdom's prophetic envoy: these are not splattered around the story in Luke-Acts indiscriminately!
8. The importance of this theme for Luke is well brought out by Franklin, *Christ the Lord*.
9. Luke does not seem to be in the slightest bit concerned about the discrepancies between the two accounts, e.g. on the exact timing of the ascension in relation to the first Easter day. (In the Gospel the ascension happens on Easter day, in Acts forty days after Easter.)
10. The theme of the delay of the parousia in Luke-Acts has been a prominent feature in Lukan study ever since the programmatic work of Conzelmann, *Theology*. See too R. Maddox, *The Purpose of Luke-Acts* (Edinburgh: T&T Clark, 1982), esp. ch. 5.
11. It is, however, perhaps surprising that Luke makes very little of Jesus' possession of the Spirit in his account in the rest of the Gospel after the Nazareth story. Nowhere else in Luke's Gospel is Jesus' activity attributed to his having the Spirit. This could be because Luke assumes it as read after his account of the Nazareth scene (so R. Brawley, *Luke-Acts and the Jews* [Atlanta: Scholars Press, 1987], p. 19); it could perhaps also be that the motif of Jesus as one anointed by the Spirit is more of a feature of Luke's source material than it is of Luke himself. On this, see my 'Christology of Luke-Acts', pp. 143–5. Nevertheless, the motif of Jesus as the mediator of the Spirit to the Christian church is an important one for Luke.

12. E.g. D. Moessner, *Lord of the Banquet: The Literary and Theological Significance of the Lukan Travel Narrative* (Minneapolis: Fortress Press, 1989; ²1998). But see A. Denaux, 'Old Testament models for the Lukan travel narrative', in C. M. Tuckett (ed.), *The Scriptures in the Gospels* (BETL 131; Leuven: Leuven University Press & Peeters, 1997), pp. 271–305, esp. 281–5. The parallels between the story of Moses and Luke's presentation are often rather allusive.

13. On this, see my 'Lukan Son of Man'.

14. For example, in Luke 6: 22 and 12: 8 Luke has the relevant saying in a Son of Man form, where Matthew has a reference by Jesus to himself using the first person. In each case it is widely agreed that Luke is more original and reflects Q more accurately.

15. For example, the eschatological sayings in Luke 18: 8 and 21: 36 are similar in general terms to Mark 14: 62; the saying about the saving activity of the Son of Man in Luke 19: 10 is similar, again at least in general terms, to Mark 10: 45.

16. The verb *sozo* ('save') is used thirty times in Luke-Acts.

17. The similarities between Luke and the Pastoral Epistles are intriguing and more substantial than one might at first sight expect. For a valuable discussion, see S. G. Wilson, *Luke and the Pastoral Epistles* (London: SPCK, 1979), esp. ch. 7 on Christology.

18. Cf. the discussion above (at n. 2) on whether Luke distinguishes between the time of the Gospel and the time of Acts in references to Jesus as Lord.

19. *Pace* e.g. Buckwalter, *Character and Purpose of Luke's Christology*. On this, see my 'Christology of Luke-Acts', pp. 149–57

20. Cf. J. D. G. Dunn, 'ΚΥΡΙΟΣ in Acts', in Dunn, *The Christ and the Spirit*, Vol. 1 *Christology* (Edinburgh: T&T Clark, 1998), pp. 241–53 (originally in the FS for O. Hofius).

21. Cf. too p. 22 above on the two uses of *kyrios* in adjacent verses in Gen 18: 12, 13, referring to Abraham and God respectively.

22. For the importance of Davidic messiahship for Luke's Christology, see M. L. Strauss, *The Davidic Messiah in Luke-Acts: The Promise and its Fulfillment in Lukan Christology* (JSNTSup 110; Sheffield: Sheffield Academic Press, 1995); also my 'Christology of Luke-Acts'.

23. Hence the idea that Jesus *qua christos* is a prophetic figure (cf. p. 138 above) seems less probable.

24. Appeals to the description of the suffering servant figure of Isa. 53 are not relevant here: the figure of Isa. 53 is not said to be a messianic figure.

25. See J. A. Fitzmyer, *The Gospel according to Luke I–IX* (New York: Doubleday, 1981), p. 200.

26. On this, see H. Räisänen, 'The redemption of Israel: A salvation-historical

problem in Luke-Acts', in P. Luomanen (ed.), *Luke-Acts: Scandinavian Perspectives* (Helskinki: Finnish Exegetical Society; Göttingen: Vandenhoeck & Ruprecht, 1991), pp. 94–114, repr. in Räisänen, *Marcion, Muhammed and the Mahatma* (London: SCM Press, 1997), pp. 49–63.

27. For this in general terms in relation to Luke's writings, see P. F. Esler, *Community and Gospel in Luke-Acts* (SNTSMS 57; Cambridge: CUP, 1987).

28. Cf. my 'Christology of Luke-Acts', and more generally, my *Luke, passim*.

29. The importance of 'theo'-logy (strictly speaking) is well brought out by J. T. Squires, *The Plan of God in Luke-Acts* (SNTSMS 76; Cambridge: CUP, 1993).

30. See Conzelmann, *Theology*, pp. 173–84.

31. The exceptions are special occasions such as Paul's conversion, or Paul's vision in Acts 18: 9 (if indeed the 'Lord' there is Jesus and not God).

32. For Matthew, cf. Matt. 28: 20; for Paul, cf. Gal. 2: 20 as well as his 'in Christ' language.

33. Cf. Moule, 'Christology of Acts', pp. 179–80.

Part 3

JOHANNINE LITERATURE

Chapter 9

THE GOSPEL OF JOHN

When we turn from the synoptic Gospels to the Fourth Gospel, we move in some respects into a different world. The differences between John and the synoptics have long been recognised, reference often being made in this context to the famous statement of Clement of Alexandria (early third century) that, whereas the other Gospel writers gave the 'bodily' facts about Jesus, 'John wrote a spiritual Gospel'.[1] Although the differences between John and the synoptics can perhaps be exaggerated, there can be no denying that at many levels John presents a radically different presentation of the life and ministry of Jesus. There are differences at the more superficial level of dates and places,[2] but there are also differences in the whole mode and content of Jesus' own teaching,[3] and the area where this is most prominent is precisely the area of Christology.

In general terms, the synoptic Jesus says very little explicitly about himself: his preaching is about God, the kingdom of God, the nature of God's demands, etc. The Johannine Jesus by contrast is far more explicit about himself so that his teaching focuses on his own person far more directly. John's Jesus makes himself the object of faith far more explicitly than in the synoptics.[4] And he teaches quite openly about himself and the importance of his own role in God's plan, supremely in the great 'I am . . .' sayings which come throughout the Gospel.[5] In line with this, the beginning and end of the Gospel focus directly and explicitly on the person of Jesus. Thus the prologue of the Gospel (1: 1–18) speaks of Jesus as the Word of God; and in what is probably the ending of at least one version of the Gospel,[6] it is stated that the book has been written 'so that you may [?come to] believe[7] that Jesus is the Messiah, the Son of God' (20: 31).

So too the figure of Jesus is portrayed in a more exalted role throughout the story. Jesus is fully in control of all the events concerned. His
miracles highlight his person, and indeed at times Jesus acts in order
to highlight even more his activity. Thus in chapter 11, when Lazarus
falls ill and dies, Jesus is portrayed as deliberately delaying going to
heal him in order apparently to make the miracle of raising him all the
more stupendous (11: 4, 15). John describes what appears to be a vestige
of the agony scene in Gethsemane (12: 27); but in John there seems to
be no real agony on Jesus' part and Jesus displays unbounded and
unquestioning confidence in God. So too, in the account of Jesus' actual
death, little if anything is made of Jesus' suffering. Jesus admits to thirst
on the cross, but only in order to fulfil scripture (19: 28); and his final
word is no agonized cry of dereliction, as in Mark, but a statement of
supreme confidence: 'it is finished' (19: 30). Above all, it is in John that
we get the two most explicit statements in the New Testament about
the divinity of Jesus. Moreover they come at key points in the narrative – at the beginning and at the end – encompassing the whole story
in a powerful *inclusio*. Thus the first verse of the prologue affirms that
the Word was not only in the beginning 'with God', but in some sense
also 'was God' (1: 1); and Thomas at the end of the story openly confesses Jesus as 'my Lord and my God' (20: 28). John thus presents
Jesus explicitly in far more exalted terms than anything we find in the
synoptic Gospels.

In terms simply of historical reliability or 'authenticity', it seems
impossible to maintain that both John and the synoptics can be presenting us with equally 'authentic' accounts of Jesus' own life.[8] The
differences between the two are too deep seated and wide ranging for
such a position to be sustainable. If there is a choice, it is almost certainly to be made in favour of the synoptic picture, at least in broadly
general terms. The Johannine picture then presents us with a view of
the Jesus tradition which has been heavily coloured and influenced by
John and his own situation.

Further, it has now become clearer in recent Johannine studies that
we should almost certainly think of 'John', the author of the Gospel,
not necessarily as some individual writing his Gospel in splendid
isolation, but as part of a community facing very real pressures and
tensions.[9] At the very least we have to take note of the existence of the
three Johannine epistles, all of which are written in an idiom very
similar to that of the Fourth Gospel and with much of the same highly

distinctive Johannine vocabulary and terminology. The epistles are probably not by the same author as the Gospel,[10] so one must postulate at the very least one other author heavily influenced by the ideas of John. But the epistles also clearly shown the existence of a community, and in the case of 1 John and 3 John it is a community where a certain amount of disagreement and division has evidently taken place. The communal aspect is probably also indicated in the Gospel by the use of the first person plural at times: for example, in the prologue the writer states that 'the Word became flesh and *we* have seen his glory' (1: 14), probably indicating that the writer is part of a larger group. Thus the trend in recent years has been to see the Gospel not so much as the work of a particular individual theological genius (though it may be that in part), but also as the product of a particular Christian *community* facing its own particular problems in its own situation.

The nature of that situation may be reflected at one or two points in the story of the Gospel itself. For example, in the story of the man born blind in John 9, the story tells of the dialogue between 'the Jews' who do not accept the reality of the miracle and the man's parents (9: 18–23). In the dialogue, the parents refuse to answer the Jews' questions. This, it is said, is because 'they were afraid of the Jews; for the Jews had already agreed that anyone who confessed Jesus to be the Messiah would be put out of the synagogue' (v. 22). Such a situation makes virtually no sense in terms of the time of the ministry of Jesus or of the earliest church.[11] Rather it seems to reflect a much later situation when Christian allegiance to Jesus and membership of the Jewish synagogue were regarded as incompatible and Christians were excluded from the synagogues. The same setting is implied by two other verses in the Gospel, one (12: 42) again purporting to be a reflection of the situation at the time of the narrative, the other (16: 2) being a prediction by the Johannine Jesus of what is in store for the disciples. The fact that this state of affairs is mentioned on more than one occasion suggests that it is of some importance for the writer of the Gospel. Thus many have argued (in my view convincingly) that these verses reflect the situation of the Johannine community itself. The Johannine Christians as a group have been put out of the synagogue and excluded from participating with Jews there. The story as it is told in John thus reflects more than one level: indeed it has become customary to speak of John as a 'two-level drama'.[12] The story is at one level a story about Jesus and his disciples in the 30s, but it is also a reflection of the situation of a later Christian community, probably in the last quarter of the first century.

The precise date of any exclusion of Christians from Jewish synagogues is debated. Much has been made in the past of a version of the twelfth of the eighteen benedictions which includes a clause cursing all heretics and which has been dated by some to a decree from Jamnia c. CE 85. In recent years more doubt has been thrown on this and it is uncertain how far Christians were ever formally banned from Jewish synagogues.[13] Nevertheless, however formal and legally binding it may or may not have been, it seems clear that the Johannine Christian community found itself thrown out of a setting where its members had thought formerly they belonged. Thus John reflects a situation of some bitterness on the part of Christians against Jews, as well as some considerable anger and rejection by Jews against Christians. It is this sense of mutual hostility that is reflected in much of John, reaching one of its most intense peaks in John 8 where the Johannine Jesus accuses the Jews of not being children of Abraham, or of God, but of the Devil (8: 44). The negative portrayal of 'the Jews' pervades the whole Gospel, and the use of the blanket term 'the Jews' to refer to Jesus' opponents in the story has led to many charges that John is in some sense 'anti-Semitic'. There is no space here to discuss the issue further, though one should simply note that John's language is the reflection of a situation of intense hostility, probably on both sides, and indeed it may be a situation which has led to deaths on the Christian side.[14] Further, as we shall see shortly, John himself is very firmly convinced of the Jewish basis of his Christian convictions about Jesus. Moreover, if Christians have been expelled from synagogues, this is probably something forced on Christians by other Jews: presumably the Johannine Christians would have been happy to stay as part of the Jewish community. To use what has become standard scholarly jargon, they have moved from being 'Christian Jews' to becoming 'Jewish Christians' but it is against their own will and maybe they would have much preferred to stay as 'Christian Jews'.[15]

The suggestion that Christians in John's community have (probably recently) been expelled from the synagogue indicates that the situation of the Johannine community is probably a changing one. Certainly the trauma of the expulsion has led to a dramatic change in their situation. So too the (probably later) Johannine epistles let us see a further point in the changing history of the community with internal splits within the community leading to some kind of 'schism' (cf. especially 1 John 2: 18–22). Thus the community behind John was clearly not a static or unchanging one.

Some scholars in recent years have tried to build on this and have, on the basis of the Gospel (and the epistles), postulated a number of different stages in the history of the Johannine community.[16] This might be correlated with the fact that the present form of the Gospel suggests at times that it has come together in stages, and not all parts fit together entirely happily as a connected whole.[17] Some quite ambitious histories of the Johannine community have been proposed, though whether we can be so precise is not absolutely certain. For some, too, this developing history is to be connected with changes in the christological beliefs of the Johannine community, so that one can distinguish between earlier and later Christologies within the Gospel.[18] Such precision may be a little optimistic, though the whole issue should make us alert to the possibility that John is at times taking up earlier traditions and adapting them so that they are significantly changed in the course of the adaptation.

On any showing John is clearly using earlier traditions.[19] One widely held theory is that John is using an earlier source which included the stories of Jesus' miracles, the so-called 'Signs Source'.[20] This is perhaps indicated by the numbering of the first two signs (the 'first' in 2: 12, the 'second' in 4: 54, though the numbering then peters out), and the conclusion in 20: 30–1 that Jesus 'did many other signs not recorded in this book'; there is also the fact that in the present form of the Gospel, the miracles are clearly taken *as* 'signs', that is as pointers to some deeper reality beyond themselves, usually focused on Jesus himself and often developed in a discourse following the account of the miracle. Thus the miracle story of the feeding of the 5000 in John 6 is followed by the long discourse about Jesus as the 'bread of life', clearly by the end leaving far behind the issue of real food and physical hunger.

All this suggests that, in terms of Christology, we may have to be alert to the possibility of different layers in the tradition in John, and that some ideas may have been changed and developed as they were taken up by the final evangelist. Perhaps though, in seeking to discover something of the Christology of 'John', we should respect the fact that the present form of the Gospel[21] was felt to make sense to the author/editor responsible for it. Thus even if the final author has used earlier traditions, these traditions were felt to be still valuable and valid enough to be included in the Gospel. In seeking to delineate 'John's' Christology I shall therefore use the whole of the Gospel as at least a potential witness to that Christology, but bearing in mind the possibility that we may see at times earlier Christologies which the evangelist may be using and which may be slightly less in tune with his own beliefs than other parts of the Gospel.

Signs and Messiahship

The fact that John may reflect a complex development of tradition history is probably shown in the use of the term Messiah/Christ. In one way, John's use of the term appears to be surprisingly undeveloped, at least when compared with some other New Testament writers. Thus John regularly uses the term as a clear title with the definite article (cf. 1: 20, 41; 11: 27; 20: 31), unlike the usage of, say, Paul and Acts where often the word Christ seems to have lost its titular sense and become virtually just another proper name ('Jesus Christ'). In one way, John thus appears to be aware of the origins of the term in Jewish expectation more than other New Testament writers. However, such an impression may be misleading and on closer inspection John's usage turns out to be rather more complex.

The usage in 20: 31, where it is said that the 'signs' recorded in John have been written so that 'you may believe that Jesus is the Messiah, the Son of God', has led many to claim that John's Signs Source (if it existed) may have been related to the idea of Jesus as the Messiah.[22] Similarly, in 6: 15 the response of the crowds to the miracle of the feeding of the 5000 is apparently that they want to make Jesus into a 'king' (cf. too 7: 31). It is clear that the miracle stories in John are intended to draw attention positively to the person of Jesus himself as the miracle worker (in a way that is perhaps rather different from the synoptics, where the focus is rather more on the power of God at work in the miracles, and on Jesus as the channel of God's activity). Thus many have argued that the miracle stories in John may reflect an earlier stage in the history of the Johannine community, at a time when Johannine Christians still belonged to the Jewish synagogues and were trying to win over Jews to their cause by claiming that Jesus was indeed the Messiah of Jewish hopes.

Such a theory cannot, however, be maintained in such a simple form without qualification. One problem is that there is virtually no evidence that any 'messianic' figure in Jewish thought was expected to be a miracle worker. It is thus hard to correlate the 'signs' of John's Gospel with an idea of Jesus as Messiah, at least in terms of Jewish messianic beliefs at the time.

In fact the word 'signs' is more evocative of the Moses tradition in the Old Testament, where Moses performs legitimating 'signs' before Pharoh and the Egyptians. From Qumran we know too of an expectation of a 'prophet like Moses'.[23] And from Josephus we know of a number of popular figures in the first century who promised to be able to repeat the Mosaic-type 'signs' of deliverance such as dividing the Jordan (*JW* 2.259; *Ant.* 20.97–8, 168–9; cf. Acts 5: 36; 21: 38).

It is also the case, however, that although the language of 'signs' may relate to the Moses tradition, not many of Jesus' miracles in John are similar to those associated with Moses himself. For example, Jesus' healing and feeding miracles may show closer resemblance to the activity of *prophetic* figures like Elijah and Elisha (cf. 1 Ki.17; 2 Ki. 4). In fact both Elijah and/or 'the prophet' (possibly the prophet like Moses, possibly simply a prophet like Elijah) are mentioned in John alongside 'the Messiah' (cf. 1: 20–2; 7: 40–2, 52; 9: 17–22). So too in 6: 14–15, when the people see the feeding miracle, their response is that Jesus is 'the *prophet* who is to come into the world', and Jesus hastily withdraws because he apparently interprets this as an attempt to make him a 'king' (v. 15).

In the light of this, many have argued that, although originally a number of rather diverse expectations are involved, we may see reflected here an amalgamation so that Jesus is seen as a miracle-working prophet-Messiah figure, summed up in the term 'the Messiah'.[24] If so, then it clearly shows that ideas of 'messiahship' have already undergone a significant shift and development.

It is, however, doubtful whether messiahship as such, or messiahship as reinterpreted via prophetic ideas (Mosaic or otherwise) and/or miracle working activity, is the most important christological idea for John. It may be that such an idea was important at an earlier stage in the history of the Johannine community, possibly at the level of the Signs Source used by John (if indeed it existed). However, by the time of the present form of the Gospel, it would seem that other ideas have been superimposed on this earlier idea. Thus the notion (and the language) of Jesus as a prophet-Messiah figure is in part retained; but it is also deepened and extended.[25] This can be seen in a number of ways.

In chapter 1, in the series of encounters between Jesus and various figures, some of whom are to become his disciples, each of the latter makes a christological statement. Thus John the Baptist denies that he is the Messiah, Elijah or the prophet, by implication indicating that it is Jesus who fits these categories (1: 20, 22); Andrew says 'we have found the Messiah' (1: 41); Philip says 'we have found him about whom Moses in the Law and also the prophets wrote' (1: 45); Nathanael says 'you are the Son of God, the King of Israel' (1: 49). Yet all these seem to be surpassed by the statement of Jesus himself at the end of this series, referring to himself as the 'Son of Man' on whom the angels will (somehow) be ascending and descending (1: 51). In the story of the Samaritan woman in chapter 4, the extended conversation between Jesus and the woman seems to reflect a steadily deepening awareness by the woman of Jesus' true identity. Relatively early on she recognises Jesus as a 'prophet', in response to his (? miraculous) knowledge about her marital affairs (4: 19); but this leads on to further developments in the dialogue whereby the woman recognises Jesus as the Messiah (v. 25 – apparently 'Messiah' is something deeper than 'prophet') and then eventually as 'the Saviour of the world' (v. 42). A similar progression takes place in the story of the man born blind in chapter 9: the man's early response is that Jesus is a 'prophet' (v. 17), but this leads on to his believing acceptance that Jesus is the 'Son of Man' whom he then 'worships' (v. 38), and it is this that forms the climax of the story and the true 'insight' which the man attains. The category of 'prophet' is thus one that seems to reflect for John at best a somewhat inadequate idea of who Jesus is.

So too messiahship on its own, be it a royal messiahship or a prophetic miracle-working messiahship, does not seem to be the most adequate category for John's Christology. If Nathanael's confession in 1: 50 of Jesus as 'king of Israel' reflects royal ideas, then he is told that he will see 'greater things than these', and that Jesus is the Son of Man of 1: 51. In 11: 27 Martha confesses Jesus to be 'the Messiah, the Son of God'. So too in the Johannine account of the trial of Jesus before Pilate, where so much of the debate and the dialogue revolves around the idea of Jesus' kingship, the true issue seems to emerge precisely when 'the Jews' bring into the discussion the claim that Jesus has claimed to be the 'Son of God' (19: 7).

Similarly, for all that there are similarities between Jesus' activity and that of Moses, so that Jesus might be seen as in some sense a

Mosaic-type prophet, there are also clear contrasts drawn between Jesus and Moses. For example, in the long discourse on the bread of life following the feeding miracle in chapter 6, John's Jesus contrasts the manna given by Moses in the desert with the true 'bread of life' which the Father now gives (cf. vv. 32, 49), which Jesus himself is (v. 35) and which is also related to 'eating the flesh' and 'drinking the blood' of the 'Son of Man' (vv. 51c–8). Similarly, in the verse at the end of the prologue in 1: 17 ('the Law was given through Moses, grace and truth came through Jesus Christ') it is hard not to hear at least an element of sharp contrast between the figure of Moses and that of Jesus.

Thus Jesus for John is not *just* a 'messianic' figure, nor indeed primarily a prophet like Moses. Rather, it is the twin categories of 'Son of God' (or perhaps just 'Son') and 'Son of Man' that are far important and seem to reflect deeper truths about who Jesus is as far as John is concerned.

It is perhaps at this point that an attempt to stick to specific christological titles, and to try to differentiate between them, probably breaks down. To a certain extent, christological categories, or 'titles', are bound to overlap in Christian usage, simply by virtue of being applied to the one person Jesus. Certainly in John, the different christological categories tend to merge into each other. Thus some of what is said of Jesus as 'Son' or as 'Son of God' applies also to Jesus as 'Son of Man', and indeed is sometimes said of (or by) Jesus without reference to any specific christological category or title at all. So too many of the things said of Jesus as Son in the bulk of the Gospel relate very closely to what is said in the prologue of the Gospel of Jesus as the Logos (Word). This is not to say that the various titles have lost all their individuality and are used with total freedom and complete interchangeability. For example, the things predicated of Jesus as Son of Man are slightly but significantly different from things said about Jesus as Son or Son of God. Jesus as Son of Man is one who 'ascends', language not normally used of Jesus as Son of God; and while Jesus as Son is often said to be 'sent' by God, this language is not used of Jesus *qua* Son of Man.

All this no doubt simply illustrates the fact that the various terms used of Jesus have different origins and hence are used to relate to different aspects of the total picture of Jesus created by the Gospel. Alternatively, we have to recognise that the final completed picture presented by John has developed out of the various constituent elements something that is very different from anything previously envisaged or (as far as we can tell) articulated. Thus we need to bear in mind here as always the distinction between how terms and/or ideas might have been used in earlier traditions and the way in which they are used in the developed presentation of John's Gospel. It may well be that the term Son of God has its origins as a royal, messianic term and that such a usage may still be visible in John: thus in Nathanael's assertion that Jesus is 'the Son of God, the king of Israel' (1: 49), the term 'Son of God' seems to be primarily (just) a royal designation. Yet in John's overall presentation it is clear that the designation of Jesus as 'Son of God' or 'Son' is intended to say far more than this as well.

It is this 'far more' that is clearly reflected in part in the obvious offensiveness which the claims of the Johannine Jesus cause to the Jews. At one point this is apparently simply connected with the idea of Jesus as Messiah. Thus in 9: 22, the reticence of the parents of the man born blind is said to be due to the fact that the Jews had decided that 'anyone who confessed *Jesus to be the Messiah* would be put out of the synagogue'. Yet it is clear that more is at stake than simply a bald claim that Jesus was a 'messianic' figure. Such a claim must have been part and parcel of Christian claims about Jesus from the very start of the Christian movement, and yet Christians were tolerated as members of the Jewish community for many years. However, it seems clear that this verse in John has in mind the more far-reaching claims about/by the Johannine Jesus, and John's use of the word 'Messiah' had already broadened out in scope considerably.

Son of God

What is evidently much more offensive to the Jews in John is related to other factors more explicitly associated with Jesus' claim to be 'Son of God' (though in any case 'Messiah' and 'Son of God' are closely related for John: cf. 11: 27; 20: 31). It is precisely because Jesus has claimed to be 'Son of God' that the Jews seek to have Jesus condemned to death by Pilate (19: 7). In part this also relates to Jesus' origins. The question of Jesus' origins recurs at many points of the Gospel, though the answer of John's Jesus is clear: Jesus comes from 'heaven', sent by his Father (cf. 6: 41; 7: 29; 8: 23, etc. and the various debates between Jesus and the Jews in these chapters). Above all, the Jews' objection to Jesus is that by claiming to be God's Son, or by calling God his Father in the way he does, Jesus has made himself 'equal to God' (5: 18), or has in fact made himself God (10: 33). The claims of the Johannine Jesus thus make him guilty of blasphemy in the eyes of the Jews and the struggle is literally a life-and-death one (cf. 10: 33). And indeed the claim that Jesus *is* 'God' in some sense is one that the evangelist himself can affirm positively (1: 1; 20: 28).

John's language about Jesus, and about Jesus as Son of God, has a number of different features associated with it. The most obvious is perhaps inherent in the word 'Son' itself. God is Jesus' 'Father' in a special way so that Jesus refers to him as 'my Father' (2: 16; 5: 17, 43; 6: 32, etc.). Further, he has been 'sent' by God, so that God is often referred to by the Johannine Jesus as 'the One who sent me' (4: 34; 5: 24, 30; 6: 38; 7: 16, etc.). Sometimes the two are combined so that God is 'the Father who sent' Jesus (5: 37; 6: 44; 8: 16; 10: 36; 12: 49; 14: 24). However, the two ideas of sonship and mission are probably originally separate.

The idea of Jesus as the one who is 'sent' certainly need not imply any very 'high' Christology. Such language is very much at home in Old Testament prophecy. Thus, for example, Isaiah offers himself as the answer to God's cry 'Whom shall I send?' with the words 'Send me' (Isa. 6: 8–9). And the idea that God has commissioned the true prophet is a fundamental belief in Jewish tradition. So too in John's Gospel itself, we may note the words of the prologue in 1: 6 referring to John the Baptist as 'a man *sent* from God'. The language of 'sending' on its own is thus probably rooted in prophetic traditions showing Jesus as a true prophet figure.

As we have seen, this idea is frequently coupled in John with the idea of Jesus as 'Son' or 'Son of God'. Whether these two phrases should be distinguished in terms of their origins is debatable.[26] 'Son of God', as we have seen, may have its roots in Jewish messianic traditions. The notion of Jesus as 'Son' may be based in Jesus' own use of 'Abba' ('Father') in addressing God in prayer (cf. Mark 14: 36).[27] Sonship language on its own need not imply any very 'high' Christology, as we have already seen in considering the synoptic Gospels, but no more than agreement with God's will and obedience to him. Sonship may imply an element of unity with God; but it is a unity based on total obedience and dependence on the part of the son to his Father. Such an idea may well be reflected in several parts of the talk of the Johannine Jesus. For example, in 5: 19–20, the language of

Jesus' words ('the Son can do nothing on his own but only what he sees the Father doing') may have as its basis a very mundane statement about human fathers and human sons: a son can only learn from his father. In this sense, and it is an important aspect for John, Jesus' sonship implies and entails his total dependence upon God the Father. Thus alongside any claim to unity between Jesus and God (e.g. 10: 30 'I and the Father are one') must be placed a note of total dependence and subordination (e.g. 14: 28 'the Father is greater than I').[28] Indeed there is an important sense in which, for John, Jesus' unity with God is shown precisely *in* dependence and subordination to God.

Yet there is clearly more to John's Christology than simply portraying Jesus as a prophetic figure 'sent' by God and who is obedient to God as a son to a father. John has clearly also enriched these ideas with further notions. One of these, as has become clear in recent years, is that of agency.[29]

The idea of agency is not necessarily a religious one at all, though it clearly has similarities with notions associated with prophecy. The basic idea is that 'an agent is like the one who sent him',[30] so that an agent can be regarded for some purposes as the same, or 'one with', the person who sends him. Within Judaism, the principle of agency applied in a number of different settings and different contexts where an agent would represent another person. The idea is reflected in some parts of the synoptic tradition, applied to Jesus as the 'agent' of God and to the disciples as 'agents' of Jesus (cf. Luke 10: 16 pars), and the same idea recurs in, for example, John 13: 20: 'whoever receives one whom I send receives me; and whoever receives me receives him who sent me' (cf. too 12: 44–5; 14: 9). In one way of course the idea is similar to that of prophecy: the prophet too 'represents' God in some way and indeed the words of the prophet *are* the words of God, so that prophetic oracles are typically introduced by 'Thus says the Lord . . .' However, the quasi-identity claimed between an agent and the sender takes the language one stage further than anything found in prophecy. In this sense, John's language about the oneness of Jesus with the Father goes further than what is implied by the prophetic model.

Nevertheless, even when an idea of agency is added to the prophetic model, and even if these are both enhanced by ideas of sonship, we have still not fully encompassed everything that John evidently wants to claim for Jesus. Above all, there is the notion that Jesus is the *revealer*, and reveals the things of God – or rather that he reveals God himself.

In the language of John, Jesus has come *from heaven* and tells of what he has seen and heard from his Father (cf. 3: 31–2, 34; 8: 26, 38; 12: 49; 15: 15; 17: 19); indeed Jesus is himself the revelation *of God*, so that to have seen Jesus is to have seen God himself (1: 18; 14: 9).

Son of Man

Some of these ideas are expressed in the Son of Man sayings which John records. As we have seen, the Son of Man sayings are firmly rooted in the synoptic tradition. The Son of Man sayings in John bear some similarity to the synoptic sayings, though it is clear that they have been developed very considerably in line with John's own ideas. Perhaps the saying closest to the synoptic tradition is John 5: 27, where it is said that God 'has given him [Jesus] authority to execute judgement, because he is the Son of Man'. The language is similar to Daniel 7: 14 where the one like a son of man is given vindication and 'justice' in the heavenly court. The saying in John 5 does go further than Daniel 7 in that the Son of Man figure is now the one who actually dispenses judgement – though the same move is made by at least some of the synoptics (notably Matthew: cf. Matt. 25: 31) and may also have been made independently by the authors of *1 Enoch* and *4 Ezra*.[31]

What is more striking about the Johannine Son of Man sayings is the idea embedded in them that Jesus *qua* Son of Man is a figure who ascends to heaven to a place from which he has previously descended. 'No one has ascended into heaven except the one who descended from heaven, the Son of Man' (3: 13); 'What if you were to see the Son of Man ascending to where he was before?' (6: 62). There is debate about whether the prime motif in these sayings is ascension alone, or descending as well as ascending. Certainly the idea of the Son of Man 'ascending' in John is not unrelated to the language used by John of Jesus as Son of Man being 'lifted up' (cf. 3: 14–15; 8: 28; 12: 34). Indeed the conjunction of 3: 13 with 3: 14–15 make the link clear. But also for John, Jesus' being 'lifted up' is identified – allusively at first but by the end quite clearly – with his being lifted up on the cross (cf. 12: 33: the language of being 'lifted up' is 'to indicate the kind of death he was to die'). As we have seen, Son of Man language in the synoptic tradition is strongly linked with Jesus' suffering and death, especially in Mark (and thence in Matthew and Luke: cf. Mark 8: 31; 9: 31; 10: 33, 45, etc.). In terms of the origins of the language, it may be then that the language of the Son of Man's being lifted up/ascending owes quite a lot to the synoptic language about the suffering Son of Man, developed by John who interprets the cross itself as Jesus' glorification and 'lifting up'.

Yet this does not exhaust the meaning of Son of Man language for John. As we have already seen, the Son of Man ascends to *heaven*, to where he has come from originally and from where he has first descended (3: 13; 6: 62). Thus Jesus as the Son of Man, by virtue of his origins, is uniquely able to fulfil the role of revealing the mysteries of heaven, and of God, to other human beings on earth. It is this idea that may also be implied by the highly enigmatic verse 1: 51 'You will see heaven opened and the angels of God ascending and descending upon the Son of Man'. The language is reminiscent of the story of Jacob's dream of the ladder, with angels ascending and descending on it (Gen. 28: 12). What seems to be implied by John is that the Son of Man acts as the link by which heaven and earth are connected, the means by which the things of heaven can be revealed to those on earth. Jesus is thus the source or means of divine revelation. Certainly, too, this idea of Jesus as the one who reveals God to others is implied by John in other sayings which do not refer to Jesus as Son of Man (cf. 1: 18; 5: 17; 6: 46; 14: 6, 8–9).

It is certainly hard to derive any of these ideas from the Son of Man tradition itself. However, one notable 'parallel' (or anti-parallel) to the use of such language, especially in 3: 13, has been noted for some years now. This concerns the claims made about others by some (or about themselves) to have made mystical ascents into heaven and hence to be able to reveal the mysteries of heaven to others. There seems to have been a strong tradition associating Moses with such an ascent into heaven,[32] as well as figures like Enoch, Abraham and others. We know too of developing interests in Judaism from around the time of the end of the first century of so-called 'merkabah mysticism',[33] a claim to be able to be transported to heaven as a result of meditating on the vision of the chariot (*merkabah*) in Ezekiel 1. This interest may be implied in *1 Enoch* 14, Sirach 49: 8, and other texts such as the *Songs of the Sabbath Sacrifice* from Qumran (4Q400–7). So, too, from a little later, we hear of some rabbis who claimed to have 'entered the garden' (*t. Hag.* 2.3–4), possibly a reference to a claimed vision of the chariot throne. One of these, Rabbi Elisha ben Abuyah, was deemed to be a heretic because he thought the glorious figure he saw on a throne was a 'second power in heaven' (*3 Enoch* 16; *b. Hag.* 15a). It thus appears that Judaism at the time of the writing of John's Gospel was developing a strong interest in such mystical visions and the claims resulting from them; but equally, this seems to have been a time when the Jewish authorities were also clamping down hard on what others evidently regarded as dangerous excesses.

It may be then that it is this background which lies behind much of the Fourth Gospel.[34] Certainly the claim in John 3: 13 that no one has ascended to heaven except the Son of Man becomes much more pointed when set against such a background: for it becomes a more polemical denial against possible claims by any other rival figure to have entered heaven and to be able to reveal the secrets there.

This suggested background may also help to explain a little more the vehemence of the Jewish reaction to the Christian claims about Jesus. If this were indeed a time when the Jewish authorities generally were entrenching and drawing tighter boundary lines about their religion and excluding some elements as unacceptable, then it is perhaps a little less surprising that Christianity came under the spotlight so harshly. If Christian claims by the Johannine community about Jesus as a revealer figure related to Jesus as one who could reveal the mysteries of heaven itself, or God himself, then similar reactions by the Jewish authorities to figures like Rabbi Elisha may have led to strong rejection of the Christian claims and the decision to exclude Christians from the Jewish synagogues.

Yet John does not present Jesus as *just* a latter day Moses or Enoch-figure, ascending to heaven from earth. Jesus is one who ascends to *where he was before*. Built into the Johannine scheme is therefore an idea of pre-existence in some sense, and of a pattern of descending as well as ascending. Two possible models have been suggested for such language.

According to the first, Jesus' role is described in terms very similar to those used of the figure of *Wisdom* in the Jewish tradition. We have already seen that language of Wisdom as some kind of pre-existent being was already present in Judaism (cf. Prov. 8: 22; Wisd. 9: 9) as also was language about Wisdom being sent from God (Wisd. 9: 16–17; Bar. 3: 9; *1 Enoch* 42). It has long been recognised that much of the language of the prologue in John 1: 1–18 can be paralleled in language about Wisdom, and the same also applies to virtually all of John.[35] Thus John's Jesus and Wisdom act as the agent in creation (Prov. 8: 22–31; John 1: 3); both are the source of light (Wisd. 7: 26–9; John 1: 5; 8: 12), or food and drink (Sir. 24: 19–21; Prov. 9: 2–5; John 6: 35, 51–8). Notably the language of Jesus as the Word 'coming to his own' (1: 11) and then 'becoming flesh' and 'dwelling' (literally 'tabernacling') among people on earth (1: 14) has a parallel in Sirach 24: 8 where God tells Wisdom 'make your dwelling [lit. tabernacle] in Jacob'. So, too, the long first-person discourses of Wisdom (Prov. 8; Sir. 24) are similar in some respects to the long discourses of the Johannine Jesus which are often developed out of an 'I am . . .' saying by Jesus.

The application of such language to a human being may well represent a quantum leap from the use of such language in non-Christian Judaism (though if John made such a leap he was almost certainly not the first Christian to do so: as we have already seen, the category of Wisdom was exploited christologically by Paul, the author of Colossians and Matthew). Thus some have suggested recently that another possible background for John's ideas may be that of an *angelic* figure.[36]

The idea of God being surrounded by an angelic retinue is one that can be traced back to the earliest stages of Israelite history, as we have already seen in chapter 1. Moreover, we have also seen the way in which an angelic messenger can apparently oscillate between being someone separate from God and being God himself.[37] It may be then that it is this idea that also informs the total Johannine picture. Jesus in John as the one who re-presents God on earth may thus be adopting in part an angelic-type role.

Against such a view it has been noted that angels are generally only short-term visitors, and certainly Jesus for John is certainly on earth for rather longer than the average angel of Judaism![38] So too, despite the real parallels which can be shown, and which justify the suggestion that John's Jesus is *like* an angel in several significant respects (and therefore 'angelo*morphic*'), there is still no real parallel in Judaism to an idea of an angel becoming 'incarnate'.[39]

Maybe all this simply shows that there is no one single category to explain the Johannine picture fully. It may be then that we have to content ourselves with the fact that, in terms of previous ideas, John has taken a number of rather different, disparate notions and combined them in his portrayal of Jesus as the Son of God/Son of Man/Logos who is pre-existent with God in heaven, sent by his Father, who reveals God to those on earth, and who eventually returns to the place where he has come from. There seems to be little doubt that in this composite picture, John has made rich and varied use of Jewish materials. Yet, as with other New Testament writers, the use made has taken John some considerable distance from the way in which such materials are used in Judaism. We have seen this in relation to John's use of the categories of messiahship and divine sonship, and his use of 'Son of Man'. Clearly for the Jewish opponents of Jesus in John's story ('the Jews', who one assumes represent the Jewish opponents of John's Christian community in John's time), this distancing has reached the point of being intolerable: the claims by the Johannine Jesus (i.e. presumably the claims made about Jesus by Johannine Christians) have become so extreme that they are regarded as blasphemous, threatening the fundamentals of monotheistic belief. Thus in John 10: 33 'the Jews' say 'it is not for a good work that we are going to stone you, but for blasphemy, because you, though only a human being, are making yourself God'.

Nevertheless, it would seem that John believes that the claims made by the Johannine Jesus can and should be contained *within* the parameters of Judaism and within a monotheistic framework. Even the momentous claim by the Johannine Jesus 'I and the Father are one' is one which he claims can be defended within Jewish presuppositions and does not deserve the charge of blasphemy (cf. the argument of 10: 31–9 and the appeal to Psalm 82: 1). Apparently then even the claim to divinity for Jesus (1: 1; 20: 28) is one which, in John's eyes, can evidently be tolerated without prejudicing the uniqueness of God. For John, Jesus is the revealer – and to a certain extent the embodiment, or 'incarnation' (cf. 1: 14) – of the one true God. Certainly John goes out of his way to emphasise that the revelation provided by Jesus far outpasses any other rival claims to be able to reveal the things of heaven (cf. 3: 13), and even God himself (cf. 1: 18), to human beings. Yet it is precisely as the one who is obedient to the Father in everything that Jesus's unity with God is to be seen.

There can be no question that the claims made about Jesus in John are qualitatively different ('higher') than those in some other parts of the New Testament. But equally, the insistence of John that his Christian claims do not breach the bounds of monotheism forbids a neat equation of Jesus with a(n other) divine figure alongside God. The tensions and complexities of the Johannine picture undoubtedly contributed to the later disputes between Christians in subsequent christological debates, with different sides being able to appeal to different parts of John's Gospel for support.[40] That lies outside our purview here. Perhaps we can simply note the way in which John's presentation no doubt sets the agenda for the subsequent discussion by insisting not only on the full humanity of Jesus ('the Word became flesh') but also on the final and definitive nature of the revelation provided by Jesus so that Jesus is the Son sent from the Father, the Son of Man who has ascended back to his place of origin in heaven from where he descended, the embodiment of God's wisdom and word: the one whom the true follower can and should acknowledge as 'my Lord and my God' (20: 28).

NOTES

1. Cited by Eusebius, *E. H.* 6.14.7.
2. E.g., in John, Jesus 'cleanses' the temple early in his ministry; in the synoptics it is much later. In John, Jesus is active for much longer in Jerusalem; in the synoptics, Jesus is in Jerusalem for only one final week of his life. In John, Jesus dies on the eve of Passover, in the synoptics he dies on the feast of Passover itself.
3. Instead of the short pithy sayings and the parables which characterise the synoptic presentation of Jesus' teaching, John's Jesus teaches in long discourses with none of the parables so characteristic of the synoptics. So too, categories such as the 'kingdom of God', which is so prominent in the synoptics, rarely appear in John; in turn other categories, such as teaching about 'eternal life', dominate the picture in John.
4. John 14: 1 is typical: 'Believe in God, believe also in me'; cf. also 20: 31. In the synoptics the motif occurs only in Matt. 18: 6 ('these little ones who believe in me') which is almost certainly due to MattR (the Markan parallel in Mark 9: 42 lacks the phrase 'who believe in me').
5. John 6: 35; 8: 12; 8: 58; 10: 7, 9, 11; 11: 25; 14: 6; 15: 1.
6. For a variety of reasons, many have argued that ch. 21 is a later appendix to the Gospel, written by another hand: the vocabulary is slightly different, and in any case 20: 30–1 bears all the hallmarks of the ending of a book and is rather anti-climactic when followed by a whole further chapter.
7. There is variation among the MSS of John at this point: some read a present tense *pisteuete*, perhaps implying that the aim is that people continue in their (existing) belief, others read an aorist *pisteusete*, perhaps implying that people should make a single act of belief (i.e. perhaps change their belief in a one-off act). The latter possibility might imply rather more of a missionary aim for the Gospel.
8. By 'authentic' accounts, I mean here historically accurate representations of what Jesus himself actually said and did. The *theological* 'authenticity'

of John's account is quite another matter.

9. Cf. e.g., D. Rensberger, *Overcoming the World: Politics and Community in the Gospel of John* (Philadelphia: Westminster Press, 1988), ch. 1. The most influential works on John's community in recent years have been R. E. Brown, *The Community of the Beloved Disciple* (New York: Geoffrey Chapman, 1979) (as well as his Anchor Bible commentary); also J. L. Martyn, *History and Theology in the Fourth Gospel* (Nashville: Abingdon, ²1979).

10. This issue is treated in all the commentaries on the Johannine epistles as well as the standard *Introductions* to the New Testament: cf. e.g. Kümmel, *Introduction*, 442–5.

11. All the evidence we have suggests that Jesus, and the earliest followers, remained – and were allowed and expected to remain – within the jurisdiction of the synagogue authorities.

12. The phrase was originally coined by Martyn, but has become very widely used now in relation to John.

13. Cf. the discussion in W. Horbury, 'The benediction of the *Minim* and early Jewish-Christian controversy', *JTS* 33 (1982), pp. 19–61.

14. Cf. John 16: 2: 'The hour is coming when those who kill you will think that by doing so they are offering worship to God'.

15. Again the terminology is that of Martyn: 'Christian Jews' refers to people who were positive in their attitude to Jesus and the Christian movement but who stayed within Jewish structures, religiously and socially. 'Jewish Christians' refers to those who had left the social structures of non-Christian Judaism. In one sense, no New Testament Christian would have regarded himself or herself as a 'Jewish Christian' in this sense since all would have thought of themselves as 'Jews' still in some sense or other.

16. See the works of Brown and Martyn already mentioned. For a useful summary of the different positions, see M. C. de Boer, *Johannine Perspectives on the Death of Jesus* (Kampen: Kok Pharos, 1996), esp. ch. 2.

17. There is of course the well-known problem of the pericope of the woman taken in adultery in 7: 53–8: 11: this is missing from most MSS of John, is stylistically quite unlike the rest of the Gospel and hence is almost certainly a later addition to the text. We have already noted the phenomenon of ch. 21, which seems to be a slightly redundant 'appendix' after 20: 30–1. There is another well-known problem with John 6 which seems to disrupt the narrative flow between chs 5 and 7 by suddenly transporting Jesus back to Galilee when 7: 1 then presupposes that he is still in Judea.

18. This is above all the view of Brown who correlates the linear progression of the story within the Gospel with the (supposed) historical development

of the community and its beliefs.

19. If nothing else one should note the common points between John and the synoptics: however they are to be explained in detail, they clearly show John's use of earlier traditions (whether of the synoptics or of the sources used by the synoptics).

20. The ablest defender of the theory is R. Fortna: see his *The Fourth Gospel and its Predecessor: From Narrative Source to Present Gospel* (Edinburgh: T&T Clark, 1989).

21. Probably with the exception of 7: 53–8: 11 which can be excluded on text-critical grounds.

22. Cf. Fortna, *Fourth Gospel*, pp. 226–8; De Boer, *Johannine Perspectives*, pp. 85–90; J. Ashton, *Understanding the Fourth Gospel* (Oxford: OUP, 1991), ch. 7.

23. In 4QTest, the text from Deut. 18, referring to the coming of a 'prophet like Moses' is quoted, apparently with respect to hopes for a future, eschatological figure.

24. See De Boer, *Johannine Perspectives*, p. 88; Martyn, *History*, pp. 102–11; also W. Meeks, *The Prophet-King: Moses Traditions and the Johannine Christology* (Leiden: Brill, 1967), p. 26.

25. See M. de Jonge, 'Jesus as prophet and king in the fourth gospel', in *Jesus: Stranger from Heaven and Son of God. Jesus Christ and the Christians in Johannine Perspective* (Missoula: Scholars Press, 1977), pp. 49–76.

26. Cf. Ashton, *Understanding*, p. 318; De Boer, *Johannine Perspectives*, pp. 113–14.

27. For discussion of this in relation to Jesus' own self-understanding, see pp. 220–1 below.

28. See C. K. Barrett, '"The Father is greater than I" John 14.28: Subordinationist Christology in the New Testament', in *Essays on John* (London: SPCK, 1982), pp. 19–36.

29. See P. Borgen, 'God's agent in the fourth gospel', in J. Ashton (ed.), *The Interpretation of John* (London: SPCK, 1986), pp. 67–78; Ashton, *Understanding*, pp. 313–17.

30. Cf. *Mek. on Exod.* 12: 3; *Ber.* 5: 5, etc.

31. Cf. p. 126 above.

32. Cf. Philo, *Mos.* 1.158; Josephus, *Ant.* 3.96; *Pseudo-Philo* 12.1. See P. Borgen, 'Some Jewish exegetical traditions as background for Son of Man sayings in John's Gospel (Jn 3,13–14 and context)', in M. de Jonge (ed.), *L'Evangile de Jean* (BETL 44; Leuven: Duculot & Leuven University Press, 1977), pp. 243–58. Also J. D. G. Dunn, 'Let John be John: A gospel for its time', in P. Stuhlmacher (ed.), *The Gospel and the Gospels* (Grand Rapids: Eerdmans, 1991), pp. 293–322, on p. 307, repr. in Dunn, *The Christ and the Spirit*, vol. 1, pp. 345–75, on 359.

33. See C. C. Rowland, *The Open Heaven: A Study of Apocalyptic in Judaism and Early Christianity* (London: SPCK, 1982).

34. See especially Dunn, 'Let John be John'.

35. See e.g. B. Lindars, *The Gospel of John* (London: Marshall, Morgan & Scott, 1977), pp. 77–9; R. E. Brown, *The Gospel according to John I–XII* (New York: Doubleday, 1966), pp. cxxii–cxxv; Dunn, 'Let John be John', pp. 314–17.

36. Cf. J. Ashton, 'Bridging ambiguities', in *Studying John: Approaches to the Fourth Gospel* (Oxford: OUP, 1994), pp. 71–89.

37. See p. 27 above. The picture of some interchange between the angel and God can be found in several texts: e.g. in Gen. 21, Hagar is addressed by 'an angel of God' in v. 17 who tells her that 'God has heard the voice of the boy [Ishmael]'; but then in almost the same breath, she is told 'I will make a great nation out of him'. (Cf. too Gen. 31: 11–13.) In Exod. 3, the 'angel of the Lord' appears to Moses in the burning bush (v. 2), yet it is God who speaks (vv. 4, 6).

38. Dunn, 'Let John be John', p. 313. Ashton's response is that John is also a short-term visitor in John's eyes (*Understanding*, p. 352)! Yet despite e.g. John 16: 16–20 and the discussion of the 'little while' that Jesus will be with his disciples, Jesus' time on earth is considerably longer than that spent by any angelic visitor in Jewish literature.

39. The one possible exception might be the *Prayer of Joseph*, a fragment of which is preserved by Origen and which appears to imply that Jacob was an angel who came down to earth and 'tabernacled' as Jacob-Israel. See the discussion by J. Z. Smith, in J. H. Charlesworth, *Old Testament Pseudepigrapha* (New York: Doubleday; London: Darton, Longman & Todd, 1985), vol. 2, pp. 699–712, with further literature cited.

40. See T. E. Pollard, *Johannine Christology and the Early Church* (Cambridge: CUP, 1970).

Chapter 10

THE JOHANNINE EPISTLES

———∝⌒———

At the start of the discussion of John's Gospel, I said that, for all the brilliant individual genius of the evangelist, John should be seen as part of a community and his Gospel as reflecting the situation of that community. Moreover, the highly distinctive vocabulary and idiom of the Gospel are shared by some other writers, notably by the author(s) of the Johannine epistles. It thus makes sense to talk in some sense of a Johannine community, or Johannine school, the members of which shared the thought world shown by John and were also influenced by John.

When we turn to the Johannine epistles, we are clearly moving in the same broad area of ideas and terminology as encountered in the Fourth Gospel. However, a number of differences between 1 John[1] and John's Gospel suggest that the two works are not written by the same author. There is no time to go into any details here on the question of authorship.[2] However, many have argued that, although the author of 1 John knows some of the language of John, he lacks the theological profundity of the evangelist. In particular, it would seem that, in some respects, the Christology of 1 John is rather less advanced or developed than that of John. Thus, for example, 1 John does not contain any of the 'I am . . .' sayings which characterise the Fourth Gospel. In addition, 1 John sometimes ascribes to God a feature which is ascribed to Jesus in John. Thus 1 John 1: 5 says that '*God* is light', whereas in John, Jesus says that he himself is the 'light of the world' (John 8: 12, cf. 1: 4, 9). Similarly, in 1 John 4: 21 it is God who is the originator of the love command, whereas in John 13 it is Jesus who gives the love command. 1 John seems rather more theocentric at points where John is christocentric.

The situation is, however, made unclear by ambiguity in the language

172

of 1 John at crucial points. Despite the deceptively simple form of Greek used by the author, his language is very imprecise and his meaning is at times uncertain.[3] In relation to Christology this applies especially to texts like 1 John 1: 1–4 and 5: 20. Thus in 1: 1–4, the language is in one way very similar to the language used in the prologue of the Gospel (John 1: 1–18) with the common reference to the 'word'; and no doubt the similarity is intentional, with the opening section of the letter echoing the opening section of the Gospel. Yet while in John it is clear that the 'word' is Jesus himself, this is much less clear in 1 John. Commentators are divided as to whether the reference here really is to Jesus or whether it is rather to the Gospel message considered more broadly.[4] So, too, the precise reference of the final clause in 5: 20 ('This is the true God and eternal life') is also unclear. Is it intended as a statement qualifying the previous reference to Jesus ('his Son Jesus Christ') or the 'his' mentioned in the previous phrase, that is God? Is it thus a claim about the full divinity of Jesus (cf. John 20: 28), or is it simply a switch back (generally characteristic of the author) from Christology to theology? Again the commentators are divided. Similar ambiguity occurs at other key points in the epistle, where as often as not a vague third person singular reference (he/him) is left undefined and one does not know if the reference is to Jesus or to God. Thus when the writer says 'You know him who is from the beginning' (2: 13, also in 2: 14), is this a reference to God, or to Jesus seen in highly exalted, pre-existent terms? Thus it seems entirely appropriate to describe the Christology of 1 John as 'ambiguous rather than high'.[5]

In one sense, the Christology of 1 John is rather monochrome. Two terms predominate in the references to Jesus (apart from some ambiguous references to the 'word': cf. 1: 1–2; 2: 14). First, Jesus is 'the Christ' (2: 22; 5: 1). Yet on several other occasions, 'Christ' is used as if it were virtually just another proper name in the phrase 'Jesus Christ' (1: 3; 2: 1; 3: 23; 4: 2, 15; 5: 6, 20) and the key issue is evidently seen in the claim that Jesus (Christ) is the 'Son of God' (4: 2, 15; 5: 5, 10). Further, the close parallelism between believing that Jesus is the Christ and believing that Jesus is the Son of God (cf. 5: 1 with 5: 5, or 2: 23 after 2: 22) suggests that for this author 'Christ' and 'Son of God' are virtually synonymous.[6]

It is, however, doubtful whether the author has any awareness of the background or significance of these terms, for example in Jewish messianic expectations. The elaboration of the meaning of the phrase 'denying that Jesus is the Christ' in 2: 22 in terms of 'denying the Father and the Son' (2: 22–3) and the mutual interdependence of Father and Son suggests that we are a long way from any ideas associated with Jewish messiahship. More likely, the immediate background of the language of 1 John is the language of the Fourth Gospel itself. Thus 1 John simply presupposes the fusion of the various terms as applied to Jesus and seems to interpret them in what he understands as the appropriate 'Johannine' way. It is though at times uncertain how far the author is really aware of the deeper significance implied by the language and how far he simply knows what he thinks are the correct words to use.

The question of the meaning of the terms does, however, arise in relation to what has evidently become one key issue for the author. It seems very likely that 1 John represents a stage in the life of the Johannine community that is later than that reflected in the Fourth Gospel itself. Moreover, it is a very specific situation of conflict and division; but, unlike the situation of the Gospel, it seems to be one involving division within the Christian community itself. Any disagreement or conflict with Jews outside the Christian community seems to have disappeared from sight. Rather, there has evidently been a major disagreement within the community which has led to one faction splitting off (2: 18–19). This is almost certainly to be related to the author's passionate insistence on the importance of confessing 'Jesus Christ come in the flesh' (4: 2, cf. 2 John 7). Related too may be the insistence on the fact that Jesus Christ has come with/by 'water and blood', not just water only, but water and blood (5: 6). Although the precise details are not absolutely clear, most would argue that what the author is insisting on is the humanity of the person of Jesus, including the saving significance of his human life *and* his death. This may well be in response to another group who were in the community (but who may now have left) who denied the full humanity of Jesus. Rather then than opposing a 'low' Christology (denying that Jesus is special at all), the author may be opposing too 'high' a Christology, a Christology that viewed Jesus as a heavenly figure whose humanity was all but denied. The opposing group may then have been 'Docetics' in some sense, claiming that Jesus' humanity was in some sense a slight sham. The author of 1 John opposes this vigorously, insisting on the importance of asserting that Jesus has come *in the flesh*, that is as a fully human being, and that this coming involved his real human death: it was a coming with 'blood' (a reference probably to Jesus' death) as well as with 'water' (perhaps a reference to baptism).[7]

It has in fact been plausibly argued that the debate reflected in 1 John may arise from competing interpretations of a common tradition consisting of the Fourth Gospel itself.[8] John's Gospel does certainly contain elements which might be seen as tending towards the view that Jesus is a divine being whose humanity is scarcely real. Thus John 1: 14 says 'we have seen his glory'; and, in parts of John 17, Jesus appears as a figure who comes from heaven and who is something of an alien or stranger in the world (cf. v. 16: 'I do not belong to the world'). Similarly, as we saw earlier, Jesus' suffering in John can be interpreted as on the point of disappearing: cf. the pale shadow of the Gethsemane tradition, in John 12, and the supreme confidence, rather than any cry of dereliction, shown by Jesus on the cross in John. Yet equally John's Gospel contains other elements that indicate that Jesus' humanity is indeed real. As well as being the revealer of the divine glory that is also *his* glory (1: 14b), the Word has truly *become flesh* (1: 14a)! Insofar as Docetism (the denial of Jesus' full humanity) is related to 'Gnosticism' (though the problems of defining Gnosticism are enormous), it seems that the schismatics of 1 John prefigure the positive way in which John's Gospel was used and valued by Gnostics in later Christian history. 1 John can then be seen as part of a counter-reaction that may have in part succeeded in rescuing John from being taken over by later Gnostics and in making the Christology of the Gospel more accessible to the wider Christian church.

Thus even if 1 John itself lacks the profundity of the Fourth Gospel and fails to grasp the full depth of Johannine thought, at times simply repeating the key words, nevertheless its achievement may have been considerable in preventing the Gospel itself from being hijacked by Gnostics and leading to the rejection of the Gospel by the 'orthodox' later. For itself, the Christology of the writer seems rather vague and imprecise at critical points. What is important above all is that, somehow or other, Jesus is the 'Messiah'/'Son of God' whose full humanity cannot and must not be compromised in any way.

NOTES

1. 2 John and 3 John are very small in extent and so I focus primarily on 1 John in this section.

2. See e.g. Kümmel, *Introduction*, 442–5; also see the various commentaries, e.g. R. E. Brown, *The Epistles of John* (New York: Doubleday, 1982).

3. There is notorious ambiguity in understanding key phrases such as 'the love of God' in 1 John: is this the love which God has for other human beings? Or the love which human beings are meant to show to God?

4. Cf. the imprecise reference to '*that which* was from the beginning, which we have heard . . .', etc. (The pronoun used is a neuter one in Greek, not a masculine.)

5. See J. Lieu, *The Theology of the Johannine Epistles* (Cambridge: CUP, 1991), p. 72.

6. Cf. M. de Jonge, 'Variety and development in Johannine Christology', in De Jonge, *Jesus: Stranger from Heaven and Son of God*, pp. 193–222, esp. 200–6.

7. This is the most widespread interpretation, though cf. De Boer, *Johannine Perspectives*, ch. 6.

8. See Brown, *Epistles*, pp. 69–115.

Chapter 11

REVELATION

We have looked at the Gospel and the epistles that now go under the name of John together. We turn now to look at the other book of the New Testament which goes under the name of John, namely the book of Revelation. The justification for considering Revelation as associated with the name 'John' is self-evident since the book itself claims to be written by a person called John (Rev. 1: 1). This is of course unlike the Fourth Gospel and the Johannine epistles, none of which makes any explicit claim about the name of their authors. Tradition has of course ascribed the Fourth Gospel and the three Johannine epistles to the apostle John. Whether Revelation is by the apostle John is very uncertain and we shall not discuss the issue here. Whether Revelation is in fact to be associated with the Fourth Gospel and the Johannine epistles is a slightly different question. Older church tradition ascribed all these texts to a 'John'; but it was very soon recognised that Revelation could not be by the same person as the author of John or the author of the Johannine epistles.[1] It is today universally accepted that, at very many levels, the author of Revelation is quite different: his style, his manner of writing Greek, including his at times highly idiosyncratic use of Greek grammar, distinguish him clearly from the author of John and the author of the Johannine epistles.

Whether there is some other kind of connection between Revelation and the other New Testament 'Johannine' writings is, however, not quite to easy to answer. It could of course be purely coincidental that Revelation is written by a 'John', and the other Johannine writings are ascribed traditionally to a 'John'. John was after all a very common name.[2] However, despite all its differences from the other Johannine writings, Revelation does show a number of intriguing points of contact and agreement with the other New Testament Johannine texts. For example, Revelation and John's Gospel are alone in the New Testament in referring to Jesus as the 'Word' (Greek *Logos*) of God (John 1: 1–18; Rev. 19: 13). Both John and Revelation also refer to Jesus as the 'Lamb' (John 1: 29, 34; twenty-eight times in Revelation), albeit with a slightly different Greek word used (John *amnos*, Revelation *arnion*) and with probably rather different overtones of meaning (cf. below). Both John and Revelation also speak of the 'water of life' (cf. John 4: 14; 7: 38–9; Rev. 7: 17; 21: 6; 22: 1, 17). As a result of some of these points of contact, several have argued that it may be sensible to think of Revelation, as well as the Johannine epistles, as associated with the Fourth Gospel and forming the literary product of some kind of Johannine 'school'.[3] It may therefore be appropriate to consider Revelation at this point in our discussion.

The book of Revelation is one of the hardest books of the New Testament to interpret (and this applies not only to our present topic of Christology). The book calls itself an 'apocalypse' (Rev. 1: 1 Gk *apokalypsis*, NRSV 'revelation') and is by common consent a text which can be described as 'apocalyptic'. There is, however, enormous debate about what is the most appropriate way to define an 'apocalypse', or 'apocalyptic' writings or ideas.[4] In the past, apocalyptic writing has often been assumed to involve primarily speculation about the end of the world. It is, however, now recognised that this is probably too narrow a definition. Apocalyptic can be just as much about the present as the future; it can then be about revealing what is present in heaven as much as about what is happening on earth (either now or in the future).[5]

In some respects, however, Revelation is rather *un*like other texts normally described as 'apocalyptic'. For example, other apocalyptic writings often claim to be written by a famous figure in the past, looking forward to the future. Revelation makes no such claims: it is written by an otherwise unknown person called John who is a contemporary of the readers. Nevertheless, Revelation shares with much other 'apocalyptic' writing a tendency to use a rich variety, if not a riot, of verbal imagery in describing what is happening, has happened or is about to happen. In the case of Revelation, the language is also deeply coloured by Old Testament terminology. Although there is not a single Old Testament quotation explicitly signalled as such (e.g. by an introductory formula), the whole book is chock full of biblical phraseology and biblical allusions, and a failure to appreciate these leads a modern reader to have little understanding of what the author may be trying to say.

The rich, imaginative and poetic use of language also makes any prosaic understanding of the text difficult. The author is quite capable of playing with language in a highly creative and original way in the descriptions he paints. To take one example at random, John says, 'I turned to see the voice which was speaking to me',[6] violently juxta-posing the visual and the aural ('seeing a voice'). There is too the fact that frequently John describes heavenly figures, that is angels or, occasionally, God himself. Inevitably such descriptions strain language to the limit and beyond. In the case of God, for example, no language is capable of giving an exact, precise description: the most that can be given is then an analogy or a claim that the figure being described is *like* something or someone else. All this means that Revelation gives no precise descriptions, and if we expect, or look for, such in the text we shall be disappointed.

This has implications for our more limited concern of this study, Christology. Further, Revelation is similar to virtually the whole of the rest of the New Testament in that Christology as such is not the author's direct concern. Like Paul or the evangelists, John does not set out to write a doctrinal treatise, on Christology or whatever. John writes here to pass on the 'revelation' (1: 1) he has received. His exact purpose in writing is disputed. Many have argued that it is a charac-teristic of apocalyptic writing to emerge from a situation of oppression, or at least what is *perceived* to be a situation of oppression.[7] The vision of the apocalyptic writer, whether it be of a present reality in heaven or of a hoped for future, then serves to give hope and encouragement to the beleaguered community. John may be writing in such a situation with Christians being persecuted, or at least fearing the threat of per-secution. An alternative model is, however, that John is seeking not so much to bring comfort and hope to a suffering community, but is rather trying to jolt a community that he considers to be over-complacent to alert it to the grim realities that are threatening it. We perhaps do not need to decide between the various alternatives here. Suffice it to say that the author's aim is not directly christological. Rather, it is to use his claims and beliefs about Jesus in such a way as to address his community, to encourage them and to exhort them.

As far as christological titles are concerned, John uses some of these relatively infrequently. 'Christ' appears seven times (1: 1, 2, 5; 11: 15;

12: 10; 20: 4, 6), Son of God only once (2: 18), 'son of man' twice (1: 13; 14: 14), though on both occasions only as part of an analogy and in each case it is disputed whether there really is a 'Son of Man Christology' in mind at all.[8] The term that occurs most frequently is 'Lamb', which comes twenty-eight times in all. However, we have already noted on several occasions in relation to other New Testament writers that a titular approach to Christology may not be the most appropriate, and this is even more so in the case of Revelation. Certainly too in Revelation, John can make his point by using a rich variety of poetic and metaphorical language in describing, or referring to, the person of Jesus quite as much as, if not more than, by using 'titles' as if the latter had fixed meanings. In any case, as we have already seen and shall see again, much of the meaning invested in any title may be provided as much by the Jesus event itself as by anything inherent in the title.

One of the most striking aspects of Revelation's Christology is the way in which at times the author uses language of Jesus which is elsewhere used of an angel. (One may note in passing that this language about Jesus does not use any christological 'title' at all.) Whether one should speak of an 'angel Christology' is very doubtful and it is very unlikely that Jesus is necessarily being identified or classified as an angel as such (cf. below). Nevertheless, the similarity is sufficiently striking for some to talk of an 'angelomorphic Christology': Jesus is perhaps *like* an angel.[9]

The most striking example of this phenomenon is the description John gives of the risen Jesus in Revelation 1: 13–16. The language here is extremely rich and evocative, full of resonances and echoes for those whose ears are attuned to the language of the Old Testament. In particular, the description of Jesus here has a number of echoes of the description of the (probably angelic) figure who appears to 'Daniel' and is described in Daniel 10: 5–6. Thus the 'golden girdle around his breast' of Revelation 1: 13 is similar to the 'loins girded with gold of Uphaz' of Daniel 10: 5; so too the 'feet . . . like burnished bronze, refined as in a furnace' of Revelation 1: 15 is similar to the 'arms and legs like the gleam of burnished bronze' of Daniel 10: 6; similarly, 'his voice was like the sound of many waters' (Rev. 1: 15) is more than reminiscent of 'the sound of his words [were] like the noise of a multitude' (Dan. 10: 6 though cf. also Ezek. 43: 2). There is no 'quotation' here, nor is the Greek word (or 'title') *angelos* used of Jesus. Nevertheless it seems clear that Jesus is being described here in terms that are quite deliberately evocative of the angelic figure in Daniel 10.[10]

As already noted, the description of Jesus in Revelation 1 is by no means a straight quotation of Daniel 10. One notable feature of the description which does not derive from Daniel 10 comes in Revelation 1: 13–14, where the risen Jesus is described as 'one like a son of man . . . his head and his hair were white as white wool, white as snow; his eyes were like a flame of fire'. The language here is clearly reminiscent not of Daniel 10 but of Daniel 7. The description of Jesus as 'one like a son of man' recalls Daniel 7: 13, a passage which has clearly been extremely influential in New Testament Christology elsewhere, as we have seen. What is also particularly striking though is that the description of Revelation 1: 14 is reminiscent not of the man-like figure of Daniel 7: 13 but of the Ancient of Days (i.e. God himself) in Daniel 7: 9–10, *to* whom the one like a son of man comes ('his raiment was white like snow, and the hair of his head like pure wool'). Some have argued that the figure of Jesus is here taking on divine attributes.[11] As we shall see, there may be some truth in this in relation to other aspects of Revelation, but it is not certain that this particular verse can be pressed as far as this. It would appear that others at about this time had also ransacked the description of the Ancient of Days and applied some of the details to an angelic figure. For example, the description of the angel Yahoel in *Apoc. Abr.* 10–11 also includes some details from Daniel 7: 9: for example *Apoc. Abr.* 11: 2 says 'the aspect of his face like chrysolite, and *the hair of his head like snow*'. Here we have clear use of imagery used previously of God now applied to an angelic figure.[12] It seems then that the description of the risen Jesus in Revelation 1 uses an array of verbal images and reminiscences which suggest that Jesus is presented here as an *angelomorphic* figure, and all the Old Testament verbal echoes can be interpreted in this way.

How far such an idea recurs in Revelation is not always clear. However, it may well be that the (only) other occasion in Revelation when there is a reference to 'one like a son of man', Revelation 14: 14, also refers to Jesus as an angelomorphic figure. The issue is not straightforward since the figure is not even clearly and unambiguously to be identified with Jesus; also it is not certain if the figure is meant to be taken as 'angelic' (or at least angelomorphic). However, the reference in the very next verse to *'another* angel' (Rev. 14: 15) suggests that the figure of verse 14 is assumed to be an angel-type figure. Moreover, the description of the figure of Revelation 14: 14 as 'one like a son of man' recalls the description of Jesus in those terms in 1: 13; and the reference to the 'cloud' in 14: 14 recalls Jesus' coming with the clouds in 1: 7. Hence most commentators assume that the figure here *is* intended to be Jesus.[13] If so then we have another example of Jesus presented as an angelomorphic (indeed all but directly angelic!) figure.[14]

Nevertheless, despite all that has been said so far, one must also say that, however 'angelo*morphic*' Jesus might be for the author of Revelation, Jesus is not (just!) an 'angel' *per se*. The Christology is at most one of an angelomorphic Christology, not an angelic Christology. Jesus is never explicitly called an *angelos* in Revelation (not even in 14: 14, though it must be admitted that, if the description of the figure in the next verse as 'another' angel is pressed, this must come very close to implying that Jesus is an angel!). It would seem that to claim that Jesus was/is an angelic figure would say too little for John.

This perhaps comes out most clearly, at least by implication, in the two scenes that occur towards the end of the book, where John meets an angel and responds by trying to worship him: each time the angel responds by forbidding such activity, claiming that he is a fellow creature with John and that God and God alone can be the object of worship (Rev. 19: 10; 22: 9). What is then so startling in one way is that Jesus clearly *is* the object of worship elsewhere in Revelation, apparently without any embarrassment.[15] Thus the scene in Revelation 5 closely parallels the scene in Revelation 4. In Revelation 4, God receives the worship of the heavenly host (4: 11 'Worthy are thou, our Lord and God, to receive glory and honour and power'); in chapter 5, virtually the same is said of the Lamb (cf. e. g. 5: 11 'Worthy is the Lamb who was slain to receive power and wealth and wisdom and might and honour and glory and blessing'). And then at the end of chapter 5, God and the Lamb are joined together as the joint recipients of the (single!) worship offered: 'To him who sits on the throne and to the Lamb be blessing and honour and glory and might for ever and ever' (5: 13), and the elders 'fell down and *worshipped*' (5: 14). The scenes with the angel in chapters 19 and 22 indicate that John is sensitive to the problems and dangers of breaching a monotheistic faith by having creatures other than God being worshipped. Yet then the very fact that Jesus *is* the object of worship in Revelation, without any apparent apology or embarrassment, suggests that Jesus is regarded by John as far greater than any angelic figure and pushing up into the realm of divinity.

The same is perhaps indicated by other features of the text. This in a way very similar to the openings of the Pauline letters, Jesus is placed alongside God (and the seven spirits) in the opening greeting which John addresses to the seven churches: 'Grace to you and peace from him who was and is and is to come [i.e. God], and from the seven sprits who are before his throne, and from Jesus Christ . . .' (Rev. 1: 4–5). So too some of the names and attributes given to Jesus overlap significantly with the names and attributes ascribed to God. Thus Jesus says in 22: 13 'I am the Alpha and the Omega, the first and the last, the beginning and the end', echoing the claims of God himself to be the Alpha and the Omega (1: 8), and the beginning and the end (21: 6).[16]

Possibly relevant too is the way in which the author may sometimes use singular pronouns and/or singular verbs to refer to God and Jesus together.[17] For example, Revelation 22: 3 says that 'the throne of God and of the Lamb will be in it [= the new Jerusalem], and *his* servants will worship *him*'. Similarly, 11: 15 talks of 'the kingdom of our Lord and of his Messiah' and then immediately says 'and *he* will reign for ever and ever'. The situation is not entirely clear, since the language could be taken as referring to God alone on each occasion; and in any case John's Greek is notoriously imprecise and idiosyncratic in its use of grammar, so that we cannot necessarily put too much weight on such details. Nevertheless, the evidence would fit with what appears clearly elsewhere in the text, namely that Jesus is placed alongside God as the object of worship, and indeed the subject of so much activity normally ascribed to God; and yet perhaps the pressures of monotheism are here exerting influence so that Jesus is brought with*in* the limits of a monotheistic godhead as an object of worship.[18]

However, this is not to say that Jesus is subsumed completely into the person of God. John is well aware that God and Jesus are separate. God is Jesus' 'father' (cf. 1: 6; 2: 27; 3: 5, 21; 14: 1); and for all the transfer of some names and attributes from God to Jesus, some are not transferred: for example Jesus is never called 'almighty' (Greek *pantokrator*), a word that seems to be reserved for God alone (Rev. 1: 8 and eight other times). Nor is Jesus ever explicitly called 'God' (Greek *theos*) as such (hence *un*like John 1: 1; 20: 28). Yet John does implicitly make some extraordinarily 'high' claims for Jesus by effectively placing him in a divine category whilst still maintaining a monotheistic framework.

Lamb of God

No discussion of the Christology of Revelation would be complete without some discussion of one particular christological descriptor, or 'title', which is applied to Jesus in Revelation. As I noted at the start of this chapter, John uses relatively few of the more 'traditional' New Testament christological titles, or if he does he uses them sparingly. The one term that does occur very frequently of Jesus is that of 'the Lamb'. Introduced in chapter 5 the term then dominates the account from this point on.

It is clearly a very important christological term in Revelation, though its origins are not at all clear. The background for the term in Revelation might be the description of the suffering servant figure of Isaiah 53 as one 'like a lamb that is led to the slaughter' (Isa. 53: 7); however, there is no other clear link between Revelation and Isaiah 53 (and even the verbal link via 'lamb' may look closer in English than in Greek: certainly the Greek word of Revelation – *arnion* – is not the same as that of the LXX of Isa. 53 which uses *amnos*). Others have suggested that the Passover lamb is in mind, though Revelation displays no interest in relating Jesus to the sacrificial cult.[19] A third possibility is an image which may have been current in Jewish apocalyptic of a fighting warrior lamb (cf. *1 Enoch* 90: 9) But the prevalence of such an image is uncertain, to say the least.

In any case it may be that John's use of the lamb imagery is intended to be *different* to what is expected. Certainly an aspect of this is implied by the very first occurrence of the terminology. In John's vision of the Lamb in chapter 5, one of the elders comes and consoles John who is looking for someone to be found who is worthy to open the scroll. The elder tells John not to weep, for 'the lion from the tribe of Judah, the Root of David, has conquered' (v. 5). The language is evocative of Davidic messianic overtones, with reference for example to the prophecy of Isaiah 11 of the root of David. Yet when John turns and 'sees', he sees *not* a warrior king, but 'a *lamb* standing as if it had been *slaughtered*' (v. 6). There may be a real sense in which the lamb imagery is intended to be *contrary* to what is expected. Certainly the vision of a slaughtered lamb seems to be the exact opposite of what the seer expects to see. The military victory looked for has been achieved paradoxically by the death of the Lamb.

Certainly elsewhere John clearly knows the tradition of the expectation of the military Davidic messiah figure. Thus Jesus is 'the root and descendant of David, the bright morning star' (22: 16, cf. Isa. 11; the last phrase alludes to Num. 24: 17, probably understood at the time as a messianic text). So too the military idea is clear in references to the sword that comes from Jesus' mouth (1: 16; 2: 2, etc.) and is used to strike down the nations (19: 15). So too the 'conquering' image is prevalent in all John's talk about Jesus and about Christian followers of Jesus (cf. the conclusions of each of the seven letters to the churches in chs 2–3, which all refer to 'the one who conquers'). Yet it is clear that the means of this victory is precisely suffering and death. The Lamb conquers by virtue of the fact that he has been slaughtered (cf. 5: 6); similarly others will 'conquer' only if they too are prepared to meet the same fate: compare 12: 11 'they have conquered him by the blood of the Lamb and by the word of their testimony, for they did not cling to life even in the face of death'.[20]

It may therefore be wrong to look for a clear unambiguous background which will 'explain' John's use of the lamb terminology as applied to Jesus. There is a real sense in which perhaps John intends that what he says about Jesus as the Lamb should go *against* normal expectations. The real 'substance' of the image is primarily provided by Jesus and his cross. Thus it may be *Jesus* who determines the meaning of the image, and in part the force of the language arises precisely from the *lack* of correspondence between what is said in the New Testament text and the expectations of readers from the thought world of the background at least in terms of any 'messianic' figure.

The book of Revelation offers a kaleidoscopic vision of past, present and future as part of its aim to encourage and exhort Christians to resist the evil that is in the world, evil which threatens them and their true faith. The author uses a rich variety of scriptural language in all that he says, not only in relation to what he says about Jesus. However, this is no exercise in scriptural exegesis for its own sake. The aim is to address what the author sees as a real crisis facing the church and, as part of his message to the churches he is addressing, he develops a richly painted picture of Jesus. At the heart of it is Jesus and the cross: for Jesus the central aspect of his time on earth is his obedience and his willingness to suffer even to the point of death, and for 'John' this is the climax and the focus of Jesus' 'victory'. It is to get across that primary idea that John develops the image of Jesus as the Lamb who conquers, but who conquers in and through being slaughtered. That is the centre of John's Christology, as indeed it is the centre of his whole message.

NOTES

1. The case for this is made as early as the third century: cf. the arguments put forward by Dionysius of Alexandria, as recorded in Eusebius, *E. H.* 7.25.

2. It was in fact quite common in the early church to try to get round the evident problems of trying to ascribe Revelation to the same author as the Fourth Gospel by positing a number of different John's.

3. See E. S. Fiorenza, 'The quest for the Johannine school: The apocalypse and the fourth gospel', *NTS* 23 (1977), pp. 402–27, for discussion.

4. See the essays in J. J. Collins (ed.), *Apocalypse: The Morphology of Genre, Semeia,* 14 (1979).

5. See especially Rowland, *Open Heaven, passim.* The different possible time references in some of the images in Revelation – some referring to the future, but some referring to the present and/or the past – are well brought out in the commentary of G. B. Caird, *The Revelation of St John the Divine* (London: A. & C. Black, 1966).

6. The NRSV 'whose voice it was that spoke to me' simplifies the text somewhat prosaically.

7. The two are of course not the same! For discussion, cf. A. Yarbro Collins (ed.), *Early Christian Apocalypticism, Semeia,* 36 (1986). Also the essays in D. Hellholm (ed.), *Apocalypticism in the Mediterranean World and the Near East* (Tübingen: Mohr-Siebeck, 1983). The traditional setting posited for Revelation has been the alleged persecution of Christians under Domitian in the mid-90s. Such a theory has come under fire in recent years, partly because of doubts about whether Domitian did in fact ever instigate a bout of persecution against the Christians: see L. L. Thompson, *The Book of Revelation: Apocalypse and Empire* (New York: OUP, 1990). However, there may still have been a localised situation of persecution; and in any case, we should remember that the threat to the Christian community was, for the writer, as much what was *thought* to be threatening, quite as much as what did actually occur. See the survey of the issue in T. B. Slater, *Christ and Community: A Socio-Historical Study of the Christology of Revelation* (JSNTSup 178; Sheffield: Sheffield Academic Press, 1999), pp. 18–63.

8. On each occasion it is clear that there is a clear allusion to the language and imagery of Dan. 7, and the phrase 'like a son of man' is all but an explicit quotation from Daniel.

9. See Rowland, *Open Heaven,* esp. pp. 94–113; Gieschen, *Angelomorphic Christology,* ch. 11; Carrell, *Jesus and the Angels, passim.*

10. The exact identity of the figure in Dan. 10 is debated. Many assume that he is to be identified with the angel Gabriel who appears to 'Daniel' in

ch. 8. Others (notably Rowland) have argued against this, claiming that Dan. 10 represents the end of a significant line of development in a tradition reaching back to the famous visions of the throne of God in Ezek. 1 and Ezek. 8, the visions of the 'chariot' that influenced so much of the later mystical tradition within Judaism (cf. Rowland, *Open Heaven*, 94–113). In this alleged development, the figure of God 'bifurcates' so that God appears in the form of an angel. Such a theory has been examined critically by others with some doubts cast on the details. (See Hurtado, *One God, One Lord*, pp. 86–90; Carrell, *Jesus and the Angels*, pp. 4–13.) But in any case, the crucial factor may be not so much the past tradition history of the text of Dan. 10, but rather how the text was read in the first century. Here it seems clear that the text was taken as referring to an angelic figure.

11. Cf. e.g. Caird, *Revelation*, p. 290.
12. Cf. too *1 Enoch* 106: 2–5. Full discussion and other parallel texts in Carrell, *Jesus and the Angels*, pp. 162–4.
13. Full discussion in Carrell, *Jesus and the Angels*, ch. 9.
14. Other examples of a similar Christology which have been suggested include the description of the rider on the white horse in Rev. 19: 11–16 (cf. Geischen, *Angelomorphic Christology*, pp. 252–6; Carrell, *Jesus and the Angels*, ch. 10), and the description of the 'mighty angel' in ch. 10, who *might* be intended to be Jesus (so Gieschen, *Angelomorphic Christology*, pp. 256–60). These are, however, more uncertain.
15. See R. J. Bauckham, *The Theology of the Book of Revelation* (Cambridge: CUP, 1993); for more detail, especially in relation to other contemporary texts, see also his earlier 'The worship of Jesus in apocalyptic Christianity', *NTS* 27 (1981), pp. 322–41.
16. Bauckham, *Theology*, pp. 23–4, 53–8.
17. So Bauckham, *Theology*, pp. 60–1.
18. Bauckham, *Theology*, pp. 60–1.
19. Bauckham, *Theology*, pp. 70–1, sees both ideas in the background.
20. See Caird, *Revelation*, p. 293; Bauckham, *Theology*, pp. 67–76.

Part 4

BEHIND THE GOSPELS

Chapter 12

THE SAYINGS SOURCE Q

In considering the Gospel tradition, we have looked at each Gospel in turn, asking about the particular features of the Christology of each of the evangelists. Behind the Gospels lies ultimately the figure of the historical Jesus. Yet between the historical Jesus and our Gospels there is a not inconsiderable gap. What lies in that gap is to a very large extent hidden from us since so little by way of concrete evidence (in texts or anything else) has survived. One such piece of possible (indirect) evidence will, however, be considered here, and that is the so-called Sayings Source 'Q'.

When introducing the discussion of the Gospels, I referred to the classic Two Source Theory as the basis which I would assume. According to this, Mark's Gospel was used as a source by Matthew and Luke. In addition, however, there is a not inconsiderable body of material which Matthew and Luke share in common and which has no parallel in Mark. The agreement between Matthew and Luke is often very close indeed (e.g. on answers to prayer in Matt. 7: 7–8/Luke 11: 9–10), suggesting either that one evangelist has used the other as a source, or that both have had access to common source material. For a variety of reasons, many have opted for the second of these alternatives, arguing that there must have existed a body of source material available to Matthew and Luke alone, and this material is usually known as 'Q'.[1]

While the existence of such 'Q material' is in general terms widely (though not universally) accepted as the best way to explain the Matthew–Luke agreements, the exact nature and extent of Q is disputed. Whether Q constituted a *single* body of material, collected and available to Matthew and Luke in *written* form (so that one could speak of a Q *text*) is less clear. So too some have argued that the Q material

191

may have grown over the course of time so that one can detect different stages, or strata, in Q (a 'Q[1]','Q[2]','Q[3]', etc.).[2] There is no space to debate the issue in any detail here and I can only summarise my own view.[3] For myself, I remain persuaded that (1) the agreements between Matthew and Luke are so extensive, not only in relation to detailed wording but also in relation to the relative order of some of the traditions they share in common, that it makes sense to think of Q as a unified body of tradition, possibly existing in written form. This is perhaps supported by the fact that (2) this Q material in Matthew and Luke sometimes exhibits a number of distinctive and characteristic features in terms of ideas which serve to mark it out as a separate 'source' within the synoptic tradition. Further, (3) there can be no doubt that the individual traditions in Q, like those in Mark, represent at times the end-point of a complex development in the history of the tradition. However, (4) more specific theories about the growth of the *literary text* of Q through clearly identifiable stages or strata may go beyond what our extant evidence will bear. At the end of the day, we have to remember that we have no text of Q itself extant! What we do (probably) have is Q as it has been read and used by Matthew and Luke. With this in mind, I shall focus here on the Q material as a whole, without necessarily seeking to distinguish a 'Q[1]' from a 'Q[2]', but rather raising the question of what the Q material as a whole might tell us about the ideas of the Christians who collected, preserved and handed on this body of tradition, looking in particular at the question of Christology.

We have already seen, in seeking to discover something of each of the evangelist's christological ideas, that the evidence is at best indirect and implicit. The Gospel writers do not present their beliefs in the form of any explicit doctrinal statements. Rather, they choose to write a story purporting to represent the things Jesus himself had said and done. In relation to the other Gospel writers, however, we were at times able to get some kind of a handle on their material by looking at some of the christological 'titles' used in their stories. Nevertheless we have also often noted that the use of 'titles' may be misleading or inadequate as a way of accessing christological beliefs. This is certainly the case in Q where christological 'titles' are somewhat thin on the ground! For the most part, Q signals the importance and significance of Jesus – or rather Q has Jesus signal his own importance and significance – via more indirect means. Almost all of Q is taken up with teaching ascribed to Jesus.[4] And, as with so much of the synoptic tradition, Jesus is rarely portrayed as referring directly to his own person with claims about his own status or role. Much of Q thus offers at most an 'implicit Christology'.

Christ

With regard to explicit 'titles', it is perhaps surprising that there is no clear direct reference, as far as we can tell, to Jesus being seen as a 'messianic' figure: the term *christos* does not appear in any Q text (insofar as we can reconstruct the wording of Q). We have already seen that *christos* became very firmly attached to Jesus at a very early date. Further, we have also seen that *christos* would be primarily at home in a Jewish context. Since Q almost certainly emanates from such a (Jewish Christian) context, Q's silence about Jesus' 'messiahship' is not a little startling.

Lord

Occasionally the term *kyrios* is used of Jesus in Q. The centurion in Q 7: 6 addresses Jesus as 'Lord' (*kyrie*) when confessing his unworthiness to have Jesus come to his house, though the use of the vocative *kyrie* may indicate that the word itself means no more here than a polite form of address, as we have seen. At the end of the Great Sermon in Q (evidently one of the sources for Matthew's Sermon on the Mount), Jesus bemoans those who call him 'Lord, Lord' but who do not obey his teaching (Q 6: 46).[5] Such a saying suggests that the use of 'christo-logical' 'titles' is considered less important than taking note of, and putting into practice, what Jesus actually preaches.

Jesus and the New Age of Isaiah

It is, however, not only Jesus' teaching that has importance for Q. Despite Q's very high concentration on the teaching of Jesus (i.e. in the amount of space devoted to it), Jesus' miracle working activity also clearly has great significance. Thus in the Q section Q 7: 18–23 the question is explicitly raised by John the Baptist about Jesus' identity. He asks whether Jesus is 'the coming one' (v. 19).[6] Jesus' reply in Q is in the form of a series of allusions to Isaianic passages, notably Isaiah 29: 18–19; 35: 5–6 and 61: 1, referring to what is happening in his own ministry: 'the blind receive their sight, the lame walk, the lepers are cleansed, the deaf hear, the dead are raised, and the poor have good news brought to them [lit. are evangelised]' (Q 7: 22). By implication, the events of Jesus' ministry – including his miracles – are claimed to be the fulfilments of Old Testament hopes for the future, classically expressed in the Isaianic passages mentioned above. It is hard to place such a claim in the context of any fixed 'messianic' expectations: the passages from Isaiah expressed hopes for the future age, but the activities mentioned were not thought to be performed by a 'messianic' figure as such. The Q passage thus presents Jesus in more general terms as the bringer of the expected new age, and as the medium through whom the conditions of the new age were being established in his own ministry.

The climax of the claims made in Q 7: 22 probably comes in the final clause 'the poor have good news brought to them'.[7] This is almost certainly an allusion to the words of the prophecy of Isaiah 61: 1: 'the Spirit of the Lord is upon me because he has anointed me, he has sent me to bring good news to the poor.' The Jesus of Q thus claims to be fulfilling the role described in Isaiah 61: 1, which is above all a *prophetic* role. Jesus is here by implication making a claim to be a prophetic figure.

The importance of Isaiah 61 within Q may also be shown by the probable allusion to that Old Testament context in the first two beatitudes which appear in Q (Q 6: 20–1). Matthew and Luke do not agree in wording at this point so the reconstruction of the detailed wording of Q here is uncertain and disputed. Nevertheless, a strong case can be made for saying that the beatitudes in Q pronounced a blessing on the 'poor' (Luke 6: 20, rather than Matthew's 'poor in spirit' [Matt. 5: 3] which may well be MattR), and promised 'comfort' to those who 'mourn' (following Matt. 5: 4, where Luke's wording in Luke 6: 21 is slightly different).[8] This then is very close to the wording of Isaiah 61: 1–2 which claims that the task of the prophet is to preach the good news to the 'poor' (v. 1) and also to 'comfort all who mourn' (v. 2). (The verbal agreement is very striking between the Greek LXX of Isa. 61 and the probable Q wording.) Thus at the very start of Jesus' preaching in Q, Jesus is made to claim implicitly that the programme set out in Isaiah 61: 1–2 is being put into practice in his own preaching and ministry.[9]

This in turn might well link with the importance evidently given to Jesus' miracles in Q. Two of the great prophets of Israel's history were Elijah and Elisha who are said to have raised a dead person to life and

cured a leper respectively (1 Ki. 17; 2 Ki. 5). Thus the reference by Q's
Jesus to the fact that the dead are raised and lepers cleansed in Q 7: 22
(along with the other activities more directly reminiscent of the Isaianic
passages mentioned above) may well be an implicit claim by Q's Jesus
to be a prophetic figure in the mould of Elijah and/or Elisha.[10]

The prophetic category is, however, also important in showing the
solidarity between Jesus and his followers in relation to the rejection
and hostility they have apparently experienced. In particular, it is
noteworthy how Q seems to have combined two motifs well attested
in Judaism at this period, but, as far as we can tell, never combined
prior to Q. These are the theme of personified, but rejected, Wisdom
and the theme of the violence suffered by the prophets.

Wisdom and the Prophets

We have encountered the theme of personified Wisdom at several
points in the course of this study. Here we may note that, in a number
of texts, personified Wisdom is portrayed as making her appeal to men
and women, but experiencing hostility and rejection (cf. Prov. 1; *1
Enoch* 42). There is, however, another stream of thought evidenced
within Judaism, focusing on the prophets. According to this the
prophets have been sent by God to call the people to repent, but all of
them have suffered rejection and violence if not death.[11] What appears
to be characteristic – and distinctive – of the Q tradition is that these
two streams coalesce so that Wisdom becomes the agent who sends
out the prophets, all of whom suffer rejection and violence, even death.
This is clearest in the doom oracle of Q 11: 49, where Q's Jesus has the
'Wisdom of God' say 'I will send them prophets . . . some of whom they
will persecute and kill'. A similar network of ideas almost certainly lies
behind the lament over Jerusalem in Q 13: 34 ('O Jerusalem, Jerusalem,
the city that kills the prophets and stones those who are sent to
her . . .'): the 'wisdom' reference is not explicit but the saying is very
redolent of wisdom motifs.[12]

Similar ideas appear elsewhere in Q. For example, in the final beatitude in Q 6: 22–3, Jesus compares his followers with the prophets of
the past in experiencing rejection and violence (cf. v. 23: 'so did their
ancestors do to the prophets'). So too the saying in Q 9: 58 ('the Son
of Man has nowhere to lay his head') may well recall the motif of
homeless Wisdom (cf. *1 Enoch* 42). Similarly the saying in Q 7: 35
('Wisdom is justified by her children') in its Q context seems to suggest

that Wisdom is associated with figures who experience hostility and rejection (cf. the criticisms of Jesus and John the Baptist which are referred to just before in Q 7: 33–4).

Much of this relates to the followers of Jesus; but equally, by implication, it clearly relates to Jesus as well. Thus although the beatitude of Q 6: 22–3 refers to Jesus' followers, the saying in Q 9: 58 is clearly about Jesus himself (as 'Son of Man', though by implication the followers of Jesus are evidently to expect the same fate as Jesus). So too the implication of sayings such as Q 11: 49 and 13: 34–5 is that the pattern that has characterised Israel throughout history in her rejection of God's prophetic messengers is reaching its climax in the events surrounding Jesus and his followers.

All this suggests (at least implicitly) that Jesus is seen in the role of a prophet, perhaps the final eschatological prophet, experiencing the fate of all God's prophets, namely rejection and violence. This also implies that, although Q may have no explicit passion narrative as such, Q did not ignore Jesus' death completely. Rather, it seems to have had Jesus interpret his rejection and suffering (and hence implicitly his death) via the idea of the rejection of God's prophets. And in this, the followers of Jesus are expected to share the same lot as their master. (In this, then, Q may not be making Jesus unique, or so different from other human beings as other New Testament writers; nevertheless the passion of Jesus is not ignored completely here.)

Son of Man

It is also striking that in many of the Q passages which seem to be influenced by this network of ideas, there is frequently a reference to Jesus as 'Son of Man'. In the saying in Q 9: 58 Jesus says that the 'Son of Man' has nowhere to lay his head. The Wisdom saying in Q 7: 35 is immediately preceded by the saying (v. 34) that it is as 'Son of Man' that Jesus is experiencing hostility to his failure to adopt an ascetic lifestyle. ('The Son of Man came eating and drinking, and you say a glutton and a wine-bibber, a friend of tax-collectors and sinners.') In the beatitude in 6: 22–3 the followers of Jesus are suffering explicitly 'for the sake of the Son of Man'.[13] So, too, in Q 12: 10 the Son of Man is (famously or infamously) the one whom the people are 'speaking a word against' (= ?defaming).[14]

Now we have already seen that, in a number of traditions, 'Son of Man' is associated with suffering. Above all this is the case in Mark and (I would argue) also in Daniel 7.[15] The Q Son of Man sayings we have looked at so far fit with such a pattern very well. Jesus *qua* Son of Man is a figure who is associated with hostility and rejection at the hands of other human beings. His followers too will experience suffering because of their association with him. Jesus *qua* Son of Man is thus by implication a suffering figure, just as he is in Mark, even if there is no explicit passion narrative in the Q nor any explicit passion predictions as such.

There is of course another side to the coin of Jesus in his capacity as being 'Son of Man'. Just as in Mark, Jesus as Son of Man will exercise an important *eschatological* role. He will act as a witness at the final judgement, speaking on behalf of ('confessing') those who have remained true to him ('confessed' him) on earth (Q 12: 8). He will come up like a thief in the night (Q 12: 42) on his 'day' which will arrive with a terrifying suddenness and which will mean disaster for those who are unready and unprepared (Q 17: 23–37). In all this, Q's Jesus seems to be occupying a role that is apparently somewhat 'higher' than that of other human beings. He and he alone will be in a position to confess those who confess him (Q 12: 8). And the 'day of the Son of Man' (in Q 17) is clearly picking up the Old Testament language of the day of the Lord himself. Thus many have seen a distinctive feature of Q's 'Christology' at this point and in this description/'title': if anything Q shows a 'Son of Man Christology'.[16]

In one way this is of course undeniable. In terms of 'titles', 'Son of Man' occurs far more often in Q than any other significant christological term and clearly has great importance for Q. Yet it is worth noting that, however prominent this language in Q is, it does not necessarily serve to distinguish Jesus from other human beings, or at least from his own followers. We have already seen that Jesus as the rejected Son of Man serves as a paradigm or example for his followers who are told that they too can expect to experience the same rejection and hostility.[17] But equally the more exalted language associated with the eschatological activity of Jesus *qua* Son of Man does not in the end serve to distinguish Jesus from his followers. For, in what was probably the final saying in Q (and hence arguably its climax), Jesus promises his followers that they say 'will sit on thrones judging the twelve tribes of Israel' (Q 22: 30). Thus the disciples will *share with* Jesus in the role of 'judging' the rest of Israel.[18] The ending of Q thus serves to align the disciples of Jesus with Jesus himself even in this exalted role of exercising eschatological judgment. If there is a 'Christology' here, it is one which serves to *unite* Jesus with his followers quite as much as to distinguish him in any way.

Son of God

The same may also be the case for the other main christological 'title' which occurs occasionally in Q, namely 'Son of God'. The term occurs in two Q passages, the temptation narrative in Q 4: 1–13, and the so-called 'Johannine thunderbolt' in Q 10: 21–2, both of which have often been seen as somewhat unusual in relation to the rest of Q (not least because of the references to Jesus as 'Son of God'). However, it may be that these passages also fit in with the general pattern emerging from Q whereby Jesus is aligned with his followers, providing an example for them to follow. Thus, in the temptation narrative, the force of the story for Q is in part to set up the person of Jesus as a paradigm of behaviour as one who is obedient to God's word and who refuses to rely on anyone other than God.[19] Thus, precisely as Son of God, Jesus is shown to be obedient to God. This then serves to align the temptation narrative with other parts of Q where, by implication, Jesus' followers are also sons and daughters of God. They are to be merciful in imitation of their heavenly 'Father' (Q 6: 36).[20] They are to address God as their 'Father' in the Lord's Prayer (Q 11: 2) and they can rely on God who as their 'Father' knows all their needs (Q 12: 30). The fact that God is the 'Father' of Jesus' followers is thus quite prominent in Q, so that implicitly they share with Jesus this relationship of the son/ daughter to the 'Father'.

The 'Johannine thunderbolt' of Q 10: 21–2 is an extremely complex passage.[21] Many have seen here a clear development, or a shift, from the rest of Q, with Jesus perhaps taking on the role of Wisdom herself as the revealer of God.[22] Thus the exclusive mutual knowledge of the Father and the Son expressed here can be paralleled in sayings in the Wisdom tradition about God knowing Wisdom (cf. Job 28; Bar. 3: 15–32; Sir. 1: 6, 8) and Wisdom knowing God (cf. Prov. 8: 12; Wisd. 7: 25ff.), as well as Wisdom revealing God to other people (e.g. Wisd. 7: 21; Sir. 4: 18).

However, the first phrase in verse 22 'all things have been delivered to me by my Father' is harder to parallel from the Wisdom tradition and is rather closer to apocalyptic thought, especially language associated with the Son of Man (cf. Dan. 7: 14 'to him was given dominion and glory and kingship . . .'). So, too, we may note that the 'title' used here is not 'wisdom' but 'son'. In fact, the language of the rest of verse 22 (i.e. after the first phrase) may have rather closer links with the sonship language used in Wisdom 2–5 (which may also have some indirect links with Son of Man language),[23] where it is the righteous sufferer and perhaps the follower of Wisdom who is the 'son' of God (Wisd. 2: 16) and who may also be thought to be claiming to have knowledge of God (cf. the taunt in Wisd. 2: 13: 'he claims to have knowledge of God'). It may therefore be wrong to look for a single christological category by which to interpret the whole of what is said in this Q saying. But in any case Q 10: 21–2 may be christologically close to other Q passages (and hence not necessarily quite so much of a 'thunderbolt' as some have suggested!) in presenting Jesus as one who remains obedient to God and also shares the status of sonship with others. In all this Q's Christology may thus show a similarity at a deeper level with Paul's Adam Christology: Jesus is presented as the one who draws his followers into a position where they share the same status and relationship to God (sonship) as he has himself.

The Q tradition lets us see a relatively early stage of the tradition, but already probably reflecting some significant developments in christological awareness by early Christians. Behind all these developments lies the person of Jesus himself. How many of all the ideas we have considered in studying the Gospels can be traced back to Jesus' own thinking? How much continuity is there between Jesus and his later followers? It is that question which will occupy us in the final chapter of this study.

NOTES

1. The theory of the existence of Q is debated, not only by advocates of the Griesbach hypothesis. Pre-eminent among questioners of the Q hypothesis in recent years has been M. D. Goulder: cf. his *Luke – A New Paradigm* (JSNTSup 20; Sheffield: Sheffield Academic Press, 1989) as well as several other publications. For defences of the Q hypothesis, cf. J. S. Kloppenborg, *The Formation of Q* (Philadephia: Fortress Press, 1987); D. R. Catchpole, *The Quest for Q* (Edinburgh: T&T Clark, 1993), ch. 1, and also my *Q and the History of Early Christianity* (Edinburgh: T&T Clark, 1996), ch. 1.
2. The theory is associated above all with the work of Kloppenborg (see previous note).

3. For more details, see my *Q and the History*, chs 1–3.
4. There is a little teaching on the lips of John the Baptist at the start; the only other real 'narrative' elements are the temptation narrative and the story of the healing of the centurion's servant in Q 7: 1–10. It is just possible, but by no means certain, that Q contained an account of Jesus' baptism by John. (A standard convention now is to refer to verses in Q by means of their Lukan chapter and verse number, without necessarily presupposing anything about whether Luke in fact preserves the Q wording more accurately. Thus 'Q 7: 6' refers to the Q tradition preserved in Luke 7: 6 and its Matthean parallel [here Matt. 8: 8].)
5. Matthew's parallel in Matt. 7: 21 is similar in general terms, including the reference to people calling Jesus 'Lord, Lord', though somewhat different in the detailed wording of the rest of the saying.
6. As far as we can tell, 'the coming one' was not a phrase used of a recognised eschatological figure, 'messianic' or otherwise, at this period.
7. The fact that it is the final clause probably indicates this.
8. For more detailed argumentation, see my *Q and the History*, pp. 223–5.
9. The case for the importance of Isa. 61 for Q would be enhanced further if it could be shown that the explicit citation of Isa. 61 in Luke 4: 18–19 also stems from Q. I believe a strong case can be made for this, despite the obvious difficulty for such a theory, namely that this is not a tradition common to Matthew as well. (See further my *Q and the History*, pp. 226–36.) It is striking that Matthew and Luke do agree in referring to the name of Jesus' home town as 'Nazara' (rather than the more usual 'Nazaret(h)') in this context (Luke 4: 16; Matt. 4: 13), and the Lukan form of the citation of Isa. 61 in Luke 4 has a number of unusual features suggesting that this may have come to Luke from an earlier tradition.
10. One should note too here the explicit comparison Jesus makes between his own role and that of Elijah and Elisha in Luke 4: 25–7 which – arguably – is also a Q passage (see previous note). Also there is now a startlingly close parallel to Q 7: 22 in a Qumran text 4Q521, which arguably presents a view of an Elijah-type prophetic figure. On this see Collins, *Scepter*, pp. 117–22.
11. Neh. 9: 26 ('Nevertheless they were disobedient and rebelled against you and cast your law behind their backs *and killed your prophets*, who had warned them in order to turn them back to you') is often regarded as the 'base' text on which later texts build.
12. The image of the hen gathering its brood has a parallel in a saying about Wisdom in Sir. 1: 15; and the motif of Wisdom withdrawing when she cannot find a dwelling place on earth is found in *1 Enoch* 42 (cf. 'your house will be left desolate' in the Gospel saying).
13. Matthew has 'for my sake', but it is widely agreed that Luke's version is more original here.

14. Notoriously, they are forgiven if they speak a word against the Son of Man. How one reconciles such an easy-going attitude with what is said in the verses immediately preceding (in Luke and probably in Q as well), where reaction to Jesus is said to have the direst, and final, consequences (Q 12: 8–9 'whoever confesses/denies me, the Son of Man will confess/deny'), is very difficult to say.

15. See pp. 112–13 above.

16. Cf. the work of H. E. Tödt, *The Son of Man in the Synoptic Tradition* (London: SCM Press, 1965), and many others who have followed him, even if there have been debates about the precise nuances of what is implied.

17. This is perhaps most clear in Q 9: 58 in its context of a quasi-'title' verse for the mission charge which follows; cf. too Q 6: 23.

18. In Q 'judging' almost certainly refers to discriminating judgement, rather than a 'ruling over' as some have maintained.

19. See my 'The temptation narrative in Q', in F. Van Segbroek, C. M. Tuckett, J. Verheyden and G. van Belle (eds), *The Four Gospels 1992* (FS F. Neirynck; Leuven: Leuven University Press & Peeters, 1992), pp. 479–507. (Q generally has very little comparable with, for example, the sabbath controversies of Mark, or the dispute about food laws, suggesting that Jesus was in conflict with the Jewish Law. Q's Jesus is notable for being thoroughly obedient to the Law.)

20. Luke's 'merciful' here is almost certainly the Q wording, and Matthew's 'perfect' (Matt. 5: 48) is probably MattR.

21. For more detail on what follows, see my *Q and the History*, pp. 276–81.

22. See for example Kloppenborg, *Formation*, pp. 198–9, and several others.

23. See further my *Q and the History*, pp. 266–76: Wisd. 2–5 and Dan. 7 may represent two lines of tradition, ultimately going back to Isa. 53, which develop the idea of the righteous sufferer(s) as one(s) who will ultimately be vindicated by God against their one-time persecutors.

Chapter 13

JESUS' SELF-UNDERSTANDING

―――⇁⇀―――

So far our discussion has been concerned with what early followers of Jesus thought about him. In this chapter, we turn to a question of a rather different kind: what did Jesus think about himself? The issue of how important such a question should be, and the problem of how normative any answer we give might be, will be addressed briefly at the end of the discussion. For the moment, I shall only be concerned with the historical question of what Jesus himself may have thought about his own role and person.

Anyone with any knowledge of the study of the New Testament will know that to venture into investigating such questions is to open up a minefield of potential problems and difficulties at almost every level. Such issues have been with us ever since the rise of critical scholarship. They have come even more to the fore in the last twenty years or so when there has been a huge mushrooming of interest in the historical Jesus in what has been called (perhaps slightly pretentiously) the 'Third Quest for the Historical Jesus'.[1] Given the enormous amount of literature now produced in studies of the historical Jesus, it will not be possible here to do more than state my own view, and that relatively briefly. Certainly it will not be possible to engage in much if any critical dialogue with the rest of the (by now enormous) body of literature on the historical Jesus. But before we can start to try to say something about Jesus himself, we need to address the question of what sources and methods we can or should be using to discover reliable information about him.

Sources

So far we have used individual texts to discover information about the views of their authors. I have stressed at a number of points that, if we are trying to find out about the christological views of the writer, the evidence available may be rather indirect since no New Testament writer writes an explicit treatise on Christology. Nevertheless, in the case of the authors of New Testament texts, we do have the texts they wrote (or at least approximations to what they wrote!).

In the case of Jesus, such direct access is of course not an option for us. Jesus wrote nothing himself (or if he did, it has not survived). What we do have is a number of collections of traditions *about* him, written down by other people, mostly some years after his lifetime. We have the evidence of 'Gospels', collections of traditions reportedly of things said or done by Jesus. We also have a little further evidence in some of Paul's letters of traditions which are attributed to Jesus. Yet we have nothing directly from Jesus' own hand or mouth.

Further, virtually all the evidence we have is preserved by Christians, all of whom (almost by self-definition) regarded Jesus in a positive light. Moreover, many, if not all, of them were convinced that the Jesus who had been active in Galilee before his death had in some sense or other been raised by God after his death. As such he was still alive in their present, he was one to whom they owed direct obedience (as their 'Lord') and who perhaps was still believed to speak to them in their present. Thus for the early Christians, any distinction which we today might make between a 'historical Jesus' of the late 20s and a 'risen Jesus' of the 60s or 70s would have been a rather unreal one. For them it would have been the *same* Jesus speaking. Hence early Christians evidently did not hesitate at times from adapting the tradition of Jesus' sayings to suit their own – perhaps changed – situations. We can see this happening quite plainly as Matthew and Luke rewrite the story of Mark, at times adapting the details – and even Jesus' words – to their own situation. And indeed we have already considered some aspects of this phenomenon in dealing with the Christologies of each of the evangelists.

How extensive this process of adaptation, and possibly creation, was is much disputed. That some adaptation occurred seems undeniable, given the evidence of our Gospels. How far Christians actually *created* sayings of Jesus *de novo* and read them back into the pre-Easter story is less clear. Nevertheless the nature of the Gospel tradition means that we cannot simply take everything recorded in all the Gospels as unquestionably genuine reports about what Jesus said or did in a pre-Easter situation.

What then should be the sources which we use to discover information about Jesus? As already noted, the primary sources within the
New Testament are the Gospels: the epistles contain only a very small
amount of anything purporting to come from the historical Jesus.
Among the New Testament Gospels, we have already noted that the
Fourth Gospel is more likely to be a primary source for the ideas of the
evangelist and his community rather than for Jesus himself. As we have
seen, the manner and content of Jesus' teaching is quite different from
that in the synoptics.[2] Thus it is widely held that John's Gospel for the
most part cannot be used to provide us with much reliable information
about the historical Jesus.[3] For that we must go to the synoptics.

The question of whether other sources could also be valuable here
has become a matter of some debate in recent years. Thus some have
argued that evidence from non-canonical Gospels should be given as
much, if not more, weight than the evidence provided by the canonical
Gospels. In particular, a number of scholars have argued that the
Gospel of Thomas may be an important source in this respect. The *Gospel
of Thomas*, the full text of which was discovered in one of the codices of
the Nag Hammadi library, contains a series of (mostly unconnected)
sayings of Jesus. For some, these sayings represent an independent line
of the tradition and preserve some very primitive, potentially authentic,
sayings of the historical Jesus independently of our canonical Gospels.

There is no space here to discuss the issue in any detail, and in any
case we have already considered it briefly in chapter 1.[4] The question
of the status of the *Gospel of Thomas* is much debated and there is no
scholarly unanimity on the issue. For myself, I would argue that a
strong case can be made for the view that *Thomas* is a relatively late
document. In places where *Thomas* has a version of a saying of Jesus
parallel to one we find in the synoptics, as often as not *Thomas* seems
to give a later, more developed, form of the saying. *Thomas* shows us a
stage of the *later*, developing form of the Jesus tradition, as sayings of
Jesus were used and adapted by Christians to serve their own needs
and situations. It may thus not be a very useful source for recovering
reliable information about the historical Jesus.

This means that we are thrown back to the New Testament synoptic
Gospels as our primary sources for information about Jesus. Of course
this does not mean that we can take everything there as a straight
transcript of things Jesus said. We have already seen, and exploited, the
way in which the later synoptic evangelists changed and adapted the

tradition as they used their earlier sources Mark and Q. Nor is it unreasonable to think that Mark and the Q editor were exempt from such a process either. Nevertheless, the relationship between the Gospels implies that we should focus on the earlier sources Mark and Q, rather than on Matthew's or Luke's adaptations of these sources, in seeking to recover information about Jesus, at least when the Gospels have parallel traditions. (Of course when Matthew and/or Luke alone preserve a tradition, this may have as good a chance of representing genuine material as other Markan or Q material.)

Criteria

In seeking to recover reliable information about Jesus, what criteria should we apply? Again the issue has been extensively debated and various criteria proposed, as well as criticised![5]

Perhaps the most famous (or infamous!) is the so-called criterion of dissimilarity. This claims that a tradition which shows Jesus to be dissimilar to both the Judaism of his day and the early church is authentic. Much has been written about this criterion, highlighting its strengths but also some of its fundamental weaknesses.[6] Thus, for example, we cannot be sure that we know enough about either 'Judaism' or about 'the' early church to be able to say with any confidence what may or may not be 'dissimilar' to these. Further, the picture of Jesus produced is likely to be a somewhat distorted one, inevitably producing a Jesus who is cut off from both his roots and also from the movement which claimed to be 'following' him and hence presumably in a line of continuity, rather than discontinuity, with him. The use of this criterion may produce some genuine traditions about Jesus but it can scarcely provide all the information we need to build up a credible picture of the historical Jesus.

A second potentially important criterion is that of 'multiple attestation'. According to this, traditions which appear in more than one of the major sources are likely to be authentic. Like the criterion of dissimilarity, this too has its strengths and weaknesses. Undoubtedly a multiply attested tradition has a good claim to authenticity (but equally a singly attested tradition may be just as authentic!); at the same time multiple attestation need only show that a tradition goes back to a very early stage in the development of the tradition, not *necessarily* to Jesus himself.

A third broad general criterion might be that traditions which cohere with Jesus' situation in Judaism are likely to be authentic. This could be applied at the level of language (does a tradition reflect use of Aramaic idioms/language?) or of social conditions (does a saying make sense in relation to the situation of first-century Galilee/Palestine?) or of other features as well. In a way, such a criterion emphasises the Jewishness of Jesus, arguing that if Jesus is to be plausibly located in a first-century context, he must make sense within a context of first-century Judaism. This may to some extent go against the criterion of dissimilarity which accepts only traditions which made Jesus different from Judaism. However, it has been the trend of much recent Jesus study (the so-called 'Third Quest') that Jesus has to be seen as *part of* his Jewish context, however, much he may have stood out from such a context.

None of the criteria proposed is foolproof and each clearly has its weaknesses. Nevertheless, some such guidelines may help us in trying to recover something of what Jesus might have thought about himself and his own role.

Implicit Christology

Earlier in this chapter I noted that we have only indirect access to Jesus since Jesus himself wrote nothing. There is, however, another sense in which, in relation to the more specific question of Jesus' self-understanding, any access we have has to be rather indirect. This is because, in the synoptic Gospels, the focus of attention in Jesus' teaching and activity is mostly not really his own self-understanding but his beliefs and claims about God. It is only in the Fourth Gospel that the issue of Jesus' own identity becomes a matter of explicit discussion by Jesus in any length or depth. And, as we have seen, this is one of the features of John that many have argued is more likely to be unhistorical. Thus if we are to try to discover something of what Jesus thought about himself we may have to deduce this from other parts of the tradition, rather than simply interpret things explicitly said by Jesus. If there is a 'Christology of Jesus', then it is, as many have said, more of an *'implicit Christology'*.[7] Thus before we get to the issue of any explicit Christology, we need to make a bit of a detour into a discussion of other aspects of Jesus' activity to see what they may *imply* about Jesus, rather than what may have been explicitly said.

One aspect of Jesus' teaching, the authenticity of which is hard to doubt, is its eschatological nature and its focus on the Kingdom of

God.[8] Jesus was preceded by the figure of John the Baptist, and it seems clear that John's preaching is strongly influenced by eschatological expectations.[9] One of the most certain facts of Jesus' own ministry was that he was baptised by John.[10] Whatever this event may have meant for Jesus himself, it must at the very least imply a willingness by Jesus to align himself with John's movement and hence to relate positively to John's teaching. This is supported by other parts of the tradition where Jesus clearly aligns himself with John and implicitly claims that in effect both stand or fall together.[11] It thus seems highly likely that Jesus saw his own ministry and message as being in a line of clear continuity with that of John the Baptist (however much difference between the two them there might have been as well).[12]

However, Jesus evidently did not simply repeat John's message which appears to have been primarily one of a threatening catastrophe about to hit the Jewish nation. If nothing else, Jesus changes the vocabulary so that what seems to be dominant in his teaching is the category of the Kingdom of God, language which (as far as we can tell) was not used by John. Further, there seems little doubt that Jesus' talk about the Kingdom is primarily eschatological.[13]

There is widespread agreement that the phrase 'Kingdom of God' does not mean a geographical place. Rather, it is a reference to the *activity* of God as reigning. A better translation of the Greek phrase in the Gospels might be rather 'the kingly rule of God', rather than 'Kingdom of God'. The phrase itself is not so common in Jewish literature (though it is not totally absent either). However, the idea expressed by the phrase is frequently witnessed in Jewish literature. The claim about the universal sovereignty of God which has been, is, and will be the case is fundamental for all Jewish beliefs about God (cf. e.g. Ps. 145: 13: 'Your kingdom is an everlasting kingdom and your dominion endures throughout all generations'; Dan. 4: 3, etc.).

Yet alongside this idea, there is at various times in Jewish history, and evidently also in the first century, an awareness that all is not right in the world as it is. The world does not acknowledge God as King, and the Jewish people are suffering oppression. Hence alongside the belief that God was, is and always would be King, there arose the eschatological hope that, at a future time, God would intervene to *establish* his kingly role afresh (cf. Dan. 2: 44: 'In the days of those kings the God of heaven *will* set up a kingdom that shall never be destroyed . . .'). Kingdom language can thus be used to express future eschatological hopes as much as claims about God's eternal and universal kingly rule.

It seems clear that Jesus' language about the Kingdom is to be placed in this eschatological context, rather than in the alternative context of a belief in God's eternal kingship. Thus the Gospel tradition is full of sayings and traditions that seemed to refer to the Kingdom of God has something future. Mark 1: 15 ('The Kingdom of God has drawn near') may represent a Markan summary of Jesus' teaching but it is surely not far off the mark in terms of substance: the Kingdom of God is something that is expected to come in the future – and perhaps very soon. The same is implied in the saying in Mark 9: 1 ('There are some of those standing here who will not taste death until they see the Kingdom of God come with power'), a saying which, by virtue of its apparent non-fulfilment, is unlikely to have been invented by later Christians. So, too, Mark 14: 25 ('I will not drink again of the fruit of the vine until that day when I drink it new in the Kingdom of God') seems to operate with the same presuppositions: the Kingdom of God is something to be looked forward to in the future. So, too, in the Q tradition, the disciples are told to pray in the Lord's Prayer for the coming of the Kingdom (Q 11: 2 'Thy kingdom come'). Many of Jesus' parables also focus on the future aspect of the Kingdom which is to come in its fullness in the future (cf. the mustard seed, the sower, etc).[14] Similarly much of the teaching of Jesus in the Gospels is concerned with warnings about what will happen in the future, with threats of judgement and punishment as well as promises of rewards.[15]

All this would, however, not serve to distinguish Jesus very sharply from John the Baptist, apart perhaps from a change in the categories used to speak about this future hope/threat. There is, however, a persistent thread running through the Gospel tradition whereby Jesus claims that this hoped-for future event is in some sense already being anticipated in his own ministry. In a Q saying relating to his exorcising activity,[16] Jesus claims that 'if it is by the Spirit/finger of God that I am casting out devils, then the Kingdom of God has come upon the you' (Q 11: 20).[17] The Greek (at least) of the saying is quite clear: unlike say Mark 1: 15 which says that the Kingdom has 'come near', which suggests that it is imminent but *not* yet present, Q 11: 20 claims that the kingdom has already arrived (by implication in Jesus' activity in exorcising).[18]

This Q logion is perhaps the most explicit saying in the synoptic tradition claiming that Jesus' own activity signals the presence of the Kingdom. However, other sayings elsewhere make a similar (implicit) claim that in Jesus' activity the longed-for future eschatological events are already happening. Thus in Mark's account of the Beelzebul controversy (the context also of the logion in Q 11: 20), there is a saying with similar implications: 'no one can enter a strong man's house and plunder his property without first binding the strong man; then his house can be plundered' (Mark 3: 27). This implies in context that Jesus as the strong man has already bound Satan and hence can now plunder his home, that is in the exorcisms. The idea of the binding of Satan as one of the expected eschatological events was a well-established one at the time (cf. Rev. 20: 1). Thus the saying in Mark 3: 27 implies the same (in general terms at least) as Q 11: 20: in Jesus' exorcisms the hoped-for eschatological events are already happening.

Jesus' reply to John the Baptist in Q 7: 22 is similar in scope. As we have already seen (p. 193 above), Jesus' words here clearly allude to various Isaianic hopes for the new age. The claim made here is that these hopes are now being fulfilled in the ministry of Jesus himself. So, too, in the Q saying Q 10: 23–4 it is made explicit that things which others in the past ('prophets and kings') had hoped to see/hear are now being seen and heard by Jesus' own disciples. In some of the parables too the same idea is implicit. For example, in the parable of the mustard seed (Mark 4: 30–2 par.) the stress in one way is on the glorious future Kingdom that is coming (cf. above), but equally it implies that this glorious future tree/shrub is already present, albeit in the form of a tiny mustard seed. The reference is almost certainly to the activity of Jesus himself.

There is thus a claim which is firmly embedded in the Gospel tradition that the eschatological future events are fulfilled in the events of Jesus' own ministry. Clearly this *implies* that Jesus occupies a very special place within God's overall plan. Jesus is by implication the agent through whom the final eschatological activity of God is actually taking place in the present. However, we should note that all of this is at most implicit. It does not spell out in any detail the precise nature of the 'special place' which Jesus occupies. It does not use explicit categories or titles. We have then an 'implicit Christology'.

The same may also be implied by another facet of the Gospel tradition which seems to be securely based and which we can reasonably confidently trace back to Jesus. This involves the choice of precisely twelve people to constitute a special group of followers around him and to be with him.[19] It seems most likely that the twelve disciples were thought of as in some way representative of the twelve tribes of Israel. Jesus' choice of precisely twelve people is thus probably an attempt to form a nucleus for a new, or renewed, *nation* (cf. Q 22: 30 where the link between the disciples and Israel is most explicit). But if this is the case, it may be significant for our purposes here that Jesus evidently chose twelve people *besides* himself. He did not choose eleven and count himself as the twelfth. The non-inclusion of Jesus within the group may thus imply a claim by Jesus to be over and above the group in some way or other. However, we should again note the at best implicit nature of the claim. Nothing is said that is explicit about precisely the role that Jesus was assigning to himself.

We have seen that there is quite a lot in the Gospel tradition suggesting that Jesus was implicitly claiming a special position for himself and his activity in relation to God's overall plan. But can we be any more explicit? Are there any categories into which Jesus might have placed himself to express that 'specialness' any more precisely? We shall consider a few possible categories here; however, we should also recognise and accept that the fact that so little in what is usually taken to be authentic material in the Gospel tradition is explicit about Jesus' own status may indicate that for Jesus himself the issue of his own status and role was less important than his claims about the nature and activity of God.

Explicit Christology?

Messiah

One of the most vexed questions in current New Testament research is whether Jesus regarded himself as in any sense a 'Messiah' figure.

We have already noted some aspects of the issue in relation to Jewish beliefs at the time as well as in relation to the application of the term Messiah to Jesus by early (New Testament) Christians. The evidence seems to show that 'Messiah' was a fairly fluid concept in Judaism in the first century with no clear single belief focused on one set of expectations for such a figure. In contrast, the early Christians clearly applied the term to Jesus from a very early date; moreover, the name became so firmly attached to him that, by the time of the earliest writings of the New Testament which we have, namely the Pauline letters, the term has become virtually just another proper name for Jesus.[20] We have also seen that, insofar as anything definite seems to have been the focus of Jewish hopes for a 'Messiah' figure, such hopes were for a Davidic royal figure, one who would restore the political fortunes of the nation.[21]

If anything is certain about Jesus, it appears that he does not appear to have shown the slightest interest in taking over any reins of political power in the present. If 'Messiah' means a royal political claimant, then Jesus clearly had no such pretensions. At the same time, we have to explain why then the earliest Christians applied the term to Jesus. We may also note that the charge on which Jesus was finally condemned to death is almost certainly reflected in the titulus over the cross: 'the King of the Jews' (cf. Mark 15: 25; John 19: 19). Such language is not Jewish, nor is it particularly Christian: hence it is unlikely to be a later invention. Jesus was thus crucified as a royal pretender, at least in the eyes of the Roman authorities.

The evidence from within the Gospels is, however, much less clear. Some clearly editorial notes by the evangelists (cf. Mark 1: 1) can be excluded from consideration here. The main passages that arise for discussion are Peter's confession (Mark 8: 29) and the reply of Jesus to the high priest in the accounts of the Sanhedrin trial (Mark 14: 61–2). Both are Markan passages: it may or may not be significant that, as far as we can tell, the idea of Jesus as a 'Messiah' figure is completely absent from Q.

Both the Markan passages have raised doubts about their authenticity. The account of the Sanhedrin trial in Mark has peculiar general difficulties of its own, partly because of the 'irregular' nature of the trial which is described, partly too because of the doubts about who could have supplied the information about these proceedings to a later Christian author. Some have also pointed to the abrupt break in the account of the trial, moving without explanation from the issue of whether Jesus had predicted the destruction (and possibly rebuilding) of the Temple to the issue of Jesus' messiahship. The last point may be less significant, especially in the light of some of the evidence from Qumran. In some of the scrolls, notably 4QFlor (= 4Q174), it is clear that the promise of Nathan to David in 2 Samuel 7 has been taken up and applied to a Davidic eschatological messianic figure who is thought of as one who will (re)build a temple. Hence the move of the high priest from the question of temple-building to the question of messiahship may in fact be quite plausible historically.[22] It remains the case, however, that Jesus' open acceptance of the term Messiah in Mark 14: 62

remains extremely odd in relation to current messianic expectations if these imply political leadership – for Jesus accepts the term at just the point where he is without any political power at all. One must say that, if Jesus did accept the term here positively, it is being used in a highly unusual way. On the other hand, the account here serves Mark's own developing story line very well. Hence many have argued that the messianic confession of Jesus owes more to Mark's redaction than to the historical Jesus.[23]

The other instance where Jesus appears to accept the term Messiah is the story of Peter's confession at Caesarea Philippi. Again the story fits into Mark's developing narrative very well (though that does not preclude its being historical!). Nevertheless, the main thrust of the whole pericope, focusing attention on the identity of the person of Jesus himself, seems somewhat alien to the rest of the authentic Gospel material, where Jesus consistently points away from himself (at least explicitly) to refer to *God*.[24] Thus each of the two passages in the tradition where Jesus seems to accept the term Messiah arouse some suspicion as to their authenticity.

At the same time, we have to explain why it was that early Christians were convinced – at a *very* early date – that Jesus was indeed a 'Messiah'. One possibility is that the origin of the Christian use of the term lies in the titulus over the cross: Jesus was crucified as a messianic claimant; the resurrection then perhaps convinced Christians that what had appeared to be something of a crude joke before was in fact profound truth: Jesus was indeed a 'messianic' royal figure.[25] This is possible though it still does not fully explain why Christians should have used the term of Jesus so positively if Jesus himself had been negative about it. Certainly the resurrection on its own is not enough to explain things: there is no evidence of a specifically 'messianic' figure being associated specifically with resurrection.

The very existence of the titulus over the cross suggests, however, that, at his trial, Jesus must have been faced with the suggestion that he was a 'Messiah' figure, that is, for someone in Pilate's position, a political claimant. The crucifixion itself may suggest that Jesus did not deny the charge outright. (Otherwise the execution might not have taken place.) All this might suggest an ambivalence on the part of Jesus to the term: it may have been a term which he did not necessarily welcome fully, but it was one which he did not deny outright if put to him.

One can certainly see some aspects of activity possibly associated with the term which might have resonated positively with Jesus, and some aspects which might have resonated negatively. On the negative side, any ideas of political leadership seem to have been no part of Jesus' programme. On the positive side, we may note again the Sanhedrin trial and the possible link between messiahship and 'temple-building'. The evidence from Qumran has now shown us how the Qumran community reinterpreted language about the 'temple' to apply it to their own community life and its activities (1QS 8). We have also seen that one key aspect of the Jesus's ministry may have been the task of trying to form a new community, focused on his twelve disciples as representatives or leaders of a new chosen nation. If this is the case, then 'temple'-building, if understood in terms of forming a new *community*, may have been the one aspect associated with messiahship which Jesus could have regarded positively. Given that, it might explain then why the category of 'Messiah' may not have been rejected outright by Jesus, even if it was not wholeheartedly accepted. This might then go some way to explaining the undeniable fact that early Christians did apply the term Messiah to Jesus unequivocally. It would mean that 'Messiah' was a category which Jesus could perhaps in (small) part accept, but one which also he would wish to modify considerably by rejecting other possible overtones of meaning in the term. Perhaps, too, the silence of Q should be given more weight here than is often the case: any idea of messiahship as encompassing Jesus' own view may not have been central for Jesus. It may also be worth noting that, on each occasion in the Gospels where Jesus appears to accept the term, he immediately qualifies it by talking of (himself as) the Son of Man, a topic to which we shall return later.

Prophet

A category that may have been much closer to Jesus' own view is that of a 'prophet'.[26] For the most part, this was not necessarily a category which early Christians found adequate to express their beliefs about Jesus. Hence positive evidence in the Gospels that Jesus was seen in a prophetic role may be all the more significant.

The category certainly seems to have been one in which others at the time placed Jesus. On two occasions when the views of others about him are articulated, one possibility expressed is that Jesus is a prophet (cf. the views of the 'others' in Mark 6: 15, or of the 'other people' in

Mark 8: 28). There are also occasions when Jesus is portrayed as comparing himself favourably with prophets: his rejection at Nazareth evokes the wry comment 'a prophet is not without honour except in his home town' (Mark 6: 4 cf. Luke 4: 24); and in the story where Jesus is warned about Herod, he says 'it is impossible for a prophet to be killed outside Jerusalem' (Luke 13: 33) to justify his onward journey to the city.

A strong case can also be made for arguing that the use of Isaiah 61: 1–2 as encapsulating the terms of reference of Jesus' mission may well go back to Jesus himself.[27] We have already seen that this may have been a prominent feature of Q's Christology – but that does not make it *ipso facto* unhistorical! The opening beatitudes in the Q sermon are probably heavily influenced by the language of Isaiah 61 (cf. p. 194 above). So too the reply of Jesus to the messengers of John the Baptist in Q 7: 22 reaches its climax in the assertion that, in Jesus' ministry, 'the poor are being evangelised', a clear echo of the words of Isaiah 61: 1 where the task of the prophet is to 'evangelise the poor'.[28] The claim is certainly not a very explicit one in terms of Christology, and hence may owe more to the historical Jesus than to later Christians. If so then Jesus may have seen himself as in some sense fulfilling the role and the task set out in Isaiah 61: 1–2. And this is clearly primarily a *prophetic* role.[29]

The category of prophet might also explain the other aspects of Jesus' activity. Prophets in Israel were known for their use of prophetic signs or actions (cf. Jeremiah breaking the pot, or Ezekiel eating the scroll). Some of Jesus' actions may fall into this category. His action in the Temple looks very much like a prophetic symbolic action (though what precisely it is a sign of is much disputed): the fact that the incident evidently created so little stir among the Roman authorities suggests, at the very least, that it must have been very small scale and at best symbolic. Similarly, Jesus' baptism by John the Baptist suggests that he was willing to take part in what was almost certainly another prophetic symbolic action, namely baptism.[30] So too some of the miracles could be seen as prophetic 'signs'. For example, the exorcisms are clearly interpreted as instances of the in-breaking of the Kingdom of God (cf. Q 11: 20; Mark 3: 27); and the accounts of the feeding of the crowds in the desert have clear echoes of the feeding of the crowds by the prophet Elisha (2 Ki. 4) as well as the giving of manna by Moses in the desert (for Moses as a prophet, cf. Deut. 18: 15).

It may be too that Jesus saw his own future suffering as in some sense part of a prophetic vocation. We have noted earlier the existence of a tradition within Judaism, asserting that all the prophets had suffered violence.[31] The question of whether Jesus foresaw his own suffering is much debated. There can be no doubt that some of the Gospel traditions in which Jesus predicts his passion represent the writing in of the details of the passion narrative by later Christians into the pre-Easter story. Thus the very accurate prediction by Jesus of the details of his passion in the third of Mark's three passion predictions (Mark 10: 33–4) looks very much like a 'prophecy after the event'. Nevertheless, it seems not impossible that in some more general sense Jesus may well have foreseen that the opposition his ministry was arousing might result in violence against himself.[32] That Jesus related the hostility and rejection he experienced to a *prophetic* self-consciousness is suggested by Mark 6: 4 and Luke 13: 33, the two texts with which we started this section.

At the same time, we must also note that, for the most part in the Gospel tradition, Jesus' future suffering is correlated with reference to himself as 'Son of Man'. This is a topic which we will turn to shortly. Here we may simply note that however much the category of prophet may reflect Jesus' own self understanding, it does not appear to exhaust it completely. Further, we should perhaps also note that some aspects of a prophetic style of activity do not seem to be reflected in Jesus' ministry. For example, it is characteristic of (at least the biblical) prophets to claim to speak in the name of Yahweh and to be the mouthpiece for Yahweh's own words. Highly characteristic of prophetic speech therefore is the introduction 'Thus says the Lord' to prophetic oracles. Of this there is no trace in the Gospel tradition. Jesus speaks of and for himself, apparently by his own authority. However theocentric his actual preaching may be (cf. above) by pointing people to God, he does not present his own teaching explicitly as simply that of God. It is true that there are claims in the tradition by Jesus to have been sent by God and that reaction to him is the same as reaction to God (cf. Q 10: 16; Mark 9: 37). But the style of preaching which we have in the Gospels suggests that Jesus claims to speak on the basis of his *own* authority.[33] This may be then another example of an *implicit* Christology. It does suggest that the prophetic category, although perhaps encompassing an important aspect of Jesus' self-understanding, does not exhaust it.

Son of Man

The possible significance of the term Son of Man for Jesus' self-under-standing is one of the most intractable problems within New Testament studies today. The secondary literature on the subject has mushroomed over the years and shows no sign of abating. Thus, to reiterate, it will only really be possible to state one's own views here and the constraints of space will not allow any full interaction with alternative views.

The first point to make is that it seems almost certain that Jesus did use the phrase in some sense or other. The phrase occurs in all the strands of the Gospel tradition, and almost exclusively on the lips of Jesus. Further, it hardly ever occurs outside the Gospels.[34] While we must be wary of assuming that our extant evidence gives a complete picture of early Christianity, the virtual absence of the phrase outside the Gospels does suggest that the term was not a very important one for early Christians in articulating their beliefs about Jesus.[35] Hence it is most likely that the use of the phrase represents language used by Jesus himself. If the term were a creation of early Christians and had no basis at all in Jesus' own speech, then it is surprising that such a christological idea should have affected all the strands of the Gospel tradition so strongly but have left virtually no mark elsewhere in early Christian literature.

We have earlier discussed something of the possible background for the use of the phrase, as well as the use of the term by the evangelists. Clearly for all the evangelists, and also for Q, the Son of Man is Jesus and Jesus alone: Jesus' use of the terms in the Gospels is always a *self-*reference. Moreover, the consistent use of the somewhat unusual Greek phrase in the Greek Gospels suggests that, for the Gospel writers at least, the phrase was regarded as a self-designation of some signif-icance by Jesus. Many have pointed out that, when translated back into Aramaic, the phrase (as *bar enash* or *bar enasha*) is much less significant: it is a fairly ordinary phrase meaning 'someone' or 'man (human beings) in general'. (Other nuances of the generic usage have been suggested by others.) If this were the meaning of the phrase on the lips of Jesus (and we must remember that Jesus probably spoke Aramaic rather than Greek!) then the use of the term as one with considerable significance and as an exclusive self-reference by Jesus must all be due to later Christians, perhaps working at the stage when the tradi-tion was translated into Greek.[36]

This is possible, but such a theory does suffer from the same weaknesses as that which would argue that all the Son of Man references are inauthentic. If all the uses of Son of Man as a significant descriptor of Jesus are inauthentic, this must imply a powerful influence by early Christians on the tradition of Jesus' sayings that affected all strands of the Gospel tradition in a very significant way but which has left its mark on virtually no other parts of early Christian literature. The fact that the use of Son of Man as a *significant* reference to Jesus alone suggests that this too is an authentic facet of the Son of Man sayings in the Gospels.

We have already seen some features of the Son of Man sayings in our study of the Christologies of the evangelists and Q. It is striking that, although there are some surface differences, our earliest sources (Mark and Q) show some important similarities in their Son of Man sayings. Both have sayings referring to the eschatological activity of Jesus as Son of Man (cf. Mark 8: 38; 13: 26; 14: 62; Q 12: 42; 17: 23–37). Mark also has a very large number of sayings relating Jesus' suffering to his role as Son of Man (cf. the passion predictions which are all in the form of Son of Man sayings, as well as texts such as Mark 10: 45, etc.). Q has no passion predictions as such, but it does have a number of sayings about Jesus' present activity and, as we noted earlier, all relate to the hostility and rejection experienced by Jesus and/or his followers (cf. pp. 196–7 above). Thus built into these Q Son of Man sayings seems to be an idea that, as Son of Man, Jesus is one who will suffer rejection, and perhaps violence and even death. Thus the idea of the 'suffering Son of Man' is not confined to Mark: it is implied in both of the earliest strands of the tradition. By the criterion of multiple attestation, it would seem then to have as good a chance as any of being an idea we can confidently trace back to Jesus himself.

The eschatological activity of the Son of Man is seen, by the evangelists at least, as relating to the language about the figure in Daniel 7, called there 'one like a son of man'. In Daniel, and in the Gospels, such eschatological language serves in part to express the belief that this Son of Man figure will receive vindication in the heavenly court. There is, it is true, a development discernible in the Christian Gospels as compared with Daniel 7, in that Jesus as Son of Man in the Gospels has a more 'exalted' status in some respects than the Danielic figure: the latter *receives* vindication and judgement in the heavenly court, whereas Jesus in some Son of Man sayings in the Gospels is becoming more pro-active in the administration of judgement over others.[37] However, this may be of a piece with the development we see of the Danielic vision in texts such as *1 Enoch* and *4 Ezra*, as we have already noted. Thus the eschatological activity of Jesus as Son of Man seems to be based on the picture of vindication as set out in Daniel 7 and as that chapter was subsequently interpreted.

Whether the picture of the Son of Man as a suffering figure can also claim a basis in Daniel 7 is much debated. As I have indicated earlier, I believe that a strong case can be made for such a view (cf. pp. 112–13 above). In Daniel 7, the vision of 'Daniel' is primarily one which is meant to give hope and encouragement to Jews who were suffering persecution under the regime of Antiochus Epiphanes because of their commitment to God and their refusal to accede to the demands of the Hellenising 'reforms'. The vision thus provides a promise of vindication for those currently being persecuted, holding out the assurance that fidelity and perseverance – even to death – would still be rewarded in a future judgement scene in the heavenly court. All this may suggest that the figure of Daniel 7 can appropriately be seen as a figure who has been/is *suffering*. It is true that the vision itself mentions only his vindication and triumph. But if that vision is to have meaning for its readers, then the figure who is vindicated must presumably be the same as (or closely related to) the suffering one(s) of the present if the message is to have any relevance. The interpretation of the vision in Daniel 7 itself identifies the 'one like a son of man' as the 'saints of the Most High' (see 7: 22), probably the loyal people of God. Just as then the vision serves to provide hope for those suffering by picturing the vindication scene so that they can identify with the figure of the vision, so by implication that figure can be identified with them in their suffering. All this suggests that fundamental to the whole vision of Daniel 7 is an idea not just of (abstract) vindication, but of vindication as a result of suffering because of loyal commitment to God.

Against this background, the phenomenon of the Gospel sayings makes considerable sense. One cannot defend the authenticity of all the Son of Man sayings in the tradition. Nevertheless, a general trend does seem clear and indeed sensible against this background. Jesus perhaps foresaw the hostility and rejection which his mission apparently aroused as spilling over into violence so that he would have to be prepared to suffer. Yet he also believed that this suffering, possibly even death, would nevertheless not be the end of the story and he could, and did, hope for vindication by God in the heavenly court. He thus expressed his beliefs about the role he believed he had to undergo in terms of the figure described in the vision of Daniel 7 as 'the Son of Man', since this encapsulated the twin ideas of suffering with subsequent vindication.[38] There is also perhaps not too much of a problem in envisaging Jesus using what was at one level a fairly ordinary Aramaic phrase to express this.[39] Every culture and sub-culture has its own jargon and shorthand to express important ideas via the use of words or phrases which, if taken in isolation, seem relatively general or insignificant. On particular afternoons or evenings in Manchester, a statement that one is going to 'the match' requires no greater precision to be fully understood![40] We have also seen that later (i.e. post-Daniel) traditions had also fastened on Daniel 7 and developed the picture of the creature who looked like a human being (i.e. the 'one like a son of man') to speak of a special individual. Jesus then appears to be in that same tradition, at least in general terms. 'Son of Man' for him expresses his total commitment to God and his readiness to stick by that total commitment even to the point of death, whilst at the same time maintaining an absolute trust in God who, as God, would not ultimately abandon his own but would vindicate them finally and reward them.

In part this may be another side of the coin of Jesus' prophetic self-consciousness: if the role of the prophet entails experiencing rejection, violence and even death, then perhaps this is also expressed by Jesus in terms of his role as Son of Man. 'Son of Man' and 'prophet' may thus be complementary terms, overlapping in some respects but expressing key ideas for Jesus' own view of his role, its consequences and its likely outcome.

Son of God

Did Jesus think of himself as in any sense Son of God? For many this is perhaps the most important question of all to ask about Jesus' self-understanding, showing some clear continuity between Jesus and later Christian claims. We shall examine the issue of continuity – and its importance – later. Here we should, however, be alert to the possibility – even probability – that, even if Jesus did think of himself as in some sense a/the son/Son of God, this may not have meant anything remotely similar to what later Christians meant in using that phrase of Jesus.

That Jesus did think of himself as in some sense God's 'son' is hard to deny.[41] Above all there is the fact that, as far as we can tell, Jesus addressed God as 'Abba', 'Father'.[42] The evidence for this is not entirely clear, as some of the examples in the Gospel tradition are somewhat suspect in relation to their authenticity. For example, the prayer of Jesus in Gethsemane (Mark 14: 36), where he addresses God as 'Abba', is unusual since no one else in the story is apparently present (or at least awake) to hear and record what is said. The so-called 'Johannine thunderbolt' of Q 10: 21–2 is unlike other parts of the synoptic tradition (it is so-called because it sounds so Johannine and *not* synoptic, and it sufficiently alien that it is a 'thunderbolt') that doubts have been cast on its authenticity. Nevertheless, it can be said that the phenomenon of addressing God as 'Abba', 'Father', is highly unusual within Judaism at the time.[43] Hence one could plausibly argue that, even if Jesus' actual prayers as recorded in the Gospels are not authentic in their present form, nevertheless early Christians may have put such prayers in a form which was congruent with Jesus' own prayers. Hence the Abba address may well be authentic, at least in general terms.

Its precise significance is, however, less clear. One of the other instances where Jesus appears to have used the term comes in the Lord's Prayer (Q 11: 2 'Father').[44] But this is a prayer which Jesus teaches his *disciples* to pray. The privilege (if that is what it is) of addressing God as 'Abba' is thus not confined to Jesus: it is something which followers of Jesus are invited to share as well. Thus the divine 'sonship' which one might ascribe to Jesus on the basis of the Abba usage does not apparently make Jesus unique. The same is implied by early Christian usage: in Romans 8: 15 and Galatians 4: 6 Paul refers to the Abba address as something which characterises the relationship which all Christians now have with God.

The precise nuances of the Abba address have been much discussed. The (by now) older view that this was a child's term for a father[45] is now held to be somewhat difficult. To use the title of a famous article by James Barr, 'Abba isn't Daddy'.[46] Nevertheless, even if 'Abba' does not mean 'Daddy', it does probably imply a closeness of relationship, and claimed intimacy, which makes it a highly unusual and distinctive mode of addressing God.[47] Thus, even if we cannot say that Jesus called God 'Daddy', we can perhaps say that this Abba address implies a closeness of personal relationship that is certainly distinctive within first-century Judaism.

Nevertheless, the implicitly *shared* nature of the term should not be

forgotten. In one sense it could be argued that Jesus' sonship is qualitatively different from that of the disciples in that he enables others to
share in this relationship.[48] This is unpersuasive, however, at least in
relationship to sonship itself. While Jesus may indeed have a special
position in relation to the disciples, it remains the case that the actual
relationship of sonship itself, and the ability/privilege to address God
as 'Abba', is something that is common to both Jesus and his followers.

Sonship here seems to imply a relationship of trust and confidence,
reflected too in some of the Q sayings about God as the 'father' of the
disciples which we considered earlier (cf. Q 11: 2; 12: 31, etc.). It probably does *not* indicate any idea of ontological being, at least at the level
of Jesus. Language of divine sonship, as we have seen, was thoroughly
at home in a Jewish context, indicating perhaps a special relationship
to God characterised by obedience and trust on the side of the human
being, and by special choice or favour on the side of God. Jesus'
God-talk seems to fit perfectly well into this mould. But it does *not*
suggest that the one referred to as the 'son' of God is in any sense a
'divine' being.

Jesus very probably saw himself as a son of God. As such he claimed
a special personal relationship with God and a closeness to God. As
such too he claimed the right to enable others to *share* in that relationship. But the latter should warn us against seeing Jesus' sonship as
'unique' in the sense that later Christians claimed Jesus' divine sonship
as unique and qualitatively different from that of other human beings.
If anything Jesus' own ideas of his divine sonship work in precisely the
opposite direction: to *unite* others to enable them to *share* in the relationship with God which he claimed to enjoy himself.

We have looked at a number of facets of the Jesus tradition to try to
recover something of Jesus' own self-understanding. One must say that,
at the end of this discussion, the conclusions may be more than a little
imprecise. So much of Jesus' ministry is *not* directly concerned with his
own person: it is focused on God and on the needs of *other* people. We
thus have to deduce possible facets of Jesus' self-understanding from
what is implied quite as much as from what is said explicitly. That there
is an 'implicit Christology', in the sense of a 'special position/role'
occupied by Jesus and implied in his actions, seems undeniable. Trying
to gain greater precision is much harder. In some sense Jesus seems to
have regarded himself as a prophet with a mission that would arouse

hostility and violence against himself. He was willing to accept that violence, convinced that he would ultimately be vindicated by God, and may have used the imagery of the vision of Daniel 7 to express this (albeit perhaps a little cryptically). He may have had *some* idea of 'messiahship' as not totally against his own beliefs about his role, though it would seem that many aspects often associated with messiahship were probably not part of a programme which he would accept as his own. In all this he claimed a close personal relationship with God, expressed through an idea of sonship, but which he hoped that others would share with him.

All this probably distances Jesus' own self-understanding by some way from later Christian claims about Jesus to be the unique Son of God, meaning by that a fully divine member of an eternal Trinity. There may be also something of a gap between Jesus' self-understanding and the views of his earlier followers (who may not quite have reached the stage of Chalcedonian orthodoxy immediately!). Does such a gap matter? It is that question which we shall address very briefly in the Postscript.

NOTES

1. For surveys of the history of scholarship on Jesus, and also on the so-called 'Third Quest' (and how it might differ from the first two 'quests'), see W. R. Telford, 'Major trends and interpretive issues in the study of Jesus', in B. Chilton and C. A. Evans (eds), *Studying the Historical Jesus: Evaluations of the State of Current Research* (Leiden: Brill, 1994), pp. 33–74; Ben Witherington, *The Jesus Quest: The Third Search for the Jew of Nazareth* (Carlisle: Paternoster Press, 1995); also J. P. Meier, 'The present state of the 'Third Quest' for the historical Jesus: Loss and gain', *Biblica* 80 (1999), pp. 526–36. I leave aside here also the question of what exactly we mean by the 'historical Jesus', and how far this relates to the 'real Jesus'. On this see Meier, *A Marginal Jew*, vol. 1, pp. 21–40. Very briefly, the 'historical Jesus' is usually taken to be the Jesus who can be recovered by means of historical methods. But how far we have then reached the 'real Jesus' (whatever that might mean!) is another matter. We shall also raise an aspect of this issue very briefly when we consider the question of how far Jesus' own ideas about himself enable us to see the 'real Jesus'. See p. 230 below.
2. See above pp. 151–2.
3. This is not to deny that there may be some genuine historical elements

in John. However, most would identify any such elements as historical precisely because they match the synoptic picture, at least in general terms. Thus any possible further information about Jesus derived from John is likely to reinforce, rather than dramatically change, the picture of Jesus we get from the synoptics.

4. See p. 4 above, and the references in nn. 6, 7 of chapter 1.

5. For a valuable critical survey of the various criteria, see Meier, *A Marginal Jew*, vol. 1, pp. 167–95; more briefly in my *Reading*, pp. 104–9.

6. A (by now) classic article is that of M. D. Hooker, 'Christology and methodology', *NTS* 17 (1971), pp. 480–7. See also T. Holmen, 'Doubts about double dissimilarity: Restructuring the main criterion of Jesus-of-History research', in B. Chilton and C. A. Evans (eds), *Authenticating the Words of Jesus* (Leiden: Brill, 1999), pp. 47–80.

7. The formulation of R. Bultmann is often cited in this context: Jesus' 'call to decision in the light of his person *implies* a christology': see his 'The significance of the historical Jesus for the theology of Paul', *Faith and Understanding* (ET London: SCM Press, 1969), p. 237.

8. Like almost all statements in New Testament studies, this claim is disputed by some. The eschatological nature of Jesus' teaching is questioned above all by members of the Jesus Seminar who would see Jesus as primarily *not* influenced by eschatological ideas. Cf., however, the discussion immediately following here; there is a sharp critique of the work of the Jesus Seminar in Ben Witherington, *The Jesus Quest*, ch. 2; also D. C. Allison, *Jesus of Nazareth: Millenarian Prophet* (Minneapolis: Fortress Press, 1998).

9. Cf. John's eschatological preaching recorded in Q 3: 7–9 ('You generation of vipers! Who warned you to flee from the wrath that is coming . . .').

10. The event clearly caused embarrassment to later Christians (seeking to explain why, if baptism were for the forgiveness of sins, a sinless Jesus needed to be baptised). The importance of *events*, rather than individual sayings (whose authenticity will always be open to seemingly endless debate), in rediscovering the historical Jesus is emphasised by E. P. Sanders, *Jesus and Judaism* (London: SCM Press, 1985), pp. 3–13. Sanders (along with many others) regards Jesus' baptism by John as one of the 'almost indisputable facts' we can assert about Jesus (p. 11).

11. See Mark 11: 27–33; Q 7: 31–5: hence the motif is attested in both Mark and Q. The element of reserve shown to John in some later Christian sources (e.g. the Fourth Gospel) would suggest that such a positive evaluation of the Baptist is unlikely to be a Christian invention.

12. Hence the view of the Jesus Seminar, which would see a radical discontinuity between Jesus and John (as indeed also between Jesus and the early Christians), is not persuasive. Such theories are effectively

based on an application of the criterion of dissimilarity, with all the weaknesses inherent in that criterion (cf. above).

13. Now relatively old, but still valuable, is the treatment of N. Perrin, *The Kingdom of God in the Teaching of Jesus* (London: SCM Press, 1963). See also the essays in B. Chilton (ed.), *The Kingdom of God in the Teaching of Jesus* (London: SPCK, 1984).

14. Cf. J. Jeremias, *The Parables of Jesus* (London: SCM Press, 1963).

15. This is the message of several of the parables of Jesus as well as the teaching in the eschatological discourses of Mark 13, or Q 12: 39–48 and Q 17: 23–37.

16. Jesus' practice of exorcising is one of the best-attested parts of the tradition.

17. The difference between Matthew's 'Spirit' (Matt. 12: 28) and Luke's 'finger' (Luke 11: 20) need not concern us here.

18. The Greek verb translated here 'has come' (*ephthasen*) is different from the Greek verb used in Mark 1: 15 (*eggiken*), translated 'has drawn near'. The latter implies something is imminent but has *not* yet arrived; the former implies that the subject is actually present.

19. See Witherington, *Many Faces*, pp. 40–5.

20. Cf. 1 Cor. 15: 3 and the discussion on p. 46 above.

21. See the discussion in ch. 1, pp. 16–19 above.

22. The person always credited with bringing 4QFlor into the discussion about the Markan account of the Sanhedrin trial is O. Betz: cf. his *What Do We Know about Jesus?* (London: SCM Press, 1968), pp. 88–9. Cf. Witherington, *Many Faces*, pp. 60–1; J. D. G. Dunn, 'Messianic ideas and their influence on the Jesus of history', in Charlesworth (ed.), *The Messiah*, pp. 365–81, esp. 373.

23. Cf. e.g. J. R. Donahue, *Are You the Christ? The Trial Narrative in the Gospel of Mark* (Missoula: Scholars Press, 1973).

24. Cf. D. R. Catchpole, 'The 'triumphal' Entry', in E. Bammel and C. F. D. Moule, *Jesus and the Politics of his Day* (Cambridge: CUP, 1984), pp. 319–34, esp. 326–8.

25. See N. A. Dahl, 'The crucified Messiah', in Dahl, *Jesus the Christ*, pp. 27–48.

26. Cf. Allison, *Jesus of Nazareth*; Dunn, 'Messianic ideas', pp. 376–8.

27. Cf. J. D. G. Dunn, *Jesus and the Spirit* (London: SCM Press, 1975), pp. 53–62.

28. I have kept the virtual transliteration 'evangelise' here, rather than 'bring good news to', if only to emphasise the clear linguistic link between the two passages. The precise nuance carried by the verb is much debated.

29. It is just possible that the concept of Jesus as an 'anointed' figure comes from here as well (cf. Isa. 61: 1: 'the Spirit of the Lord is upon me, because he has *anointed* me . . .') and hence possibly the language of

Jesus as a 'messianic' figure has its roots here. If so, however, one might say that Jesus as 'messianic' in this sense must be seen primarily as a *prophetic* figure rather than a royal figure. However, while this might explain in one way the origin of the term 'Messiah' as applied to Jesus, there is still a problem of how specifically *royal* messianic ideas were applied to Jesus, not only by later Christians but as early as the time of the crucifixion itself: cf. the titulus over the cross mentioned above.

30. For the popular view that John was a prophet, cf. Mark 11: 32.

31. In Q this is linked with the Wisdom tradition so that Wisdom becomes the agent who sends out the prophets. However, this distinctive combination of two traditions seems characteristic of Q and is not witnessed elsewhere in the Gospel tradition: it is thus harder to trace back to the historical Jesus.

32. In this respect, the second of Mark's passion predictions (Mark 9: 31), which is couched in much more general terms, has a better claim to authenticity.

33. The 'but I say to you' in the antitheses of Matt. 5, and the ubiquitous 'amen amen, I say to you' in John may well be redactional. But there are many other uses of 'I say to you' elsewhere in the Gospel tradition: cf. Q 7: 9, 26, 28; 10: 12, 24; 11: 51; 12: 22, 27, 44; 13: 35; Mark 2: 11; 3: 28; 8: 12; 10: 15, 29, etc. So too the use of (perhaps a single) 'amen' may be characteristic of Jesus and indicative of the authority he claimed for himself.

34. Outside the Gospels, see Acts 7: 56; Heb. 2: 6; Rev. 1: 13; 14: 14. However, the two occurrences in Revelation are all but quotations of Dan. 7, as we have seen. Heb. 2: 6 is a quotation of Ps. 8: 4 and in context the phrase simply refers to human beings in general (even if what is said of humans in general is then claimed to apply to Jesus alone). The occurrence in Acts 7: 56 comes at the end of Stephen's trial scene, which is clearly intended by Luke to be closely parallel to the trial of Jesus: hence the Son of Man saying in Acts 7: 56 is a clear echo of the Son of Man saying in Luke 22: 69.

35. The proviso we must always bear in mind is of course that the Gospel editors – the evangelists and the Q editor – may be the exception to this general claim!

36. Cf. the varying, but related, views of e.g. G. Vermes, *Jesus the Jew*; M. Casey, *Son of Man*; B. Lindars, *Jesus Son of Man*.

37. This development is probably most evident in Matthew's Gospel: see the earlier discussion.

38. For such a view of the Son of Man sayings on the lips of Jesus, see e.g. Moule, *Origin*, 11–22, as well as others.

39. This is a standard criticism of the view I have outlined by those who

would argue that the meaning of the phrase on the lips of Jesus must reflect the meaning of the phrase in 'ordinary' Aramaic usage. The trouble is that it is difficult to define what is 'ordinary' usage in any language as used by any particular social group.

40. The other example I have used elsewhere is the use of the term 'the war' which, in contemporary England at least, is almost always taken as referring unambiguously to the 1939–45 war against Germany (despite the prolongation of that war until at least 1946 against Japan, and the presence of many wars since then): hence, e.g., a statement to the effect that someone was born 'after the war' in England today pins their date of birth down for most people very precisely to be being post-VE day in 1945!

41. Cf. in more detail, Dunn, *Jesus and the Spirit*, pp. 11–40; *Christology*, pp. 22–33.

42. A classic study remains J. Jeremias, *The Prayers of Jesus* (London: SCM Press, 1967), despite some overstatement of the evidence.

43. Whether we can call it 'unique', as Jeremias did, is now accepted as more doubtful: certainly there is now Greek evidence of Jews addressing God as 'Father' (Cf. Wisd. 2: 13, 16; Sir. 23: 2, 4; 3 Macc. 6: 3, 8). Dunn, *Christology*, pp. 26–7.

44. Luke's plain 'Father' here is almost certainly more original than Matthew's stereotyped 'Our Father who art in heaven', and probably reflects an original 'Abba'.

45. So Jeremias.

46. J. Barr, 'Abba isn't Daddy', *JTS* 39 (1988), pp. 28–47.

47. Matthew's opening to the Lord's Prayer 'Our Father who art in heaven' is closer to the more formal flowery periphrases that tend to characterise liturgical usage.

48. So too Paul, as we have seen, may be making slight distinctions between Jesus' absolute sonship and Christians' adopted sonship. See p. 65 above.

Chapter 14

POSTSCRIPT

—⊃⊂—

Between Jesus and the early church, there was undoubtedly something of a gap. However, much continuity there may have been, there was clearly also an element of discontinuity. This gap has been evident ever since the rise of a historical critical approach to the Gospels. It can, and has been, expressed in different ways. Loisy's classic dictum that 'Jesus preached the Kingdom of God, it was the church that came' expresses it in relation to one facet; Bultmann's epigrammatic summary 'the proclaimer became the proclaimed' is similar.[1]

In relation to Christology we have by implication seen something of this in the course of our discussion. The very existence of the differences between John and the synoptics highlights the issue very clearly. As we saw earlier, these differences force us to drive a wedge between John and the synoptics, at least in relation to the extent we can use these texts as sources for discovering information about the historical Jesus. The very explicit, and very exalted, claims made by the Johannine Jesus can hardly be squared with the picture in the synoptics which is christologically much more reserved. And it is the synoptic picture that most have accepted as providing us with our primary evidence for discovering Jesus' preaching, his concerns, as well as his self-understanding. The claims made by the Johannine Jesus thus represent beliefs of later Christians which develop considerably any ideas which we can confidently trace back to Jesus himself. Similarly, many of the beliefs about Jesus expressed in Paul, in Hebrews, in the deutero-Pauline writings, in Revelation, etc. go considerably further in their claims than anything we can claim to be ideas of Jesus himself.

Does such a gap *matter*? Such a question is clearly of a rather different nature to any we have discussed so far in the study. For the most part,

227

our discussion up to now has been primarily historical, trying to determine the ideas or beliefs of a particular person, or group of people, in
the past. We have not so far raised any questions about the *validity* of
such beliefs or ideas. We were simply trying to discover what those
ideas were.

To raise the question of whether differences between people's ideas
matter is to raise a rather different kind of question. It is more of a
theological than a strictly historical question. As such, some may think
it is outside the remit of this study. It may well also be outside the
competence of the present writer! Nevertheless, the particular issue
here is one which many feel as an acute difficulty and, hence, some
attempt will be made to try to address it in this final section.

At the risk of making a sweeping generalisation, one might say
that the existence of a possible gap between Jesus' self-consciousness
and later Christian claims about Jesus has been felt to be more of a
problem for English-speaking scholarship and/or theology than it has
been for German-speaking theology. On the one hand, in the first half
of the twentieth century, and especially within Anglican theology, it
was felt to be a matter of prime importance to show that Christian
claims about Jesus could be rooted in Jesus' own ideas about himself.[2]
Any discontinuity here was felt to undermine the validity of those later
Christian claims. An assertion about Jesus was not felt to be theologically valid unless Jesus himself had subscribed to it. On the other hand,
German-speaking theology has generally been much more willing to
countenance a possible disjunction between Jesus and later Christians.
One can see this in its most pointed form in Bultmann's *Theology of
the New Testament*, where the ideas of Jesus himself are regarded *not* as
a part of New Testament Theology itself but only as prolegomena to it.[3]
One can see this difference reflected too in the reaction to the book of
William Wrede on the messianic secret, which argued in part (in one of
its corollaries) that Jesus never claimed to be Messiah. English-speaking
scholarship tended to rephrase this in terms of Jesus not *thinking* of
himself as Messiah (which is not quite what Wrede actually said!) and
gave Wrede's book a very bad press for many years.[4] Wrede's book was
regarded as not only historically wrong, but also theologically dangerous,
in positing such a break between Jesus and later Christians.

We should, however, note the dangers of too facile an attempt to
solve the problem. For example, some might wish to argue that, if it
can be shown that Jesus thought of himself as in some sense 'Son of

God', then this shows that later Christian claims about Jesus as the 'Son of God' are justifiable. We must, however, remember that the same words can mean different things in different contexts. Certainly in relation to key christological terms, the same phrase can mean widely different things in different contexts. Hence, for example, 'Son of God' on the lips of Jesus probably meant something quite different from what the same words meant when used by fourth- or fifth-century Christians as applied to Jesus. Indeed the approach of this book, focusing in part on some of the more traditional christological 'titles' as used by New Testament writers, has been to try to highlight such differences. We cannot then solve the problem of continuity or discontinuity between Jesus and later Christians simply by focusing on one or two words or phrases which they might share in common.

There is no space here to discuss the whole issue with any attempt at completeness. All that can be offered is a few random remarks. First, it must be noted that, if there is something of a mismatch between Jesus' ideas about himself and later beliefs about him, then this is simply part of a much broader field of the whole series of 'discontinuities' between Jesus' own ideas and later developments. There is no space here to defend the case in detail, but it would seem that many of Jesus' ideas were in one way 'wrong'.[5] Jesus probably expected the end of the present world order within the lifetime of his contemporaries, and in this case his expectations were not fulfilled. He may well have anticipated his own suffering and also expected that his disciples would share in this with him.[6] In this too he was disappointed, and the disappointment of such expectations may explain something of the agony in Gethsemane as well as the feeling of apparent abandonment on the cross. Jesus may also have expected a fairly speedy end to the present world order, and judgement on his opponents – again something that probably failed to materialise in the way Jesus himself may have believed.

Yet the very fact that Jesus was 'wrong' may be precisely the reason why he might appropriately be the focus of religious commitment. A Jesus who knows exactly what is going to happen, a Jesus who has no doubts about anything, a Jesus who is sustained by companions, human or angelic, is not a figure who plumbs the depths of the human condition to the full. A Jesus who is in perfect communion with God at all times is not a Jesus who shares the human condition of alienation from God in anything but a superficial way. An all-knowing, all-powerful

Jesus makes the agony of Gethsemane and the cross into something of a sham, and the resulting Christology is verging on being docetic (as is in danger of happening in John, where for example the Gethsemane story is all but obliterated by the all-knowing power of the Johannine Jesus: cf. John 12: 27ff.: the seriousness of the danger was perhaps appreciated by the author of 1 John, as we have seen). It has always been a non-negotiable claim within (at least 'orthodox') Christian theology that Jesus' suffering and humanity were real and never compromised. Precisely then in order for that claim to be maintained, it may be not only acceptable but also entirely necessary that Jesus was, at the level of consciousness, 'wrong' in some of his beliefs. Precisely at the point where those beliefs may have been shattered, there Jesus' commitment and obedience to God may have been put to the supreme test. And precisely because it is in the context of those prior beliefs being broken, Jesus' obedience and commitment are qualitatively different and deeper than if no such a process of the shattering of beliefs had happened.

We should perhaps also note that personal identity may not be formed entirely by an individual's own self-consciousness.[7] A person is not just who they think they are: a person is as much formed by their relations to others. The 'real Jesus' thus may not be *just* who Jesus thought he was. The 'real Jesus' is quite as much the person relating *to* others, and to whom his followers related and reacted. A belief by any individual to be a 'prophet' or a 'Messiah' figure is certainly not unprecedented or unparalleled in human history. Yet such claims will be evaluated by many as much on the basis of the reactions they evoke in others as on the claims taken in isolation. For many, such claims are a simple delusion if no one has ever taken them seriously.[8] They can become a danger and/or a disaster if taken seriously by some in particular ways. So too perhaps in less profound ways we can all no doubt think of figures of the past whose value and standing in the eyes of others goes far beyond what they themselves thought of themselves and their work. Few 'great thinkers' really believe that they are necessarily great thinkers at the time. Indeed we might well feel more inclined to be dismissive of those who had such a high view of their own importance! Writers, composers, thinkers, preachers, etc. may become 'great' quite as much because of how later people have reacted to them. Their own ideas about themselves and their own importance may be irrelevant to, if not quite the reverse of, what later people might wish to claim about them.

All this is simply to suggest that, if we are asking about the *validity* of any claims about Jesus' identity, then Jesus' own claims or beliefs about himself may be only one part of the evidence which we will want to use. Certainly the possibility of an element of discontinuity between Jesus' ideas about himself and the ideas of others about him should be no bar to accepting the latter if they conflict a little with the former! Thus the model of the Jesus' followers taking up some of the language which he himself had used and, in the light of his whole life and death (and resurrection!), developing their own beliefs about him which went at times further than he himself had gone, is not something which should necessarily surprise or alarm us. The fact that Jesus has become the focus of a new religious movement makes such a process all but inevitable. And even if some of us do not subscribe to that movement, we cannot and should not criticise the development in Christology simply on the grounds that later developments are alien to Jesus' own original teaching. The Christian claims about Jesus are far more than just a repetition of Jesus' claims about himself. They represent an attempt to react to, and to interact with, the whole event of Jesus' life, death and resurrection, and to put it in terms of their overall 'theo'-logical beliefs, that is their beliefs about God and the universe.

In this book we have looked briefly at the earliest responses to Jesus, highlighting in this last section briefly the possible gap between Jesus and the earliest Christians. Another story to write would be about the differences, or gaps, which exist between early responses to Jesus and later developments. As I have already indicated, the New Testament evidence falls some way short of what was later deemed to be christological 'orthodoxy' in the Chalcedonian Definition. Maybe this only goes to show that the process of seeking to articulate one's reaction to Jesus, in part by trying to say who Jesus was, is one that has been a developing one and which probably must continue to be so. Each new generation has to work out its own answers to such questions.

In seeking to articulate some answers, those who wish to remain within a 'Christian' tradition will have to relate what they wish to say to that tradition in some way or other. And within that tradition, the New Testament will always have a key role to play, as we have seen (cf. p. 3 above). But we cannot necessarily simply repeat that New

Testament evidence as providing the definitive statement of contemporary Christology. We have to bear in mind the changes which have taken place at so many levels – linguistic, cultural, social – between the time of the New Testament writings and our own day. Least of all can we necessarily repeat one part of the New Testament evidence, for example by focusing on what we think we can discover about Jesus' own self-understanding. As I have tried to argue, the undoubted development which takes place between the pre-Easter Jesus and his post-Easter followers is not something to be regarded negatively.

Nevertheless, any claims we might wish to make about Jesus' self-understanding may not be entirely irrelevant to attempts to work out a contemporary Christology. If such a Christology is to claim to be in any sense 'Christian', then, as I noted at the very start of this book, it must relate positively not only to the Christian tradition but also to the historical figure of Jesus himself. When I said then that 'the person of Jesus is absolutely central to Christianity', and 'a Christianity without Jesus would be really impossible to conceive' (p. 1 above), the 'Jesus' concerned is not a meaningless cipher, but a real historical figure of the historical past. A 'Christian' theology or Christology which seeks to make 'Jesus' central thus cannot show complete discontinuity with the historical figure of Jesus himself.

In looking to the historical figure of Jesus, it may be appropriate to note that, for Jesus himself, the 'christological' question was perhaps *not* the most pressing issue. For him, what was perhaps more pressing was the question of *God*, of God's care for the world, and of how human beings can and should appropriately relate to God and to each other. So too any ultra-exclusive claims by later Christians, asserting that theology can only be understood in terms of Christology (along the lines of the Johannine Jesus' claim in John 14: 6 that 'no one comes to the Father except through me') must be put alongside the story of the strange exorcist in Mark 9: 38–40 and over the (theologically much more open) words of the Markan Jesus that 'whoever is not against us is for us' (Mark 9: 40).

Any focus on Christology at the expense of the 'theo'-logy (strictly speaking) is perhaps a slightly dangerous one. 'Who do people say that I am?' (Mark 8: 27) is the question I have sought to answer to a limited extent in this book. It is a question that many people – Christian and otherwise – seek to answer for themselves. For those seeking to be followers of Jesus of Nazareth, it may, however, be one stage removed from the ultimate questions about God and the nature of human existence. Christology must at the end of the day be subservient to theology.

NOTES

1. A. Loisy, *L'évangile et l'église* (Paris: Bellevue, 1902), p. 111; R. Bultmann, *The Theology of the New Testament* 1 (ET London: SCM Press, 1951), p. 33.
2. See Robert Morgan, 'Non angli sed angeli: Some Anglican reactions to German gospel criticism', in S. Sykes and D. Holmes (eds), *New Studies in Theology* (London, 1980), vol. 1, pp. 1–30.
3. Bultmann, *Theology*, vol. 1, p. 3: 'The message of Jesus is a presupposition for the theology of the New Testament rather than a part of that theology itself.'
4. W. Wrede, *The Messianic Secret* (ET Cambridge: James Clarke, 1971). The English translation was not produced until seventy years after the original German publication in 1901. See my 'Introduction' in Tuckett (ed.), *Messianic Secret*, pp. 1–28. The reaction in England to Wrede's book contrasted markedly with that given to the work of A. Schweitzer, whose *The Quest for the Historical Jesus* (London: A. & C. Black, 1906) was published very quickly after its original appearance in Germany (also 1901).
5. See the very valuable Postscript in C. K. Barrett, *Jesus and the Gospel Tradition* (London: SPCK, 1975), pp. 103–8.
6. Such seems to be the implication of Mark 10: 38–9.
7. On this, see especially W. A. Meeks, 'Asking back to Jesus' identity', in M. C. de Boer (ed.), *From Jesus to John* (FS M. de Jonge; JSNTSup 84; Sheffield: Sheffield Academic Press, 1993), pp. 38–50.
8. But I would not want to advocate a sort of 'argument from success', as if the validity of a claim is assessed solely on the basis of whether that claim 'wins through' and is 'successful' in terms of the number of positive responses. In terms of Christianity, such an argument would be fraught with danger, especially for any Christian theology which wishes to put the cross at its centre and which would regard, say, 1 Cor. 1 and Paul's language about the foolishness of the cross and of the Christian message in the world's terms as in any sense a positive statement about the nature of the Christian Gospel and its claims.

BIBLIOGRAPHY

The following suggestions for further reading make no claim to be exhaustive or comprehensive: they are simply offered as some of the items which have been found valuable in the writing of this book. The list is restricted to those in English. No attempt has been made here to include commentaries on individual New Testament books, or individual journal articles or individual essays in volumes of collected essays. References to some of these can be found in the footnotes.

GENERAL BOOKS ON NEW TESTAMENT CHRISTOLOGY

Brown, R. E., *An Introduction to New Testament Christology* (London: Geoffrey Chapman, 1994)

Casey, P. M., *Son of Man: The Interpretation and Influence of Daniel 7* (London: SPCK, 1979)

Cullmann, O., *The Christology of the New Testament* (ET London: SCM Press, 1959)

Dahl, N. A., *Jesus the Christ: The Historical Origins of Christological Doctrine* (Minneapolis: Fortress Press, 1991)

De Jonge, M., *Christology in Context: The Earliest Christian Response to Jesus* (Philadelphia: Westminster Press, 1988)

Dunn, J. D. G., *Christology in the Making: A New Testament Inquiry into the Doctrine of the Incarnation* (Grand Rapids: Eerdmans, ²1996)

Dunn, J. D. G., *Christ and the Spirit*, Vol. 1, *Christology* (Edinburgh: T&T Clark, 1998)

Fredriksen, P., *From Jesus to Christ* (New Haven: Yale University Press, 1988)

Fuller, R. H., *The Foundations of New Testament Christology* (London: Lutterworth, 1965)

Hare, D. R. A., *The Son of Man Tradition* (Minneapolis: Fortress Press, 1990)

Hahn, F., *The Titles of Jesus in Christology: Their History in Early Christianity* (ET London: Lutterworth, 1969)

Hengel, M., *The Son of God: The Origin of Christology and the History of Jewish-Hellenistic Religion* (ET London: SCM Press, 1976)
Hengel, M., *Studies in Early Christology* (Edinburgh: T&T Clark, 1995)
Hurtado, L., *One God, One Lord: Early Christian Devotion and Ancient Jewish Monotheism* (Philadelphia: Fortress Press, 1988)
Lindars, B., *Jesus Son of Man: A Fresh Examination of the Son of Man Sayings in the Gospels* (London: SPCK, 1983)
Marshall, I. H., *The Origins of New Testament Christology* (Leicester: Inter-Varsity Press, 1990)
Moule, C. F. D., *The Origin of Christology* (Cambridge: CUP, 1977)
Pokorny, P., *The Genesis of Christology: Foundations for the Theology of the New Testament* (ET Edinburgh: T&T Clark, 1987)
Witherington, Ben, *The Many Faces of the Christ: The Christologies of the New Testament and Beyond* (New York: Crossroad, 1998)

JEWISH BACKGROUND

Charlesworth, J. H. (ed.), *The Messiah: Developments in Earliest Judaism and Christianity* (Minneapolis: Fortress Press, 1992)
Collins, J. J., *The Scepter and the Star: The Messiahs of the Dead Sea Scrolls and Other Ancient Literature* (New York: Doubleday, 1995)
Neusner, J., W. S. Green and E. Frerichs (eds), *Judaisms and their Messiahs* (Cambridge: CUP, 1987)
Nickelsburg, G.W.E., and J. Collins (eds), *Ideal Figures in Ancient Judaism* (Chico: Scholars Press, 1980)
Oegema, G. S., *The Anointed and his People: Messianic Expectations from the Maccabees to Bar Cochba* (Sheffield: Sheffield Academic Press, 1998)

PAUL

Dunn, J. D. G., *The Theology of Paul the Apostle* (Edinburgh: T&T Clark, 1998)
Hooker, M. D., *Pauline Pieces* (London: Epworth, 1979)
Hooker, M. D., *From Adam to Christ: Essays on Paul* (Cambridge: CUP, 1990)
Kramer, W., *Christ, Lord, Son of God* (ET London: SCM Press, 1966)
Wedderburn, A. J. M., *Baptism and Resurrection* (Tübingen: Mohr-Siebeck, 1987)
Ziesler, J., *Pauline Christianity* (Oxford: OUP, ²1990)

DEUTERO-PAULINE LETTERS

Barclay, J. M. G., *Colossians and Philemon* (Sheffield: Sheffield Academic Press, 1997)
Davies, M., *The Pastoral Epistles* (Sheffield: Sheffield Academic Press, 1996)

Wedderburn, A. J. M., and A. T. Lincoln, *The Theology of the Later Pauline Letters* (Cambridge: CUP, 1993)

Young, F. M., *The Theology of the Pastoral Epistles* (Cambridge: CUP, 1994)

HEBREWS

Hughes, G., *Hebrews and Hermeneutics: The Epistle to the Hebrews as a New Testament Example of Biblical Interpretation* (Cambridge: CUP, 1979)

Lindars, B., *The Theology of the Letter to the Hebrews* (Cambridge: CUP, 1991)

MARK

Achtemeier, P. J., *Mark* (Philadelphia: Fortress Press, [2]1986)

Hooker, M. D., *The Son of Man in Mark* (London: SPCK, 1967)

Kingsbury, J. D., *The Christology of Mark's Gospel* (Philadelphia: Fortress Press, 1983)

Räisänen, H., *The Messianic Secret in Mark's Gospel* (ET Edinburgh: T&T Clark, 1991)

Telford, W. R. (ed.), *The Interpretation of Mark* (London: SPCK, 1985)

Telford, W. R., *The Theology of the Gospel of Mark* (Cambridge: CUP, 1999)

Tuckett, C. M. (ed.), *The Messianic Secret* (London: SPCK, 1983)

MATTHEW

Allison, D. C., *The New Moses: A Matthean Typology* (Minneapolis: Fortress Press, 1993)

Bornkamm, G., G. Barth and H. J. Held, *Tradition and Interpretation in Matthew* (ET London: SCM Press, 1963)

France, R. T., *Matthew, Evangelist and Teacher* (Exeter: Paternoster, 1992)

Kingsbury, J. D., *Matthew: Structure, Christology, Kingdom* (Philadelphia: Fortress Press, 1975)

Luz, U., *The Theology of the Gospel of Matthew* (Cambridge: CUP, 1995)

Stanton, G. N., *A Gospel for a New People: Studies in Matthew* (Edinburgh: T&T Clark, 1992)

Stanton, G. N. (ed.), *The Interpretation of Matthew* (London: SPCK, 1983)

Suggs, M. J., *Wisdom, Christology and Law in Matthew's Gospel* (Cambridge, MA: Harvard University Press, 1970)

LUKE

Buckwalter, H. D., *The Character and Purpose of Luke's Christology* (Cambridge: CUP, 1996)

Conzelmann, H., *The Theology of St Luke* (ET London: Faber, 1960)

Franklin, E., *Christ the Lord* (London: SPCK, 1975)

Green, J. B., *The Theology of the Gospel of Luke* (Cambridge: CUP, 1995)

Moessner, D., *Lord of the Banquet: The Literary and Theological Significance of the Lukan Travel Narrative* (Harrisburg: Trinity Press International, ²1998)

Strauss, M. L., *The Davidic Messiah in Luke-Acts* (Sheffield: Sheffield Academic Press, 1995)

Tuckett, C. M., *Luke* (Sheffield: Sheffield Academic Press, 1996)

JOHANNINE WRITINGS

Ashton, J., *Understanding the Fourth Gospel* (Oxford: OUP, 1991)

Brown, R. E., *The Community of the Beloved Disciple* (New York: Geoffrey Chapman, 1979)

De Boer, M. C., *Johannine Perspectives on the Death of Jesus* (Kampen: Kok Pharos, 1996)

De Jonge, M., *Jesus, Stranger from Heaven and Son of God: Jesus Christ and the Christians in Johannine Perspective* (Missoula: Scholars Press, 1977)

Fortna, R., *The Fourth Gospel and its Predecessor* (Edinburgh: T&T Clark, 1989)

Lieu, J., *The Theology of the Johannine Epistles* (Cambridge: CUP, 1991)

Martyn, J. L., *History and Theology in the Fourth Gospel* (Nashville: Abingdon, ²1979)

Smith, D. M., *John* (Philadelphia: Fortress Press, ²1986)

Smith, D. M., *The Theology of the Gospel of John* (Cambridge: CUP, 1995)

REVELATION

Bauckham, R. J., *The Theology of the Book of Revelation* (Cambridge: CUP, 1993)

Carrell, P. R., *Jesus and the Angels: Angelology and the Christology of the Apocalypse of John* (Cambridge: CUP, 1997)

Court, J. M., *Revelation* (Sheffield: Sheffield Academic Press, 1994)

Gieschen, C. A., *Angelomorphic Christology: Antecedents and Early Evidence* (Leiden: Brill, 1998)

Rowland, C. C., *The Open Heaven: A Study of Apocalyptic in Judaism and Early Christianity* (London: SPCK, 1982)

Q

Kloppenborg, J. S., *The Formation of Q* (Philadelphia: Fortress Press, 1987)

Jacobson, A. D., *The First Gospel: An Introduction to Q* (Sonoma: Polebridge Press, 1992)

Tödt, H. E., *The Son of Man in the Synoptic Tradition* (ET London: SCM Press, 1965)

Tuckett, C. M., *Q and the History of Early Christianity* (Edinburgh: T&T Clark, 1996)

JESUS

Allison, D. C., *Jesus of Nazareth – Millenarian Prophet* (Minneapolis: Fortress Press, 1998)

De Jonge, M., *Jesus, the Servant Messiah* (New Haven: Yale University Press, 1991)

De Jonge, M., *God's Final Envoy: Early Christology and Jesus' View of his Own Mission* (Grand Rapids: Eerdmans, 1998)

Dunn, J. D.G., *Jesus and the Spirit* (London: SCM Press, 1975)

Meier, J. P., *A Marginal Jew: Rethinking the Historical Jesus* (2 vols; New York: Doubleday, 1991, 1995)

Sanders, E. P., *Jesus and Judaism* (London: SCM Press, 1985)

Witherington, Ben, *The Jesus Quest: The Third Search for the Jew of Nazareth* (Carlisle: Paternoster Press, 1995)

INDEX OF MODERN AUTHORS CITED

239

INDEX OF BIBLICAL REFERENCES

off